DOMINIC HOLLAND

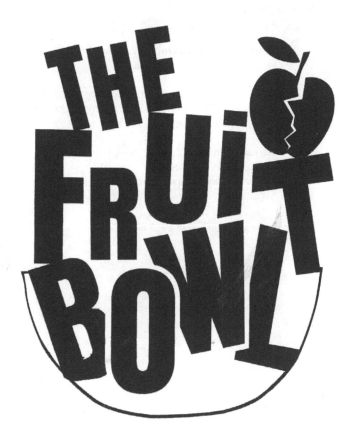

For Nikki

and

our boys

About the Author

Dominic Holland has been a professional comedian for almost 30 years and remains one of the most regarded and respected comedians of his generation (just). Described as 'the UK's master of observational comedy' by The Sunday Times but this was when Michael McIntyre was still at school.

His favourite quote hails from the late, great Bob Monkhouse – *'Dominic Holland is the UK's funniest not-yet-famous comedian.'* Years on and despite his best efforts, the not-yet-famous remains and being realistic, the odds are now firmly against.

He has made countless TV and radio appearances, published six books but is best known for being a dad and specifically the dad of Tom Holland, who is better known as Spider-Man. A detailed explanation of how this madness came to pass is explained in Dominic's only non-fiction book called *Eclipsed*.

The Fruit Bowl was formerly published as **A Man's Life** in 2013. The reasons for this new edition and title change are explained in a blog titled, The Fruit Bowl – at **www.dominicholland.co.uk** where Dominic blogs weekly and where you can sign up to his life changing newsletter.

Dominic lives in London with his wife. They have four boys and a dog called Tessa. Dominic is frequently tired.

Dominic is on all major social network channels without really understanding their power or how they work. You are welcome to message him via these channels, but if you don't get a response, then you should assume that he hasn't seen your message and it is not because he is being rude.

Dominic is lots of things but he is not rude.

Chapter 1

It was one of those mornings; so cold that weather forecasters feel duty bound to offer their advice as well as just the facts; so cold that merely informing listeners that the overnight temperature had plummeted to 'minus fifteen!' and would barely get back to zero all day would somehow feel irresponsible. And so, this morning, even the sober announcer on Radio 4 felt the need to sign off the bulletin with a helpful entreaty to *wrap up warm today, should you be brave enough to venture outside.*

Beth couldn't hear the radio over the noise of the machine and nor could she feel the cold, standing in her kitchen with its heated marble floor. She eased the plastic plunger into the juicer, which made little fuss, pulverising the large carrot into a thin line of orange juice. In the four years that she'd been making her Fruit Bowls, this was her third and most expensive juicing machine. It gave the impression of working well below capacity and despite its intensive usage; she never ceased to marvel at its efficiency. She decanted another full glass of orange-coloured juice into the crystal jug and turned the machine off. She put the jug in to the enormous American style fridge ready for husband, Tom, who would be in the shower already and for her three boys a few hours later before they all headed off to school. With her first daily chore completed, Beth quickly headed back to bed.

...and at 5.05, Pauline is here with a first look at the business pages... It was nothing personal, but Tom wasn't terribly interested in what Pauline had to say. Built into the wall of his en-suite bathroom were two screens, one with financial data that was collated for him every night and another tuned to a Japanese business channel with English subtitles.

'Morning, darling.' Beth called out as she slunk back in to their warm bed. Tom returned the greeting as best as he could manage as he finished up brushing his teeth. He wiped his mouth and re-entered his bedroom to kiss his wife on his way to their communal dressing room where his clothes for the day had been laid out for him by their housekeeper Naisi.

'There's a Fruit Bowl for you.' Beth added, her head already buried in fine Egyptian cotton and he smiled. The Fruit Bowl was a tradition that Beth had conceived and insisted on continuing on with and in her way. Tom had suggested that Naisi might assume the role of fruit juice extractor but Beth firmly rejected this and also the suggestion of preparing it the night before because don't vitamins and general goodness diminish with time? Beth enjoyed making her fruit concoctions and they were appreciated also by Tom and their boys.

Tom poured himself a full glass of juice which consisted of apples, usually a handful of red grapes, oranges, spinach, carrots and, this morning, by his reckoning a beetroot. Occasionally, Beth liked to surprise the boys with something a little bit left-field: a cucumber or fennel bulb and he imagined them trying to guess as Beth stood over them to make sure they each finished their glass.

Naisi appeared in the kitchen doorway. She had arrived at the Harper household over ten years ago and was still there, graduating from au-pair to live in housekeeper. Originally, she had stayed in the hope that a fourth child might be added to the clan – and hopefully, a girl – but Daniel, their eldest boy, announced that further siblings would be environmentally irresponsible. This had seemed radical at the time but now less so with the former Prince Harry agreeing with this sentiment and a part-time school girl from Sweden becoming the world's most deferred to commentator on the fiendishly complex issue of climate. Young Greta was Daniel's hero and all-time pin up and Tom often wondered if there was any point paying exorbitant school fees for a boy who had set his sights on becoming an eco-warrior and nothing else.

'Morning, Naisi. You needn't get up you know.'

'I know. I go back to bed soon.'

Tom laughed; it was an exchange they had most mornings. He gestured to the jug.

'Do you want yours now?' He didn't wait for an answer and handed her a full glass.

Beth was almost asleep again as he kissed her gently goodbye.

'Bye, love.'

'Yeah, I'll call you after Daniel's match – or before, if he scores.'

'It'll be cancelled I reckon. Apparently, it's freezing out there.'

Tom skipped down the broad and winding staircase with the usual sense of excitement that he felt as he left for work. He resented the term workaholic because of its negative connotations about dependency; he was just fortunate that he happened to enjoy what he did to make his handsome living. Above and beyond the call of duty, Naisi was waiting for him with his cashmere coat and scarf.

'Jerry's here and I've given him his cup of tea.'

'Thanks, Naisi. OK then, see you tonight.'

Tom opened the heavy oak door and was hit by a wall of freezing air that grabbed at him and easily penetrated his various layers of clothing. No matter how much Daniel had protested, the underground heating throughout their newly completed house had been a bloody marvellous idea. He hopped across his frost-covered drive and was upon his waiting Jaguar before his driver could react. A screen in the back of the front passenger seat was tuned to the same Japanese channel as the one in the kitchen, and copies of the *Financial Times* and *The Times* were laid on the back seat ready for him.

'Morning, Jerry. Jesus!'

'Morning, Tom. Cold enough for you?'

'Bloody freezing.' Tom settled into his heated leather seat and loosened his scarf.

'It's currently minus nine – twelve when I left,' Jerry chuckled.

Tom winced, thinking about Daniel's match this afternoon. 'Whatever happened to global warming, eh?'

The driver jabbed his foot on the accelerator. 'Doing my best, sir, honest.'

'Yeah, well don't. Daniel's probably watching. He's already on at me about the size of the bloody house.'

Jerry laughed as he looked at the magnificent pile that had taken nearly four years to fully complete.

'He tells me that under-floor heating is not carbon efficient.'

'Oh, is that right?'

'Bloody comfortable though and this car is all wrong, apparently.'

'What, not electric?'

'He asked me why it's got two exhaust pipes. Any answers for that one?'

'Er, how about because his dad is a very important man and one exhaust pipe is just not enough?'

Tom scoffed and tried to imagine using such logic on his defiant son. In fact, maybe it was time and he should get with the programme and buy something more eco and sustainable.

'Jaguar do an electric car, now, right?'

'Yeah, the E Pace. Much more cramped than this, mind.'

'But is it embarrassingly conspicuous?' Tom asked.

'You what?'

Tom chuckled. 'According to Daniel, this car is "embarrassingly conspicuous".'

Jerry grinned. 'Blimey. How old is he?'

'Fifteen,' Tom answered proudly.

They passed the old stable yard, which had been retained with a view to converting it into a studio of some kind, but for now housed Beth's bright orange Smart car. The thirsty Jag waited impatiently for the electric gates to open, like a powerful sprinter crouching for the gun, its two exhausts billowing out smoke. The back wheels crunched on the frozen gravel as the car pulled through and onto the road. Destination – the City of London.

As usual, Tom waited until they had got out of Gerrard's Cross and onto the M40 before he opened his work files or consulted any of his screens. He had realised that he didn't want to be a chartered accountant long before he had qualified as one and founded his telecommunications company, Tel-Com, just ahead of his twenty-fifth birthday. But, since taking the business back into private ownership almost eight years ago, the firm had diversified and expanded into many different areas, and most successfully, into the murky world of financial services. This morning, as usual, the motorway was empty, but each year he was forced out of bed a little bit earlier in order to enjoy a clear run. The Jag flew by the famous graffitied wall, running at ninety degrees to the motorway just outside the M25 border, and it always made him smile. Over the years, the wording had changed as the farmer or the council painted over the scrawl, but the message was always reassuringly anti-car or anti-establishment. This morning was a new and simple message: *What is the Point?* Tom shrugged at the question and surmised that none of his answers would have been very satisfactory. He enjoyed what he did, his company employed over two thousand people in eighteen different countries and with that comes a certain responsibility, not to mention pride. He reasoned that the question was aimed more at the later motorists caught in the inevitable gridlock each morning and evening of the week. But such misery didn't apply to him as he whizzed by at speed – and, if ever congestion reached such levels that not even the earliest start time could ensure him a free run, then he would reach for the helicopter brochure along with the other captains of industry and masters of the universe. Predictably, Daniel had explained that taking the train to London was the only responsible mode of transport and it did prick his conscience because he had fleetingly considered the idea, even if he hadn't actually tried it. He would rather lose an hour in bed than stand on a wet platform and hope for a seat. And of course, it wouldn't be fair on Jerry either, which was the reason he actually gave.

Forty minutes after leaving home, Tom was delivered at the front door of his office on Lombard Street at the heart of one of the busiest cities in the world. The streets were deserted with no parked cars at all and not just because it was so early. Heavy red lines daubed the city's streets and concrete bollards had appeared overnight like spring daffodils, only these were permanent and part of the world war against terrorism.

He pushed his way through the heavy, revolving glass doors.

'Morning,' he greeted the two security guards on duty. 'Another quiet night?'

'Yep. We slept straight through.' They joked.

Tom hadn't given much thought to which careers he would encourage his sons to pursue, but security was not one of them. A job where literally nothing happened constituted a good day? Tom shuddered at the thought as he pushed open the fire door to the stairwell. At forty-eight, he had a growing awareness of his mortality. He had managed to reduce his alcohol intake to what was officially considered safe but hadn't managed to increase his physical activity, a source of increased guilt because he now had a gym at his home as well as the one in his office. Lack of time was his constant excuse but as one of his few New Year's resolutions, he had started to use the staircase at work instead of the lift. Three hundred and seventy-three steps each morning had to be a good thing?

Although the ascent was becoming easier, it was fortunate that Tom was always the first to arrive because he still looked grim when he finally reached his office, gasping for breath and holding his chest. He laid his hands on the reception desk of Tel-Com and bent over at the waist, breathing heavily. He might well have been getting fitter but he was still exhausted each morning because he was ascending the stairs in less time; and so, he reminded himself that he needed to start timing himself as he headed through the open-plan workspace to his own private office. He sighed at the number of computer monitors left on standby overnight and immediately heard Daniel's voice in his head.

'If all the computer terminals and televisions in the world that were left on standby were switched off, the electricity saved would be enough…'

Naturally, Tom had the corner office with its views of St Paul's and the modern buildings huddled around it. He turned on his computer, congratulated himself for his smaller carbon footprint and sat down rather heavily. Family photos of Beth and the kids playing in the snow last year in France competed for attention with the photo of himself and Tiger Woods on the first tee at Augusta National Golf Club in Georgia. A photo that held mixed emotions for him, not just because of how badly he'd played, hardly bothering with a fairway as the golfing maestro smiled as politely as he could, but more at how he had acquired the right to play in such a golf match. Against his better instincts, at a city awards ceremony, he had become embroiled in a bidding war for the star lot and ended up outbidding a tax exile famed for his grandiose benevolence. The eye-watering cost would probably make it one of the most expensive rounds of golf ever played, and that was without the cost of keeping his name out of the trade press. It was a few years ago now and Tom looked at the picture and reflected on what lay ahead for Tiger: a plethora of trophies but a whole heap of pain also and then his miraculous and heralded comeback. For all his talents and achievements, Tom was glad that he wasn't Tiger Woods.

Chapter 2

Beth poured out the juice for herself and the three boys.

'Naisi, have you had yours?'

'Yes, with Tom, before he left.'

'Right, OK. Boys, come on, drink up.' It was always a bit of a struggle.

'There's a secret ingredient today,' Naisi announced as she emerged from the utility room with a bundle of laundry. 'Prizes for the first one to guess.'

Beth smiled as she finished her drink.

'What's the prize?' Luke always wanted to know what he was playing for, so as not to waste his time.

'Dad's love,' Beth replied and he tutted loudly before he guessed anyway.

'Carrots.'

Daniel sneered at his little brother. 'A *secret* ingredient, you idiot. It's always got carrots in it; that's why it's always orange.'

'Yeah, but it's not orange, is it you dick.' Luke scolded his, jabbing his finger at his glass.

'Luke, don't use language like that.'

'Sorry mum. But he is. OK, pineapple then.'

'You're just guessing,' Daniel said as he took his first mouthful and let it swill around his mouth like a sommelier.

'Mango,' Jack chipped in.

'Naisi, is it pineapple?' Luke asked.

'I don't know.' She grinned, looking to Beth.

'Yes, you do. I can tell! Mum told you, didn't she?'

Naisi laughed.

'Fine. Bagsy pineapple. I'm saying pineapple,' Luke shouted loudly.

Jack had gone with the rather unlikely lemon and Daniel had

yet to decide, enjoying keeping his brothers waiting.

'Come on, what's your guess, smart-arse?' Luke demanded.

Daniel took another mouthful before confidently announcing that he was going with papaya.

'What?'

'Eh?'

Daniel smiled at his little brothers. 'Papaya. Which I hope it isn't because they are native...'

'OK, that's enough with the secret ingredient,' Beth interrupted, keen to head off another environmental lecture. 'Just drink it, please. Now, what cereals do you want?'

'Sugar Puffs, please,' Luke asked with a cheeky grin.

'Do we have any Coco Pops?'

Beth emerged from the walk-in larder with an armful of boxes and a defiant grin of her own. 'Weetabix, Shredded Wheat or Honey Nut Loops?'

'Honey Nuts!' three voices chorused in unison.

Honey Nut Loops were usually the compromise between oats or bran versus sugar and E numbers. They never lasted very long and wouldn't be replaced until the less palatable alternatives had been munched through. Beth poured out three bowls and drenched them in milk before arming the toaster with four crumpets. 'Naisi, Daniel's got a rugby match today. If it isn't called off, that is.'

'No, it won't be,' Daniel said confidently. 'They've got underground heating. Can you believe that?'

'Just eat your cereal,' Beth pleaded, 'and make sure you've got your mouth guard or you won't be allowed to play.'

'Yeah, I know.' He hopped down off the stool.

'Where are you going?' Beth asked.

'To get my gum shield.'

'Get back here and finish your breakfast. I've got crumpets coming.'

'But I don't want a crumpet.'

Beth just pointed at the stool and Daniel reluctantly sat down.

'Right, twins, come on, eat up. Where are your homework diaries? I need to sign them. And your spellings as well; both of you get them ready so that we can do them in the car.'

Filling the kids with food and getting them presentable with school bags emptied of yesterday's essentials and replaced with todays was always a mad half-hour, no matter how many Naisi's were on hand to help. Lost diaries, gloves, odd socks, arguments, teeth being brushed (or not), bickering, dirty shirts, shouting and finally threats of telling Dad; it was the same every morning with Beth standing at the front door, urging her boys to hurry up because they were going to be late and that she was leaving *now*. Luke was the first to appear with everything intact.

'Good boy, Luke. Go and get in the car; it's open. You too, Jack. Hurry up. I'll be out in a second.' Beth sighed, her breath billowing like a vaper in the cold. Where the hell was Daniel? 'Daniel!' she called quickly and finally her eldest son emerged and Beth grimaced. 'Where's your coat?'

'I don't need a...'

'Just go and get your bloody coat,' she shouted. 'I'll be in the car.'

The little car steamed up the moment the doors were slammed shut and Beth grappled to get the key into the ignition. She turned the key quickly and the engine spluttered a little and then coughed reluctantly into life. The car's fans, on full tilt from the previous school pickup, blasted Beth's with a shaft of freezing air. Quickly, she shut them off, where they would remain until the engine had sufficiently warmed up and until then she would have to make do with the hot air spouted by her eldest son.

'How come Dad's car is always warm when we get in it?' Luke demanded.

'Because, dad's car is...'

'Daniel!' Beth cut him off.

As he did most mornings at 8.00 a.m., Tom was chairing a meeting of his senior management team. It was usually just a quick catch up on the previous day's events plus an airing of any views, but today it was more serious because Tel-Com was amidst, what the financial press had called, an 'audacious' attempt to acquire a mineral mine in Brazil. Under Tom's stewardship, Tel-Com had fared relatively well during the previous economic downturn, although not as well as the few financial journalists who'd become famous from reporting it even though none of them had seen it coming. Tom was not a fan of financial experts and ranked only the famous offspring of celebrities as more irksome. This morning the press had produced an array of financial strife and woe ahead, which Tom was quick to dismiss.

'Economists? I don't know why we bother.'

None of the twelve people seated around the glass table responded. They knew that Tom hadn't finished.

'I mean… Is there another profession where you can get things so completely wrong and yet still call yourself an expert?'

Tom let this hang a moment. Jeremy, his Managing Director was the first to take the plunge.

'Er, politicians?'

Tom pursed his lips. It was a reasonable suggestion and probably correct. Jeremy Dyson ranked a close second behind Tom in running the business. He had a meticulous eye for detail and was fiercely loyal and competent, but remained happy thriving in the shadow of his more talented friend. They had met during their first week together at Exeter University. Jeremy's real skill was to recognise that Tom was going places and that his coat tails might well prove more valuable than a first-class degree (which he achieved anyway, just to be on the safe side).

'What about football pundits?' James Baker, the newest and youngest member of the board added with some defiance.

'Football pundits?' Tom repeated as he thought out loud.

'Yeah, they get it wrong all the time and we still listen to them drone on. And critics?' James added, warming to his theme. 'Critics get it wrong. Case in point: *The Greatest Showman*.

'Haven't seen it.' Tom parried even though he tended to agree with James.

'Critics panned it. Made half a billion at the Box Office. Eight times more than it cost.'

'Blimey James. Never had you down as a musical fan. You do surprise me.'

'Full of surprises, me. And what about art critics? Those twats call everything wrong. That blinking unmade bed.'

General agreement and derision spread through the room and at this, Tom held up his hands in submission.

'OK, fine. Economists are not alone. But you see my point. If these people were in fact *expert*, then they wouldn't just be writing, would they? They'd be actually out there, doing it.'

Jeremy nodded enthusiastically at this, like the loyal number two that he was.

'The media loves doom and woe. But life goes on. We haven't actually moved, have we? People will still eat Mars bars and have sex and watch films and buy clothes and praise the Lord; they will still talk to each other.' Tom held up his iPhone for extra emphasis.

'Or FaceTime,' Jeremy joked.

Tom nodded. 'Speaking of which, where are we with Sao Projene?'

Projene was the Brazilian mining company that Tel-Com had spent considerable time and money trying to acquire. A deal in which Tom was fast losing patience.

'They rejected our offer at four dollars.'

Tom groaned and shook his head. He glanced down at his screen and noted an email from Michael Millhouse, his lawyer, which was almost certainly about this deal. James shifted awkwardly in his chair. He had been the last member of the team to visit Brazil and had been charged with getting the deal over the line.

'So, let me try and understand this…' Tom began. 'This is a parent company, apparently in crisis, rejecting an offer of eight hundred million US for an asset it paid almost half this sum for less than four years ago?'

None of his team spoke.

'During a time when their economy is in freefall…' Tom gestured to his copy of the *FT*, '…and furthermore, this is an asset that as yet they have failed to operate at a profit?' Tom gestured for a suitable explanation and only Jeremy was willing to respond.

'They've suggested a price that would be of interest to them.'

'Oh, have they?' Tom beckoned Jeremy for the information.

'Four dollars thirty.'

Tom chuckled to himself and gestured to James for his calculator and quickly began plugging in numbers as an awkward silence hung in the room.

'Tom, last night I spoke with Michael and the tax implications...'

Tom waved his hand. 'What is it now? Two years we've been on this...'

'Seventeen months.'

Tom shook his head. 'And around this table, who's visited? Who's been to Brazil?'

Four furtive hands registered their failure.

'Right. Four of you. And how often? Two, three times each? OK, so let's say that is three weeks of man hours. No offence, Martha.'

'Plus, they've been here twice,' Jeremy added.

'Right then, so taking all of this effort in to account then, Jeremy, what do you think?' Tom asked.

'Er...'

'What's our play here?'

All eyes were now on Jeremy. The number two after all and paid considerably more than anyone else, so only fair that he was first in line.

Jeremy dithered a little before plumping for a number.

'Er, four fifteen.'

Tom looked at his friend with a face of pained confusion. 'You think we should increase our offer?'

Jeremy didn't answer this time. He didn't know how to and he suspected that Tom did anyway. This was usually how things played out.

'Anyone else?' Tom opened it out more generally, but James felt that it was a question directed specifically at him. And now offering firm support for his immediate boss, Jeremy, would be the sensible if conservative play. And so, he took the plunge.

'Well? It's certainly worth more than four dollars. So, I like Jeremy's four fifteen.'

Tom looked a little surprised. He eyed his watch, knowing that he had another meeting to get to.

'Jeremy, offer three ninety-five.'

James bit his lip. Damn it.

'We're reducing our offer?' Jeremy asked.

'Precisely. And only until Friday. After that, we're out. That's it. Three ninety-five or it's off.'

James winced. At least he'd supported Jeremy which would count for something. But what he really wanted to do was to impress Tom.

Three nine five. Jeremy jotted the figure down on his notepad and underlined it as if he was going to forget it. The meeting was over and Tom got up. James, though, wanted to add something, perhaps to redeem himself, but Tom stopped him.

'James, don't worry about it. Your call was fine. And if we lose it at three nine five then you and Jeremy can tell me so. And besides, no one else had an opinion anyway. What was it you read at Cambridge?' he asked mischievously.

James laughed, grateful for the release that his economics degree gave the whole room.

Beth knew instantly what lay ahead the moment her car lost traction with the road. It was most likely black ice but it didn't matter. The affect was the same. The car's brake pedal was completely unresponsive but instinctively she stabbed at it angrily as her car slid to and fro before finally opting for one single direction which she could do nothing to arrest. With an eerie sense of knowing, she eyed the ugly truck ahead that was directly in her path and closing rapidly. Totally impotent she could only wait and with absolute clarity, Beth knew the outcome that awaited her and her boys. Still the car's steering wheel and brake pedal refused to respond and at that devastating moment, when everything froze still, she could assess things with clinical precision. How could this happen? Such a waste of so much ahead. And how could such a small gap, the tiny space between tarmac and rubber, wreak so much pain and devastation? No one in her small and fibre glass car was going to survive. Her attention quickly focussed on her husband and she wanted to scream about what horrors lay ahead for him.

The lorry too had lost control; its wheels locked and screaming in what sounded like a dreadful advance apology. And still the moment of stillness and silence lingered. The screaming rubber, her cries and those of her children were somehow muted. Still Beth pondered with an almost unnatural detachment. Of course, accidents happen every day – heart-wrenching stories of such sadness that people stop momentarily to consider their own good fortune before inevitably resuming their hurried and hectic lives. Their insulating bubbles reforming around them. And still she kept thinking of Tom, who was in a much worse place than her. At least she was with her boys. She wondered how he would cope and his broken image hurt her as much as anything the truck could visit upon them. This was the last thought seared onto her mind as the tranquil moment finally burst and real time erupted angrily in the form of a screaming truck smashing through and obliterating her tiny car.

The twenty-tonne lorry barely registered the impact of Beth's car and continued sliding along the carriageway for another eighty feet before eventually scraping and grinding to a halt. The driver, plunged into shock, failed to notice his shattered shin bone as he jumped from his cab, phone in hand, emergency services already dialled.

'Which service do you require?'

With his leg so badly damaged, he collapsed onto the wet road as other motorists swerved or screeched to stop, fumbling with their mobile phones, most of them calling the emergency services; others, later, no doubt, taking photos. The driver tried to heave his body upright and looked confused as to why it kept crumpling beneath him. A young man in a dark suit abandoned his Audi TT and quickly caught the driver under the arm and around his back.

'Jesus, man! Fuck! Seriously, stay still...'

'Call an ambulance!' the truck driver wailed, over and over.

'Yeah, it's done, mate. I've done it. Jesus, man, don't move.'

Having witnessed the whole thing, the young man was also succumbing to shock. He glanced around at strewn wreckage and the inevitable crowd that was already gathering, secure now in the knowledge that the backed-up traffic in either direction made them safe from any other incoming sliding vehicles. The truck driver was still unaware of his injury and peered hopelessly down the road, searching for some reassurance, to see the people from the little orange car dusting themselves down and thanking their lucky stars. But there was no such movement. He could barely make out the remains of the tiny car and it was clear that no one had survived. He leant back onto the wet and cold road and managed to turn his body sideways as he vomited violently.

'Which service do you require?'

His mobile phone was still connected. An ambulance was needed but they needn't rush anymore; it was too late for that. There was nothing any medic could do for these poor souls, the driver thought as he slipped into unconsciousness. It was a priest and God himself they needed, if indeed he existed.

Eight minutes later, the road had been cordoned off by the police as the emergency services set about clearing the carnage and getting the road open again for the impatient build-up of motorists. Space was cleared for the air ambulance to land and a doctor quickly and efficiently pronounced and recorded the deaths of Beth, Luke and Jack Harper. Sheets were drawn over their broken corpses. Daniel had survived for a few minutes after the services arrived, but another doctor quickly established that the little boy was not going to survive and just concentrated on making him as comfortable as possible. He was already blue and had lost at least half of his blood. Against protocol, the young female paramedic cradled the young boy until he finally took his last breath. She was now being comforted by her colleague in the back of an ambulance. No amount of experience or training could adequately prepare crews for such a scene. Steam from both vehicles billowed, mixing with the water spray from the fire crews, and the sheen of petrol on the road made a beautiful and ironic reflection. Police officers began taking photographs and measuring skid tracks and other markings on the road for the insurance wrangling that would no doubt ensue with various lawyers sniffing a payday also. Another officer encouraged on-looking motorists to move back to their cars and a tent was hastily being erected over the wreckage of Beth's car and her family. The driver of the lorry was now delirious, in the back of an ambulance, shaking uncontrollably, his own injury dawning on him but still having little impact. A paramedic worked to stabilise his leg and didn't answer his questions about the fate of the other motorists.

Chapter 3

Barbara had been Tom's PA since he founded his company and she ran his office with a calm efficiency. Barbara loved her God as much as she loved her three sons. Two years ago, her eldest son, Jamal, had become another crime statistic and Tom was on hand to support her. He paid for the funeral and a family holiday back to Kingston to visit relatives, but Barbara was never really the same again. She was unable to concentrate at work for a long time after his death and so Tom sent her home on full pay. He told her to take as long as she needed and he put up with temps, none of whom could adequately replace her. Barbara returned before her grief had abated but at a point when it was easier being at work than being at home alone. And now it was her turn to support him. Tom was in constant demand in his business life and one of Barbara's primary roles was to act as a protective barrier for him. She liked to think of herself as a no-man's land that had to be negotiated to get to her boss. It gave him the space he needed to get on with his job. But the phone call from the Berkshire Constabulary was different. A call from the police is always alarming but just from the tone of the officer's voice, Barbara understood the gravity of the situation before anything was said and she was barely able to hit her console to finally end the call. She said nothing to her colleagues as she slumped back into her chair, the officers on their way to the office. Images of Beth and the boys competed for her attention but she kept her focus on Tom, staring at his back through the glass of Jeremy's office. He was standing nonchalantly, apparently, a man without a care in the world.

In total contrast, the mood in Jeremy's office was convivial and celebratory, with Tom leaning against the wall as Jeremy sat with his feet on his desk and his hands behind his head.

'As soon as I got out of our meeting, I faxed their lawyers.'

Tom smiled.

'And guess what? They must have been pulling an all-nighter because fifteen minutes later, I get a phone call from Alfonse.'

Tom looked thoughtful, imagining the panic that must have gripped their office in Sao Paulo and the recriminations that would follow.

'Damn, we could have probably gone lower,' Tom joked.

'Michael said it was a masterstroke by the way. He's going to Rome today; he's going to call you later.'

Tom nodded. His desk diary was already full and he wondered if he would have time to speak to him. No doubt, Barbara would find him fifteen minutes and get Michael on the phone.

'So, you're both off to Brazil?' Tom asked.

'Yep, tomorrow I expect, or the day after. Hey, why don't you come? We can check out that football team of yours. Michael said he'd join us, and with you and James, we could play five-a-side against them.'

Tom chuckled at the prospect of a trip that was becoming ever more attractive. 'Sure, why not?' He rubbed his chin. 'Bloody hell, Jeremy. Three ninety. That is a bloody great price.'

'Absolutely and I can see it hitting five bucks just on the announcement.'

Jeremy resisted the temptation to grab a calculator and plug in some crude figures.

'You've done a press release?' Tom asked.

Jeremy shook his head. 'No. I wasn't going to bother.'

Tom looked at him quizzically.

'Yeah, you know? What's the point of the press and all that?'

Tom laughed loudly. 'Yeah, well, I didn't say they don't have their uses.'

'Sure, I'll get it drafted right away.'

Tom considered the deal again, smiling contentedly as his attention was drawn to the door behind him.

The veneered oak door opened a fraction after a cursory and barely audible knock, and Barbara appeared in the room, her broken face a study in fear. A policewoman was behind her and Tom could see the outline of a further male officer just outside the room.

Jeremy sprang up from his chair.

'Barbara, what is it?' Jeremy asked. She didn't answer, her pained eyes remained fixed on Tom.

The WPC looked down as she shut the door behind her, leaving her colleague outside. Tom, with a growing sense of gravity, placed his hands-on Barbara's shoulders appealing for information.

'Barbara, what is it?' he asked. 'Is it Junior? Or Dwight?'

Barbara shut her eyes as heavy tears ran down her ample round cheeks. She shook her head, her throat full and aching with pain for the man and his family that she loved. She was unable to speak and was panicking now. Tom's eyes left hers and appealed to the WPC.

'Mr Harper...' the WPC began. 'I am afraid there's been an accident involving...'

'Beth...' Barbara managed to whisper.

'They've been in a road accident,' the female police officer continued.

Tom stared at her in horror.

'But they're OK?' he shouted as panic held him. He moved Barbara back so that he could consider her eyes more fully, searching for some hope, something to cling to, and in that instant, he knew.

'No...'

Barbara slumped down in front of him.

'Not my boys?' Tom's head shook from side to side. 'Not my boys. No, no, please, tell me,' he pleaded, his breath shallowing as the horror wreaked havoc. 'Not my boys!'

Barbara sobbed and Jeremy looked aghast, unable to take in the news. Quickly he closed the blinds to his office, suddenly aware that the entire floor was staring directly at them.

'Barbara,' Jeremy snapped. 'They've been in an accident and they've been injured?'

The police officer looked at Jeremy and shook her head. She turned to Tom again and uttered the dreadful words.

'I'm so sorry.'

Tom slumped at his hips as if he had been winded, his brain wrestling against what he had been told. He said nothing, staring from place to place and rocking uneasily on his feet. Suddenly, he was cold and his mouth was dry; so, dry that he couldn't swallow and then his knees buckled and Jeremy lurched forward to catch him. Tom crumpled into his colleague's arms, his dead weight more than Jeremy could cope with and he needed Barbara's help to heave him onto the sofa. Tom started moaning quietly and Barbara reached over to the desk for the phone until Jeremy stopped her.

'I'm going to phone his doctor,' she protested but Jeremy shook his head. He had to take charge now.

'Which hospital have they been taken to?' he asked the officer urgently.

'Gerrard's Cross General,' the WPC answered. 'We'll have someone there waiting for you.'

Tom continued to moan, his face contorted with hurt and confusion. Jeremy grabbed for his keys. 'Barbara, I'm going to drive Tom there now. If you could get me an address? Actually, a postcode. Get me a postcode. And, yes, call his doctor. And Michael as well. Call Michael.'

Chapter 4

Tom was silent in Jeremy's car, in a state of catatonic shock. The traffic was stubborn and Jeremy was doing his best to negotiate a way through, but it wasn't easy. He glanced at his friend in his mirror. Tom was vacant and staring at nothing ahead of him. It wasn't lost on Jeremy that he had just taken delivery of his brand-new car and he had been pestering Tom to come for spin but never in such circumstances. He felt embarrassed now because the car was the latest and most powerful Aston Martin ever made, capable of speeds almost three times as fast as was considered safe for pedestrians and drivers alike. 'It'll probably kill me,' he had even joked to Tom the day he took delivery, an expression which now made him wince.

An hour into their journey, Jeremy forced a right turn very late at a traffic light to get access to Maple Street and to the hospital. Ignoring the inevitable blaring horns and angry stares that his car usually attracted anyway, he pulled up outside the hospital entrance, which was heavily daubed in yellow paint. Two police officers, male and female, were standing outside and it became apparent that it was Tom whom they were waiting for.

'Mr Harper?' An officer asked kindly.

'Yes, this is Tom Harper,' Jeremy explained on behalf of his boss, who hadn't said a word since leaving his office. Jeremy's eyes instinctively scanned the place for any prying eyes and in particular for any photographers.

'I'm PC O'Connor.'

Jeremy left Tom in their care, mindful that he would need to move his car. Smokers in dressing gowns loitering outside the hospital stared at the handsome, smartly-dressed man emerging from the Aston and being handed over to two police officers.

'I'm so dreadfully sorry, sir.'

Tom didn't react. Still he didn't say anything. Jeremy had been right. He just wanted to be with his family.

Like most parents, Tom had spent considerable time in various children's accident and emergency departments over the years, mostly for false alarms and the odd sprained ankle. He had always been touched by the efforts taken to cheer the hospital wards and departments up. The colourful murals of Disney characters; a scene from Scooby Doo; jolly Teletubbies parading around the walls; a cheery Snow-White dancing with her dwarfs who all seemed to be Happy. But this was Tom's first visit to a hospital morgue, euphemistically known as a 'Fatalities Holding Area'. No such attempt had been made to brighten up this department. It was cold to start with, in stark contrast to the generally overheated wards for the sick and every wall and floor had been painted dark grey, perhaps an appropriate backdrop for the deceased.

The enormity of the situation had now made its indelible impression on Tom's consciousness. Just a few nights ago, on television, he had caught the end of a programme where a child had survived a liver transplant; surely a modern miracle, whether or not God actually exists. But for all the success stories that a hospital can muster, surely any jubilation would come a distant second to the grief and misery that hospital's witness as Tom stood in a cold and stark room with just four beds, each one covered with a white sheet. The sheets were pristine and he wondered if they would be laundered and used again.

The chilled air pierced his skin. Minimalist furniture and a few shelves were the only other things in the room: no medicines or machines that one associates with a hospital. What would be the point? Nothing on the walls either: no posters or notices. PC O'Connor was present along with the duty nurse, both waiting awkwardly for an identification before they could leave this poor man alone. Tom knew the drill or he assumed that he did. He'd seen enough TV shows and he didn't want anyone else pulling the sheets back for him. PC O'Connor was coming up for retirement and had attended many identifications before, but never in such circumstances and given the injuries of the deceased, he was fretful as to how the man might react.

Tom could identify each of his family by the size of the bed and he wondered in a moment of idle lucidity if they had been deliberately ordered in size for aesthetic reasons: Beth first, lying next to Daniel, and then little Luke and Jack. His vision blurred as he stood next to his wife and recalled the last time he had seen her early that morning, wrapped up warm in bed in their newly completed wonder home. It was just the start of another day. And now she lay in a freezing room under nothing but a thin sheet.

He took hold of the sheet in his quivering right hand and with a quiet urgency, he pulled it back gently, almost tenderly, just enough to see Beth's eyes. For a moment, he stood and forced his swollen eyes shut. When he opened them again, he quickly nodded over at the waiting officials. The nurse started to approach, but he gestured for her to stop. He didn't want anyone near him. O'Connor shifted nervously. Protocol stated that all bodies needed to be identified but, in such circumstances, he was happy to dispense with such officialdom. Understanding Tom's needs, he and the nurse bowed their respects and left the room. Tom watched them leave and when the door finally closed behind them, he turned his attention back to Beth. Controlling himself as best he could, he pulled the sheet gently down, revealing the whole of Beth's beautiful face. He groaned loudly at what he saw and stroked her hairline. Then he moved on to his eldest son, his vision now completely blurred by the hot tears running down his face. Carefully and tenderly, he withdrew Daniel's sheet, his shoulders shaking uncontrollably as another disastrous image took up its place in his mind. He took a short moment before he did the same to Luke and to Jack. Fumbling behind him for the chair, he slumped down heavily, hung his head in his hands and the tears came in earnest.

As well as being a senior partner at Singletons, the city law firm, Michael Millhouse was Tom's family lawyer, confidant and closest adviser. At City Airport, the plane doors had been shut so his mobile phone should really have been switched off when he received the frantic message, and he caused some consternation when he requested that he be allowed off the aircraft. Fortunately, he only had hand baggage and he was seated at the very front of the plane. Still, phone calls needed to be placed and checks made before the captain agreed, and then, much to Jeremy's relief, Michael was off the plane and on his way. After a frustrating taxi journey, Michael burst through the double doors of the hospital with two assistants who had joined him en route. Despite being desperately shaken and upset, he managed to maintain his professional aura of authority and calm. Michael was one of those striking men who appear to become more handsome with age. Tall and slim, with a full head of silver hair and the permanent tan that comes with a house in the South of France, he fixed his stare on Jeremy as they held hands firmly.

'Bloody hell,' he murmured. 'Where is he?'

Jeremy gestured to a set of double doors with obscured windows off to his left.

Michael too had been bereaved. He was Daniel's godfather and he practically regarded Beth as a daughter, but now he needed to be lawyerly and effective. He knew exactly what Tom would want him to do; his own grieving would have to wait. He had already called Artemis, the public relations firm that handled Tel-Com's publicity and more importantly, guarded Tom's privacy. Keeping Tom's name out of the press was key and it irked Michael that they couldn't make any promises. He'd also spoken to Tom's older sister, Nell, who was on her way from Hampshire and was due to arrive shortly. He hadn't reached Beth's parents yet and he didn't want to leave them a message. He had an idea that they were holidaying somewhere; the Bahamas, he thought, and he instructed his team to find them and organise their immediate passage home, chartering a jet if need be. His legal team back at the office were charged with studying Beth's will and reviewing any of their insurance policies that would apply and he was waiting on a return phone call from the head of traffic police to provide him with an accurate account of exactly what had happened. Tom would want to know this. His iPhone pinged. It was Dr Steven Collier, Tom's private doctor, returning his call and despite the many and prominent injunctions to turn off mobile phones all about the hospital, Michael answered the call and made no attempt to do so surreptitiously either.

'Dr Collier, thank you for phoning...'

An hour after Tom had entered the sparse room, he was still sitting with his family. The nurse watched through the mirror from the observatory room. By now, Tom had completely removed the sheets so that he could hold and touch each member of his family. Despite their injuries and burns, they all still looked perfect to him. The boys were handsome and strong. Daniel looked defiant. He had a puzzled and inquisitive look on his face, as if he was trying to work out why such a terrible fate was being visited on his brothers and on his mum. Beth's golden hair still shone brilliantly from her broken body, which felt eerily cold as he hugged her tightly. But despite his pleas, she couldn't respond or hug him back. He wondered if she could hear him, telling her over and over how much he loved her and the boys, and the plans that he had had for them all.

He kissed Beth's forehead again, his tear falling onto her face and loosening a spot of congealed blood over her shattered cheekbone. With his thumb, he gently rubbed the blood away, careful not to damage the splintered bones of her face any further. He studied her face carefully and how even in death, she remained an impossibly beautiful woman. Momentarily, he chuckled as he recalled the moment he first saw her and how it wasn't her looks that had caught his eye all those twenty-two years ago. This was something that Beth constantly teased him about. She used to joke that, if ever he traded her in for a younger model, she would want it officially stated on the divorce papers that she had been the inspiration behind Tel-Com and that, as such, she would fully deserve half of the estate, at least. At the time, Beth had been working for IBM, a newly qualified, high-flyer from their graduate training programme to which Tom was a new recruit. She was standing in the foyer of the head offices in Bracknell, talking into a telephone which didn't appear to be connected to anything. Tom had heard about mobile telephones but he had never seen one before and he was beguiled by it, not to mention the girl holding it to her ear. Already a manager and older than him and extremely attractive, Tom would normally have been intimidated by her, but technology was a worthy distraction. He marched up to introduce himself and in doing so, bagged himself a wife and a career. They married in Bristol, far too young according to their friends and Beth gave up work when Daniel finally arrived after nearly four years of trying. And when the twins arrived two years on, Beth decided to put her career on permanent hold, a decision made easier because of Tom's meteoric success with Tel-Com. Two house moves and three children completed the family with just a dog missing to complement the perfect Sunday supplement family.

Beyond the double doors with the rubber apron, in the warmth of the waiting room, a frantic Nell had arrived and Jeremy had told her all that he knew. Her large brown eyes were reddened and her delicate face looked desolate. She was a well-groomed woman who made the very best of her looks. With some determination and equal sacrifice, she had remained slim, which made her look considerably younger than her actual age of fifty. Understandably, Nell wanted to join her little brother in the room with her relatives, but Jeremy suggested that she should wait until Tom was ready. It was better to let him beckon her in.

'Where's Michael?' Nell asked, a little needily, knowing that Michael couldn't be far away and would be assuming control.

'He's here, somewhere. On the phone I imagine,' Jeremy answered.

Understandably, Nell was bewildered and in a state of complete shock. Nervously, she constantly looked at her watch, as if she had something more important to attend to. She refused to sit down and paced constantly, looking at the doors, hoping that Tom would emerge so that she could console him. She had cried on the way to the hospital but oddly, she didn't feel like crying now. Denial perhaps but also, she wanted to appear strong, which seemed rather pathetic and ridiculous because how could it possibly help? What she really wanted was to see her little brother who was just through the ugly grey doors, dealing with the unimaginable and possibly the first genuine crisis in his charmed life.

A police officer had been in to see them both to offer his condolences and also to explain a little more about what had happened. A terrible piece of bad luck it seemed, with tragic consequences that would last a lifetime.

Jeremy's phone vibrated every two minutes or so but he didn't answer it unless it was Michael. He had set himself the task of dealing with Beth's family. Tom's parents had long since died and so his entire family was already present and nothing else really mattered. Again, Jeremy's phone sprang to life. It was James at the office and again, he let it click to answerphone. What could he say to anyone anyway? He wasn't going back to the office today. He had intended to shut the office entirely until Michael advised against it, warning that it would draw unwanted attention to Tom. It made good sense and Jeremy was grateful that Michael had got off that plane. With uncanny timing, Michael appeared through the door of the waiting room and rushed over to embrace Nell who, having finally just sat down, now leapt up again. They hugged closely and Nell sobbed momentarily, a release of pent-up emotion, just as Tom emerged through the bleak double doors, a puff of cold white air accompanying him. Nell, Jeremy and Michael, the three closest people left in his life, all stared back at him.

Understandably, he looked dreadful; as though the life had been sucked from his body. What stood before them was a completely broken man. Nell rushed forward and grabbed her brother to her, her tears flowing freely now. Tom leant down and sobbed gently into her breast as Jeremy and Michael joined the group huddle with no words uttered at all. Michael broke off first, his face strong and defiant like an officer in the field with a frightened sentry. His eyes moistened but his jaw muscle bulged and he was not going to cry.

'Tom, when you and Nell are ready, I'm driving you both home. Nell, I think you should stay with Tom this evening. I've spoken with Jonathan; he's on his way to the school now to get Ben and Ella.'

Nell agreed, her mind racing. Of course, she would stay at Tom's. Of course, he couldn't be alone. It was lucky that her husband, Jonathan could collect their kids but she worried about her car being parked at the hospital. She admonished herself for being so practical and even thinking of such a thing, a feeling compounded when Michael went on.

'If you let me have your car keys, I'll have your car driven back to Tom's.'

Nell managed a half-smile, which Michael seemed to appreciate, mistaking it for stoicism.

'Tom, take as long as you need here, and when you're ready to go, then we're ready too.'

Tom listened but he didn't respond. His eyes fixed open, barely blinking at all. His mind completely mired in confusion and unable to process or make sense of his reality. But it was real all right. It was happening. With each person he encountered, none of them could tell him otherwise.

Michael held both of Tom's hands and looked at him very directly. The older man tried to assess whether he had his attention so that he could explain what he needed to tell him.

'Beth and the boys are going to be moved to the mortuary in Slough and you'll be able to visit them later today, after you've been home.'

Tom continued to stare blankly and then turned to look at his sister. He stared at her for a moment. 'Nell, would you like to see them?' Tom asked quietly.

Nell didn't know how to respond. She glanced at Michael for help and he nodded gently.

'What do you want, Tom?' she replied gently.

Without answering, Tom took her hand and beckoned her forward. He pushed the door open and took her inside with him. In the middle of the floor she saw the four beds all pushed together and covered by a series of white sheets overlapping to form one complete cover. His family was together again.

Michael had liaised with a bereavement expert and had instructed Naisi not to do any housework at all, and especially not to do any laundry or to touch the children's bedrooms. Tom refused any medication that Dr Collier suggested and the moment he arrived home, he silently visited each of his children's bedrooms and gathered up their pyjamas. Clutching them to his chest, he undressed and slipped into his own bed on the side where Beth usually lay and closed his eyes.

Chapter 5

The next morning, Michael convened a meeting for himself, Jeremy and Angus Waddington, Tom's accountant. Angus was a fat fifty-something and an emotional type. He still couldn't believe what had happened and rather unhelpfully insisted on asking pointless questions that immediately grated on the more pragmatic Michael.

'Have you seen him today?' Angus asked.

Michael pulled at his facial stubble, a rare thing for a man normally so preened. 'No. But I spoke with Nell first thing.'

'And?'

Michael sighed a little. 'He wasn't up when I called, which is probably a good thing. Although it was early.'

Angus fretted a little more and drew his chubby hand through what remained of his curly hair. 'I just can't believe it.'

'No, neither can any of us,' Michael responded flatly. 'Now then, for the foreseeable future, we should assume that Tom won't be functional and until he is, it is our responsibility to run his affairs.'

Jeremy nodded, aware that he was drawing the shortest of the three straws in running Tel-Com in his absence. Rather selfishly, he wondered how long it might be before Tom could resume his reins. Michael, ever practical and equally competent, didn't seem as perturbed and, why should he?

'...and between the three of us, we must see to it that everything pertaining to Tom should continue as normal and function as best it can, until he makes a recovery.'

'Or *if*,' Angus added, full of foreboding. 'I mean, who's to say that –'

Michael scowled at Angus as he interrupted him. 'Yes, thank you Angus. If he does – and key to his recovery is that Tom can take just as long as he needs, because we have everything covered.'

Jeremy and Angus agreed.

'Six months, a year, however long it takes,' Michael added.

Jeremy blanched a little. 'A year? Do you really think it could be a year?' He asked, beating Angus to it.

'I don't know, Jeremy. None of us do. That's the point.'

Nell assumed responsibility for arranging the funerals. It gave her a much-needed distraction and it needed a woman's touch anyway. It was five days since the accident and yesterday, the mortuary had contacted her and tactfully suggested that Tom shouldn't visit again so that final arrangements could be made. Tom didn't agree but crucially he didn't object either. Apart from his mortuary visits, he hadn't done anything since the fateful day except sleep, which everyone agreed was a good thing. Doctor Collier provided some sedatives and visited each day but it needed Nell to make sure that he took them. He refused to eat though, which was apparently quite normal but still Nell worried and so she lost herself in all that needed organising. The worst part was liaising with Beth's parents and she felt a relief that her own parents had passed and so were spared such a tragedy. Nell had accompanied Michael to meet Beth's parents at Heathrow, cutting short their holiday. Michael explained what had happened on the phone and Nell could only imagine their grief and longing to get home, to be near their only daughter and their only grandchildren. As they emerged into the arrivals hall, Theresa Marshall, Beth's mum, collapsed as Nell went to greet them. People waiting at the airport stared at the scene. Reunions are normally such happy events but these were not tears of happiness and quickly people averted their eyes, intuiting that this was a private moment that they had no right to share in. They had lost everything in that one phone call and no words could ever console them. They visited Tom briefly, now their only connection to their previously solid and normal life, but he hadn't been much help or solace to them. He looked gaunt and unshaven, and was hardly ready for visitors. He made a brave exception in their case and they all three cried and sat in stilted silence. They didn't stay very long. Nell made apologies on his behalf and assured them that they would always be welcome back in time, when Tom had sufficient strength again.

The 11th of February was a beautiful winter's day and exactly three weeks after the fateful day. It was biting cold but with brilliant sunshine bouncing off the frostbitten ground, it would doubtless fool people into thinking that spring had arrived early and even that a round of golf was a good idea. With the blinds still drawn, Tom sat in his bedroom, still clutching his boys' pyjamas and Beth's nightshirt. He had barely put them down since he had arrived home. He had hardly left the house either. He wore the dark suit that Nell had left out for him, still in its dry-cleaning plastic. Next to it was a brand-new white shirt which Nell had ironed, and a black tie that he had owned since university. His shoes felt too big as he slipped his feet into them. He peered into the mirror that ran the length of the wall on the way into their dressing room. Beth had insisted on a full-length mirror and he hadn't objected, allowing her free reign on all the finer design points of the house. Their walk-in closet off the dressing room was like a small clothes shop, with sections for formal wear, casual and sports clothes. Since the accident, Tom had endlessly run his hands over the rails, recalling Beth and how beautiful she looked in each item. He didn't know what he would do with it all. He had heard of people keeping personal items of loved ones forever, or was he just imagining that he had? He didn't know. He didn't want to think what he would do with the physical reminders of his wife and his children. He pulled his jacket sleeves down out of habit rather than for any practical reason. The suit fitted him perfectly and so it should, having been made for him. He looked at himself in Beth's mirror and he saw only her, wearing something beautiful: the peach dress she had worn to his company ball with her hair tied up and a string of pearls he had bought for her in the Seychelles. And then his mind wandered and he couldn't avoid the haunting image of Beth now in a box somewhere and the purpose of his day ahead. He swallowed hard. Today was going to be the most difficult day of his life.

Downstairs in the kitchen was a nervous and awkward gathering of people, most of whom hadn't seen Tom since the accident. Nell knew that Tom would feel uncomfortable at seeing them all and listening to their stilted and difficult expressions of sorrow. Ted and Theresa, Beth's parents had just arrived and were doing their best also, but were clearly struggling. Two caterers worked quickly and quietly as Nell glanced anxiously at her watch. The first of the cars would be arriving soon to take family and friends before the hearses arrived, followed by the car for Tom and herself. That was the only thing that Tom had stipulated for the day: that he wanted to travel to the church with Nell and nobody else, and that he was happy for people to return to the house afterwards for a wake. Nell kissed her husband, Jonathan, and hurried him along towards the front door and the fleet of waiting cars.

'Nell, you've done brilliantly,' he said, hugging her briefly as he left her fussing over her hair and feeling silly for doing so.

The last funeral she and her brother had attended together was their mother's. Beth was pregnant with the twins at the time. Nell closed her eyes and pressed her temples gently. It was going to be an awful day for everyone but an unbearable one for Tom. She looked up the beautiful staircase, the centrepiece of the enormous hallway that the architect had pompously called his signature. She called softly up to her brother and was relieved to see him emerge from his room. He must have been watching the cars coming and going and he knew that it was time to leave.

He looked handsome but his strong, closely shaven jaw quivered and his large brown eyes blinked heavily under the obvious strain. His thick hair was almost dry and the grey specs across his temples and ears seemed to have spread a little or were certainly more prominent than she had noticed before. Brother and sister considered each other a moment. He descended the staircase and looked over her shoulder, through the large leaded and bowed window at the waiting hearses, each with a coffin. Nell stepped forward and they embraced.

St Pius's didn't look like it was going to be big enough to cope, as car after car negotiated the narrow country lane running along the cemetery up to the old eighteenth-century church that had been built without any concessions for cars or where to park them. Michael had negotiated with the local farmer to open his field as an impromptu car park. And even then, some cars had to improvise parking spaces of their own along the lane. Michael scanned the congregation gathered outside the church, huddling from the cold and shifting about to remain in the few weakening beams of winter sunshine. Given the circumstances, things had proceeded well so far and he gestured his approval over at Marcus Holt, the head of Artemis. *The Daily Express* – a newspaper specialising in grief – had got hold of Tom's story and was going to print until Michael, with some help from a friendly high court judge, had prevented them from doing so. Further prying eyes had also to be suppressed or deterred but after the funeral, the story would fade and Michael reasoned that he could worry a little less. The story had been reported in the trade press but with no photos and only a simple explanation that Tom Harper was taking time away from the running of Tel-Com while he recovered. A security firm had been brought in to sweep the grounds for any hacks with long lenses and also to discreetly vet the congregation as they arrived. All was in order. All that was needed now was the arrival of Tom and his family.

Father O'Brien hadn't seen his church so full for a very long time, perhaps ever, as the organist began Mozart's familiar funeral cortege and he processed slowly up the aisle. The congregation stood in absolute silence as the coffin bearers finally arrived at steps to the altar, closely followed by Nell and Tom walking arm in arm. All eyes were on them, wondering how Tom could be coping. He didn't avoid eye contact but he didn't seek it out either, acknowledging people as he spotted them in his peripheral vision. Father O'Brien waited for a similar acknowledgement from him so that he could begin what would be the most difficult address of his forty-year clerical career.

Father O'Brien glanced briefly at the congregation before he began.

'In the name of the Father and of the Son, and of the Holy Spirit, Amen. Welcome to all of you to this church, the church of St Pius. On behalf of Tom and Nell, I thank you all for coming here today to pay your respects and demonstrate your love and kinship for the Harper family – Beth, Daniel, Luke and Jack – in what are truly terrible circumstances.' The priest paused for a moment to gather his composure and to allow everyone else a moment also. 'At times such as this and during the last three weeks, every single person in this church, including myself, will have questioned the very existence of a God. And if there is a God, then what kind of a God is He to let something like this happen? To let this beautiful mother and her children perish in this cruel way? This is an understandable and terrifying question, and a question which is frequently and inadequately answered by the fact that God works in mysterious ways. But this isn't answer enough for us here today because what has happened to this family is not mysterious; it is tragic...'

The priest looked up once again. There was utter silence in the church.

'...but sadly, today, I don't have a better answer for any of you either. I wish that I did. But the truth is that no one amongst us can explain why such a thing could have happened. But I put it to you also, that as human beings we need the presence of God. To know that there is something greater than us and especially at times like this, to feel that a mightier help is at hand. And that our God's help is needed and that it starts to work here today. So, I encourage you to consider that judging God or blaming God is not the way to occupy your thoughts now. These are not the thoughts that will help and sustain Tom or his family, Nell, Ted and Theresa, and nor Beth or her boys either. So, I ask you to pray in whatever way you know, to whomever or whatever God is your God, both for the future of Tom and his family being buried here today and for ourselves and for our own place in this kingdom on earth and beyond. Let us pray.'

Of all the advice given to Nell in the lead up to the funeral, either professional or amateur, the one thing that did become clear was that there was no consensus or agreement on what part Tom should play in the service. Some argued that he should give a eulogy and that he would regret it if he didn't. Others advised firmly against. This was Nell's instinct and although she had raised the matter on a few occasions with Tom, he was uncommunicative and she hadn't managed to get a definite response. And so, it was left open. In the car on the way to the church, she had gently reminded him that he was doing a reading. Just a short passage from St Mark's Gospel, and that it didn't matter if he didn't feel able to do so. Michael was always on hand.

Nell allowed herself a little smile as Tom approached the pulpit for his reading. She should have known. Early in her childhood, she had established that it was far easier and more agreeable to be proud of her brother rather than jealous, something she continued into adulthood. Tom read the words of St Mark without faltering and then looked up at the congregation, picking out a few specific faces. He then removed a sheet of folded paper from his breast pocket and carefully laid it on the cold stone lectern. He had written a eulogy. Nell clenched her jaw. Of course, he had written a eulogy. Of course, he was going to speak.

'Thank you,' Tom began, his vision blurring such that he couldn't make out his own words. He blinked quickly and rubbed his left eye with his hand. 'Thank you all for coming here today.' He smiled and paused again to gather himself and to think about what he had just said. 'That might seem like a silly thing to say, my saying thank you for you being here. I am sure that none of you feel a need to be thanked, and that you all wanted to be here, for me and for my family. But, nonetheless, I wanted to say thank you because I wanted all of you to be here today with me and with Beth and with our boys: Daniel, Luke and Jack. But I also wanted to say thank you for the roles that you played in my family's life and for helping to make their lives so full and so happy – and for the roles that many of you will continue to play in my life, alone now, without my family.

Nell held her handkerchief to her face. She could hear other sobs from behind her. Sitting beside Jonathan, she clutched his hands tightly. Tom too could hear and feel the grief and he felt the need to pause again for everyone, himself included.

'All of us in this church are struggling with what has happened. And for some of us, things will never be the same again.' Tom glanced quickly and shared a moment with Beth's parents. Her mum looked utterly broken, her face pinched in pain. The loss too much for her, clutching at her husband's arm who was sitting ram-rod straight, staring proudly at his son-in-law, his eyes burning red and his face wet with tears. They knew how much Tom loved their daughter and how much he loved them for creating her.

'...and we shouldn't need to pretend otherwise so that we

appear brave and stoic. Because I am confident that anyone who knew Beth and was a friend to any of my boys will not be able to forget them and nor will they want to. I'm sure that many of you have been sending me messages and offering your time and support in whatever way you can, to which I haven't responded, but please understand that I am grateful whether you hear from me or not. But now I would like to say a much greater thank you – an impossible thank you – to my family, to my wife Beth and to our boys.'

Tom looked at the four coffins laid out in front of him. He hated the way that they were separated and was irked that protocol wouldn't allow for one big communal coffin. Jack and Luke's coffins were the smallest and he imagined his little men inside and alone. They were twins and they hated being separated and so this configuration seemed unduly cruel. His tears that were welling suddenly breached his defences and fell down his smooth face. His throat swelled and physically hurt. The priest stood up and was about to approach, until Tom stopped him with a gesture and quickly caught himself.

'Of course, we should not be here this morning because my family should still be with me. And this is a loss that will always remain with me. Because the only thing that really matters in my life is what I achieved with Beth. In every way, Beth was a beautiful woman, a friend to so many people here. A wonderful wife to me but most of all, she was an extraordinary mum to her boys and that is how I will remember her. And from this, if there can possibly be an upside, then it is this… that it is me who is left behind without our boys and not Beth; that Beth is still with her boys and that they are with their mum. Because, strong though she was, and impossibly difficult though this is, I will cope better than Beth could have done. Some of you will know that Beth was also brilliant. She gave up her career when Daniel was born and would have done so whether I had been successful or not. And it was the right thing to do, because she was a better mum to the boys than I could have been a dad, and I don't apologise for how unfashionable that makes me sound.'

The congregation sat spellbound in silence, save for the unavoidable sobs and sniffles which even Michael was contributing to, his stiff upper lip eventually buckling. He couldn't recall the last time that he had cried, not even at his dad's funeral – given his good innings and full life that he had had. This was different though, because, as well as for his own grief, he was moved with admiration for Tom, without doubt the only client whom he loved.

'And so, to my boys.' Tom continued. 'The world was quite literally their playground. But now their accomplishments will remain in the past which is a shame for us all and for the world, if Daniel had been allowed to continue...'

People seized on the comic allusion to Daniel's green interests and a small chuckle and much-needed relief spread through the tiny church.

'And I hope that your individual memories of my boys will remain vivid for you also, and that each of you will keep their memories alive. And to do that, I would like to ask a favour from each of you here today.' Tom looked up to make his appeal and this time, he took more time and could make more individual eye contact with people, who each felt privileged for just the slightest of moments. He particularly noticed the school friends in their smart uniforms with their parents, teachers and their headmaster. Now addressing the young boys in particular, Tom went on.

'Please... if you would, I'd like each of you here today to write down something about each of my boys: something perhaps that is unique to you and to your friendship.' He faltered a little and wiped his eyes as he noticed a tiny boy sitting in the first pew. He didn't know his name but he must have been a friend of one of his twins and so he addressed him directly. 'If you were Jack's friend, or Luke's...'

The little boy reacted, his eyes flashing at the mention of their names.

'...or probably both? Then write down something about them. You can get your mum and dad to help you. Write something down about them, something that you and my boys did together...' Tom was openly crying now and needed to use his handkerchief for the first time. It would have been perfectly understandable if he had stopped at this point but he couldn't. This was the most important part of what he had to say and the only chance he would have to say it and so, he continued. 'It could be anything: an incident or something that was just said – good or bad. It might even be an argument you had, just so long as it is real and unique and not just something you've made up. Please write it down and keep it somewhere safe. And from time to time, get it out and look at it and recall the incident. Because that would make me happy to know that that memories of my boys are being kept alive. And I hope that this will help me, because I am heartbroken. I am truly broken and some people here today are going to need to put me back together again.' He glanced up at Nell as she still clung to her husband. 'And knowing that you'll remember Beth and my boys is a good place to start. Thank you.'

He folded the piece of paper, which he hadn't consulted once, and walked the few steps from the pulpit, past his family to the front pew. Jonathan broke Nell's grip and shifted along so that Tom could sit next to her, his quivering hand searching for hers. He squeezed her hand tightly and she could feel the energy and emotion coursing through his body. As he sat down, his body slumped, limp with exhaustion, as if it had been gearing up for something difficult and now that it was complete, he was spent. Nell squeezed his hand back. She tried to appear strong to reassure him, but she was scared and fretful.

Tom didn't attend the wake and dragged his exhausted body upstairs as soon as he arrived home. He had greeted everyone at the church after the service. He had smiled and shaken their hands, young and old, and said 'thank you' and 'of course' repeatedly.

'Well done, Nell,' Michael comforted her in a quiet moment in the kitchen. She had hoped that Tom would be at the wake but understood why he wasn't. He would have enjoyed seeing that everyone had been given a Fruit Bowl.

'What's with the fruit juice?' Michael asked.

Nell shook her head. 'It was my idea; silly really. Beth used to make it each morning for Tom and the boys. She called it the Fruit Bowl.'

Michael raised an eyebrow.

'It's a long story. Tom and I used to laugh about it. I'll let him tell you.'

'Of course.'

'I'm so proud of him, Michael.'

Michael just shrugged. 'He's a remarkable man.'

Nell nodded. He'll need to be. Michael made to move.

'He knows where I am, so I'm not going to call him for a day or two. But before I do, should you need anything, anything at all, day or night, you know where I am.'

'Thank you.'

Tom lay on his bed. It was dark outside and he could hear the last of the guests leaving. He was relieved that the funeral was over, but devastated also. It felt final, like a departure from his old life and the start of the unknown. He remembered reading somewhere, that the bereaved often enjoy the funeral; enjoy being the focus of everyone's attention and concern; people they hadn't seen for ages suddenly reappearing to offer their love and to express their sympathy. But Tom hadn't experienced this sensation at all. One thing that he had been warned about and he now understood to be true was that the immediate time after the funeral was the hardest of all. Being left alone in a house full of memories. He had asked Nell and Naisi to leave the house ostensibly as it was. None of the laundry had been washed, nor the boys' bedrooms tidied. The house was largely as they had left it that morning, as if they were on their way home, but of course they weren't. They were never coming home. And this was Tom's new life.

Exhausted, he closed his eyes and wondered whether he might be able to sleep properly now that the funeral was over. In the days since the accident, he honestly didn't think that he'd slept at all. His sleep patterns had altered dramatically and he now lay awake each night, unable to find much peace or any solace. Beth and the boys filled his mind wherever he went. And with the additional image of his family now in the freezing ground, Tom opened his eyes widely. There wasn't any prospect of him falling to sleep.

Chapter 6

Tom pounded up the flights of stairs to his city office. It was now almost three months since the accident and his first time back at work. He realised that he had to use the constants in his life as an anchor and that work was a useful distraction. He crashed heavily into the empty office lobby. He was much less tired than he expected, given that he still wasn't sleeping, hardly at all in fact. He slumped in his chair and waited for his screen to come to life and fill with numbers and icons. Usually this information would already be familiar to him, having studied it at home and then again in the car on the journey in. But, this morning, he hadn't consulted anything and nor was he inclined to do so now. The screen blurred and he just sat in silence. It was just after 6.30 a.m. People would be arriving soon enough and the thought of seeing colleagues again suddenly made him nervous.

The date of Tom's return to work had been much debated by Jeremy and his colleagues. Jeremy didn't know and hadn't pushed it with Tom, and Michael too was vague about it. When he's good and ready but the sooner the better was the consensus. But this bright April morning, Tom had taken everyone by surprise. James was the first to arrive and was startled to see the lights on in his office. As he approached, he quickly ran over what he might say in his mind.

'Hey, Tom. It's great to see you.'

Tom looked up rather vacantly. After a moment, he nodded 'Hey, James, thanks.'

'How are you?' James asked, immediately wishing he hadn't. Tom just shrugged, adding to the sense of awkwardness. He didn't look great. He looked exhausted, his eyes ringed with black and his cheeks sunken from what looked like a large loss of weight.

'It's been quiet without you: much less fun,' James staggered on. 'The Brazilian deal went through. I know that Jeremy emailed you...'

Still Tom didn't register. The office had hoped that this enormous South American coup might have buoyed him and catalysed his comeback. But they heard nothing from him and he didn't look very excited about it now.

Later that morning, Jeremy sat with Tom in his office, to welcome him back of course but also to brief him on developments and to review the future. But Tom was uncommunicative and the atmosphere was strained. It felt awkward and inappropriate for Jeremy, strategizing for profit with a man who had so much and yet had nothing at all. Tom pulled at his face and stared out of the window at something that had caught his eye. The pair of peregrine falcons that were resident at St Paul's perhaps or a plane on its way off to somewhere far flung?

'So, going forward then; how do you want to play this?' Jeremy asked, feeling that he needed to force the issue, but still Tom didn't respond.

'Tom?' Jeremy called, his voice slightly raised, startling Tom who just shook his head.

Jeremy took a moment.

'Tom, if you feel ready to come back, then that's great, but if not...' Jeremy trailed off unwilling to say anything he might regret. Tom stared at a picture on his desk. Jeremy couldn't see which, but he could guess. He averted his eyes downward and looked under Tom's desk. He was startled to see that Tom was wearing a pair of running shoes.

The next two days followed a similar pattern. Tom sat in his office and attended a couple of internal meetings, and it was apparent to everyone that he should not be back at work. He was distracted and unable to focus and in stark contrast to the man they knew, his presence was now a hindrance. And with each day, he appeared to be getting worse, not better, which rather dented the universal 'give him time' argument. Unintentionally, he was making his colleagues feel awkward. No one knew what to say to him or how to behave. There was no right thing to say. Should they be sombre or upbeat? Neither felt appropriate and in to the second week of his reappearance, Jeremy was aware that Tom was a problem that he needed to address.

The following day, a meeting was scheduled with a series of fund managers that Tom would ordinarily have chaired, but in the current circumstances, Jeremy didn't want him to attend. It was 10 a.m. already and Tom hadn't yet arrived at work and Jeremy hoped that he wouldn't. His face fell then when he saw Tom push through the entrance door, sweating and out of breath as usual. Jeremy sighed as he watched his boss stagger through the open-plan office as colleagues averted their eyes. Jeremy picked up the phone. He needed to speak with Michael Millhouse. He would understand and more importantly, he would know what to do.

Tom insisted on attending the meeting, his first external meeting since the accident. Jeremy quietly relented and assured his colleagues that this situation was not set to continue. At the meeting, Tom's appearance hadn't helped and his contributions were confused and inappropriate. Jeremy could feel the confidence ebbing from the room every time he spoke and he contacted every client afterwards to apologise and to give his assurances also. Then he called Michael again and insisted on a hastily convened meeting that very afternoon, having been fobbed off earlier in the day.

In Michael's office, along from Liverpool Street Station, he listened carefully as Jeremy explained the situation. He paused in his customary manner once Jeremy had finished.

'Right,' Michael began. 'Just so I'm clear? Tom's behaviour is erratic and possibly unhelpful…'

'No, Michael, not possibly. Definitely, I'm afraid.'

'Sure. But I'm less clear on what you want to do about it?'

Jeremy bristled, irritated that Michael was playing the ignorant card when it was perfectly clear what he was asking for.

'Because it sounds to me that you might want Tom to resign.'

Jeremy reacted quickly. 'No, that's not what I'm suggesting…'

'Well, good. That is good to hear, because this is the firm that Tom founded.'

'Yes, thank you, Michael,' Jeremy snapped angrily, 'but I am well aware of this because I was bloody well there with him when he did.'

Michael took the hit which he probably deserved.

'We want him back at work, of course we do. Jesus, why wouldn't we? It's what I want more than anything because it's me having to fill his bloody shoes.'

Michael nodded, feeling a little guilty now for being obtuse.

'But not in his current state of mind,' Jeremy continued. 'What we need is the old Tom back at work.'

'Yes, quite, but therein lies the problem,' Michael agreed. 'How long will it take for the old Tom to re-emerge, if at all?'

'What? You don't think...'

'I don't know. I've talked to his doctors and to his various counsellors. But there's no certainty about anything. Psychologists? They're like bloody economists.'

Jeremy smiled ruefully at the reference which reminded him of Tom before the accident and he looked at Michael, appealing to him to understand.

'Michael, the real problem here is – and I apologise if this sounds callous, but the reality is...' he paused for a moment. 'Only Tom lost his family. No one else did. And whilst we all care deeply about him and we all want to help him; people's sympathies have limits. And these limits are normally financial.'

Jeremy glanced up at a sober Michael.

'Tom's family isn't coming back and there isn't anything any of us can do. But people care about their own families, too. And so, they need to worry about their numbers and frankly, so do I.'

Michael was pensive, listening to a petition that was upsetting but perfectly reasonable.

'Because, Michael, you know how competitive –'

Michael now had heard enough and held up his hand in surrender, which came as a great relief for Jeremy.

'But of course, as soon as he starts to recover...'

Michael nodded. He knew the rest. 'OK, Jeremy, I understand and I appreciate your candour.'

'Thank you.' Jeremy hoped he was thanking Michael for what he was agreeing to do. It was implicit and didn't need explaining. 'I have some papers that I need him to sign anyway so I'll have a word with him. I don't know quite what I'll say, but I'll put it to him.'

Chapter 7

With his lungs bursting, Tom pressed on, sprinting as fast as he could, crying out with the pain of his exertion. He fixed his attention on a tree in the distance and speeded up, his knees pounding as his whole body screamed in pain and for him to stop. Finally, he crashed to the ground, rolling onto his back, his chest heaving in huge gulps of air to ail his stricken body. His hands covered his eyes and raked at his sweat-soaked hair.

Michael thanked Naisi and made himself comfortable in Tom's warm and chic drawing room.

'Do you know how long he'll be?' he enquired.

Naisi shook her head awkwardly. Tom was usually a man of such routine but there was no telling anymore about anything that he did, especially with his increasingly regular and manic runs.

'Sometime, he very long. Sometime, can be two hour,' Naisi said with alarm in her voice. She clearly disapproved and was worried about him too.

Michael looked at his watch and wasn't best pleased. When he had called to make the appointment, Tom had been evasive and distracted but he had been insistent and managed to pin him down to a time, even agreeing to come to his house. He fingered a couple of his client files but he couldn't really concentrate on them because he didn't know how long he had; a little like starting to read a long article in a doctor's waiting room. He looked at his watch and wondered whether he should call Tom's mobile but decided not to. Since his meeting with Jeremy last week, matters concerning Tom's behaviour had rather come to a head. Angus, his accountant, had been to see him on a similar mission, forcing Michael to act immediately. Angus was particularly concerned at some of Tom's recent financial transactions; amongst them he had liquidated most of his personal equity portfolio and requested that Angus set up a charitable covenant for a local children's hospice. Nothing wrong with philanthropy, but there was also news from his personal broker of some extraordinary financial trades that Tom had recently made.

Tom was now back on his feet again and running hard, faster and faster in order to reach complete and utter exhaustion. It was a wet morning and his crashing through the puddles, not to mention his time lying on the sodden ground, meant that he was soaked through and covered in mud when he burst through the heavy wrought iron gates of his house. He spotted Michael's BMW and scowled, recalling that he had agreed to a meeting. He nodded at Michael's chauffeur and registered the shock on his face. He had met him before but he couldn't remember his name. He pushed at his mighty front door. It had taken four strong men to hang it, as heavy as it was, and now it glided to and fro so effortlessly and closed with a reassuringly expensive click. Michael was quickly up and out of his chair to greet Tom in his own hallway. Given the state of him, it was fortunate that it was tiled and not carpeted.

'Bloody hell, man,' Michael said, unable to hide his shock at Tom's appearance. 'What are you doing, training for the marathon?' he added: an attempt at some levity which failed badly.

'Michael, I forgot you were coming.'

Not even a hello, then.

'It's a magician I need, Michael, not a lawyer. Know any magicians?'

Michael smiled as best he could, cross with himself that he hadn't visited sooner.

'Look, I'm in no hurry... so you go and have a shower and freshen up. Whatever?' Michael said helpfully, but Tom ignored him and guided him back into the sitting room.

'No, that's OK. I'm running again this afternoon anyway.'

Immediately, Michael resolved to meet with Nell as soon as he had finished here with Tom. His phone beeped: it was Angus again, probably with more worrying news.

Tom slumped heavily into his beautiful cream sofa, seemingly uncaring about leaving muddy wet stains. He hadn't taken his shoes off either and they had left a tell-tale trail across the oak floor. Naisi was certainly earning her money and was evidently under some considerable strain watching her boss disintegrate before her own grieving eyes. She had a worn expression as she entered the room with a pot of tea and one tall glass of fruit juice, presumably for Tom. Tom looked at the documents Michael had placed on the table, each immaculately typed and with little yellow stickers protruding from the sides where Tom's scrawl was needed.

'Nell's gone home, I hear?'

Tom sighed heavily, a viscous line of spittle that he hadn't bothered to remove dripping from his chin. 'I think it's best.'

'And, how are you?' Michael asked, feeling silly for doing so because the answer was glaringly obvious. 'Getting very fit I see.'

Tom grinned. Both men knew that his running wasn't a quest for fitness.

'Stuff you want me to sign?'

Michael noted that he hadn't asked what the papers were, something he would never have done before the tragedy.

'And work? Jeremy tells me that you're back.'

Tom shifted his vision beyond Michael.

'He's worried about you,' Michael added.

'Is he?'

A moment passed between the two of them.

'Worried for me? Or worried about me?'

Michael didn't respond, which was an answer in itself.

'Well, you can tell him not to worry,' Tom said flatly. 'I'm through with work.'

It was an emphatic statement which took Michael by surprise and which Tom picked up on.

'It's the knowing I can't take,' Tom stated, his tired eyes now suddenly angry.

'I'm sorry?' Michael asked.

'People knowing about it: knowing what has happened to me but not knowing how to cope. Not knowing what to say or what to do.'

Michael nodded, understanding now and rebuking himself. 'They're all doing their best, I'm sure.'

'Yes, no doubt. But it's no good. It's not working. Not for me anyway.'

Michael sighed heavily.

'Do you say nothing or do you say sorry? And how long do you keep telling someone that you're sorry?' Tom asked rhetorically. There was no answer and although Michael tried to explain that his colleagues were also struggling with his loss and that they all wanted him to recover and get back to work, his words seemed hollow up against what Tom was facing.

Tom motioned for a pen. He wanted to sign whatever it was and get on with the rest of his day. It was an awkward moment for them both but Michael understood and he decided to leave the matters that Angus had raised with him for the time being.

Chapter 8

Tom tugged at his beard and stared at Agatha Rayner, counsellor to the stars. She had come highly recommended. She'd written books and had appeared on television, but what really marked her out was that she had counselled the young princes, William and Harry, after their mother's death. Her golden ticket because since then, the heartbroken and troubled rich had beaten a path to her expensive Hampstead door. But Tom wasn't convinced and his cynicism might well have been the obstacle to his accessing her healing powers. In truth, he was only there to satisfy Nell because she had arranged it for him, but their current session together had not gone well.

'It'll be the twins' birthday next week: the fifteenth.'

Agatha nodded. She never answered immediately and seldom asked questions; hers was more of a listening service. Great work if you can get it.

'Do you have anything planned?'

Tom ignored her. 'God, they were beautiful boys. But I expect you must hear that all the time? Every kid that ever dies, they're always beautiful and the life and soul of the party: the popular kid that everyone loved. Never the ugly kid, huh? Have you noticed that?'

Agatha didn't respond. She just sat there impassively, an empty vessel into which her client could pour his grief and anger.

'We were going to go to Portugal. We have a place there. I was going to play golf with the twins. Daniel didn't approve of golf, nor the villa. Apparently, the Algarve is a drought zone. Daniel was brilliant. Maybe, even a genius. I think that *genius* is overused, don't you?'

Still, Agatha didn't respond.

'Apparently, I'm a business genius,' Tom spat angrily.

Agatha nodded. Expressing anger was a good thing, signalling progress even. 'Are you sleeping any better?' she asked.

Tom looked at her, his eyes heavy and reddened. Der!

'And the medication?'

'Look, I don't want to sleep, OK, because if I do then I have to wake up and start all over again. I have to realise that it's all true and not just some hideous nightmare.' He closed his bloodshot eyes until his anger quelled. And then suddenly, he looked afraid and needy. 'Please...' he pleaded. '...when is this going to start getting easier?'

Agatha shifted awkwardly at such a definitive question.

'I know, you don't know, not really; no one does, right?' he asked.

And the pressure on her eased a little because he was right.

'But the thing is...' Tom leaned forward pulled at his beard again. 'If time is the great healer and all that? How come it's getting harder?'

Agatha felt the spotlight again. 'Tom, what you're asking me is – are you ever going to recover? And the answer is, yes.'

Tom didn't look convinced.

'But that is not to say that things will ever be the same. Recovery might just be a place where you can accept what has happened and are able to cope with it. But things will always be different for you now.'

Tom looked at her gratefully and nodded. 'That's right, what you just said.'

'But this doesn't mean –'

'No, no, it's OK.' Tom was keen to reassure her. 'It's a good thing because this way I won't ever forget them. Because this pain I have is a reminder of them.'

Agatha protested. 'But this pain is hurting you as well.'

Tom laughed at this and nodded his head vigorously. 'Oh, yeah, it hurts. Jesus, it hurts all bloody day, like it's in my blood, coursing right through me.'

Agatha reverted to silence again. The wall clock chimed and she was as relieved as Tom.

Chapter 9

An apprehensive Nell sat in Michael's office with its grand furniture and fresh coffee, neither of which offered much comfort. Michael let her air her worries and fears about her brother. It rather played into his hands for the drastic move he was about to suggest and the reason for convening this meeting.

'All he does is bloody well run – middle of the night, all day long – so he's completely exhausted and yet he still can't sleep. According to Naisi, he grabs an hour at most and then he's off again.'

Michael shared her worries and it only galvanised his determination to step in.

'He's lost heaps of weight and he looks awful. He's shouting at Naisi, which he's never done before; scaring her so that she wants to move out.'

Michael held his hand up in his customary way. 'Nell, I'm as worried as you are, and not just about his health.'

Nell straightened. 'What do you mean?'

'Well, frankly, I'm worried about his state of mind and in particular, what impact this could have on his means.'

Nell was shocked and a little offended. It was vulgar that Michael should concern himself with money, which seemed to be the least of his problems. 'Michael, I'm surprised at you. Do you really think that's what's important here?'

'Yes, Nell. I'm afraid it is.'

'Right, well, given that Tom is clearly inordinately wealthy, I really don't think –'

'Nell, please…'

Nell wiped a tear from her face and looked to Michael for an explanation.

'His wealth might seem to be a crude concern, but nonetheless - as wealthy as he is, he won't remain so if he continues on as he is.'

Michael now had her full attention. 'What do you mean?'

Michael breathed out heavily. 'Tom has been making some quite alarming financial decisions.'

Nell gestured for him to continue.

'Charitable contributions…'

'Right. But he's always been generous –'

Michael interrupted by placing a sheet of paper in front of her. Nell didn't need to read it. She just saw a figure at the bottom of the page and it stopped her immediately.

'And there are others of equal amounts.'

Nell shook her head with worry.

'Plus, recently he's made some disastrous financial trades with some terrible losses – cavalier plays, equities, foreign exchange – trades he would never normally have made. Which makes Angus and I wonder if they haven't been deliberate?'

Nell shot him a look.

'What do you mean?'

Michael shrugged. 'You tell me?'

'Michael. You're his lawyer, you always have a theory.'

'Well, as a matter of fact I do. But it's not pleasant, I'm afraid.'

'Well, what is it?' Nell snapped.

'I have an idea that Tom might be trying to punish himself.'

Nell heard the words but couldn't fully grasp their meaning.

'Because maybe he's feeling guilty?'

Nell looked angry now on behalf of her brother. 'Guilty? Why? What the hell has he got to feel guilty about?'

Michael tried to remain calm but it wasn't easy, given what he was about to suggest. 'Nell, please, understand that I'm just theorising here. But Tom did mention to me, quite frequently actually, that he wanted to spend more time with his boys.'

'Right. And don't all dads?'

Michael ignored this. 'So, perhaps now that this possibility has been taken from him. He's feeling guilty that he might have been a better dad.'

'How dare you?' Nell raged. 'Tom was a great dad and his boys loved him!'

'Yes, of course, I know, but that's not the point, is it?'

'Well, what is your bloody point because your theorising is lost on me.'

Michael bit at his thumb. 'We both know that Tom was a great dad. Of course, he was. But maybe Tom doesn't realise this anymore. That's my point. We have no idea what he is thinking or feeling right now and he's certainly not of sound mind, you've said so yourself.'

Nell nodded: a small concession and enough for Michael to clutch to.

'I don't know; maybe he associates his wealth with the reason he saw too little of his boys. Or maybe he just wants to punish himself because somehow, he feels responsible for their deaths, which is completely irrational, but maybe not to him. And it is only his perspective that matters right now. And why I must protect him. We both must.'

Nell held her hands together and considered these words.

'Whatever his confused thinking, the fact is, he is squandering his wealth, which is against his best interests, and he will definitely not thank me if I allow him to continue. Far bigger fortunes than Tom's have evaporated.'

Nell nodded.

'And when he is of sound mind again, then of course, he can do what he wants with his money. But until then, as his lawyer and his friend, I would be negligent if I allow him to continue.'

The penny finally dropped for Nell and she looked at him, wide-eyed. 'And that's why you've invited me here, to stop him?'

Michael gestured his agreement.

'Because I'm his kin and his executor?'

'Precisely. In the event of his passing or being considered unfit –'

Nell shook her head, immediately uncomfortable. 'But you'll need medical evidence...' She stopped. From Michael's expression, she could see that he had already spoken with his doctor. 'Oh, Michael, you haven't?'

Michael snapped now. 'Nell, I'm sorry if you don't approve but what would you rather happen here? That he just gives it all away?

And the house too? He's had estate agents around already?'

A reckoning now hit Nell. 'So, what are you suggesting? To deny him access to his own money?'

'Unless you have a better idea,' he answered curtly, annoyed now at her tone.

'Well, for how long?'

'I don't know? That's what all of us want to know. Until he's back, at least to a point that we both feel comfortable to trust him…' His voice trailed off.

Nell rubbed her face as she considered her bleak options.

'But I can't do it without your approval.'

Nell shook her head. She was tired and upset, but she could see his reasoning. Her incredibly capable little brother now needed to be protected.

At eight miles, Tom thrust his arms above his head and began to scream as he settled into one of his lung-bursting sprints, his teeth bared in pain and his head flailing from side to side. He made a disturbing sight to anyone watching and this early spring morning an elderly lady walking her dog stared at the seemingly deranged man charging through the park. Instinctively, the woman clutched at her handbag. Just the presence of the man and his mania was unsettling. With his lungs already straining, Tom pushed on even harder towards his target, a familiar oak tree, at some eighty metres ahead. The dog walker probably considered whether to call one of the emergency services. An ambulance certainly and possibly even the police because he looked like he'd escaped from somewhere. She was a good distance from him, a safe distance, but given the rate he was running, he could make up the ground between them in no time and she anxiously fingered the mobile phone that her daughter had insisted she carry. Some thirty metres short of the tree, Tom's legs gave out and he collapsed heavily to the ground, relieved that he had achieved his point of complete physical exhaustion. His stomach heaved and quickly he forced himself onto his side as he retched painfully as bile dripped from his mouth. In the near distance, the old lady had gathered her spaniel in her arms and was quickly making for her car. Tom spat on the ground, his throat burning as he stared at the grey sky above with absolutely nothing in his mind. Watching a film, reading a book, conducting a conversation; it didn't matter – nothing could distract him and empty his mind better than being physically exhausted. He was literally running himself into the ground, sometimes in the middle of the night, and physically pounding his conscious mind into submission. Quelling his mind because it was infected with his unbearable sense of loss. As he lay on the ground, he waited for the cold dew to seep through the various layers of his clothing and to chill his skin. The cold felt good as it attacked the small of his back but it didn't remain cold for long: either until his body became accustomed to the cold or the heat of his body had warmed the water; he didn't know which. He reflected on the irony that his frenzied exercising was possibly extending his life expectancy which would prolong his time apart from his family.

As he got stronger, he needed to run further distances to fully exhaust himself and so he had taken to adding star jumps, boxing and press-ups to his regime, anything to speed up the process of allowing him to forget who he was.

Tom rolled onto his stomach and pulled his legs up under him so that he rested on his knees and then onto his haunches, before finally springing aggressively to his feet and charging off in the direction of the car park. The elderly lady had been observing but was now frantically fighting to open her car door.

Chapter 10

Tom never revisited his counsellor again, as running became his main coping mechanism despite the disapproval of Nell and Naisi, but it wasn't long before the wooded area flanking his house became off limits to him. As he recovered in the parkland one day, he got chatting with a dog walker: an attractive woman; she was a teacher in Reading but had been signed off work for more than a year with stress at having been verbally assaulted by a pupil. Unperturbed by his manic running, she had approached him which at first, he had enjoyed. He liked the fact that she knew nothing about him, but on meeting her for the third and fourth time he suspected that their encounters were not just coincidence. She started to look more made up and perfumed. She was obviously lonely and began sharing personal details, which made him uncomfortable. He certainly did not reciprocate. Tom felt embarrassed and worried that he might have misled her. And he felt disloyal to Beth as well, so he would need to find another place to run and exhaust himself.

Another advantage of running was that it got him out of his house and away from the memories it held for him in every room and with every object. The school mugs that the boys had decorated and the cracked one that Jack had dropped, chipping the marble floor into the bargain. Tom had shouted at him when it happened, but replacing the tile was now struck from his to-do list. The tile and the memory would both remain. The garden was a particularly cruel place with its swings and tree house. Tom couldn't decide whether the vegetable plot that Beth and the boys had sewn was a good or a bad thing. When the carrot shoots first appeared, he was pleased he could nurture the plants, but then he worried that the crop might perish just like his family had done. So, late one night, he dug the whole plot up before charging off on yet another run. Dirty and inappropriately dressed in a smart shirt, chinos and trainers, he cut an unusual figure for a recreational jogger and he gained the attention of a group of boys hanging outside a chip shop. It was a little after midnight as he charged towards the canal at full speed. He looked as if he was running away from something, which he was, but the boys could never have known what. Finally, he slowed and came to a stop under the stone bridge, bending over to begin his recovery. The kids smiled at the prospect of easy pickings.

Tom could sense that he was not alone as the youths fanned out around him and instinctively, he understood their intentions, so he didn't look up.

'What happened, mate? D'you miss your train?' one of them asked with a derisive air.

Tom heard a cackle of laughter. A scruffy boy stared down at him. He was wearing a tight pair of velour type trousers and a sleeveless puffer jacket over a hooded top. Tom faced the youth without a flicker of fear but plenty of anger. The boy cleared his throat and spat menacingly on the ground, as if marking his territory.

'What you got for me bro?' The young man asked with a nonchalant sneer, a question Tom chose to ignore, forcing the boy to react. He was committed now and had his crew to impress. He looked left and right to make sure that he was OK to proceed and then took on a more menacing tone. He was sixteen, possibly older, but still much too young to have a neck full of tattoos.

'Gimme what you got, bro. Seriously, fam, gimme your fucking wallet? The boy stepped forward and shouted in Tom's face, 'What, cunt? You deaf?'

Tom instinctively shoved the kid backwards. His face was covered in the boy's spittle, which he didn't bother to wipe off. The kid sneered and grabbed into his pocket to produce a small blade, which glistened faintly under the gaze of the street lamp. Knife crime fills the news bulletins and now it visited Tom personally. But still, Tom didn't flinch and the first doubts appeared in his assailant's mind. Tom hated him. He loathed his presence and his cavalier malevolence. He wondered how many other people he had assaulted and he hated that he was alive and that his boys had been taken. And then he saw how this could perhaps serve him. How this miscreant kid might even do something useful.

Without another thought, Tom stepped towards the kid and the blade. He grabbed at either side of his own shirt and snapped it open, buttons firing off in all directions. He stepped forward again, pushing his exposed chest at his assailant.

'Go on then, tough guy!' Tom shouted, thrusting his pained face into his personal space.

Some of his gang immediately began backing away. There's was a straightforward mugging crew and certainly hadn't factored in murder as part of their strategy. They all backed away further.

The boy with the knife was the last to leave, trying to salvage some seniority at least.

'You're a fucking loon, man,' he snarled as a parting shot, turning to join his crew. Tom watched them leave. The cool air wrapped around his bare chest and made him shudder. Adrenalin coursed through his body and a tear ran down his face. He felt ashamed because what if the youth had been more brazen and fulfilled his request. Losing his own life had some appeal but without ruining the life of some lost delinquent also.

Predictably, Christmas was difficult. On Tom's insistence, Naisi returned to Brazil for the holiday. He assured her that he could cope and that he would call her if he needed to. He spent Christmas day with Nell, Jonathan and their children and Nell thought to invite Beth's parents as well, which was a good idea on paper but made the occasion even more strained. Tom lavished his nephew and niece with presents and strained to control himself when little Ella asked why her big cousins had left her.

Nell left out some clean towels and a brand-new shaving kit for him, as a hint for him to freshen up his appearance. He had run in the morning without showering afterwards and his wild and unkempt hair added to the look of a man who had all but given up. He was too thin and barely touched his dinner.

Nell drove him home on Boxing Day and was alarmed to see the state of the house. The absence of Naisi was plain to see. The bedrooms were untouched but the kitchen and drawing room were chaotic and she quickly got to work clearing things up. She expected that he would protest but he didn't even seem to notice and busied himself with finding something or other. Nell wanted to say something but managed not to and then she heard the front door shut. Through the kitchen window, she caught him disappearing off on yet another run. He had barely said a word to her all morning.

Into February, a year on from the accident, and things continued to spiral downwards. Most surprising and worrying to those closest to him, Tom made no mention of the new financial arrangements. Michael reasoned that matters might even revert to normal in due course without Tom ever knowing. With Nell's persuasion, Naisi had returned from Brazil and quickly wished that she hadn't. She was harrowed to see that Tom looked even worse on her return as his depression subsumed him. He had taken to not bothering to dress appropriately, even walking around the house almost naked; cutting a pitiful figure with his emaciated frame.

One morning, she heard the front door close after him and his heavy panting and moaning in the hallway, another gruelling run completed. After five minutes or so, she heard him drag himself off the floor and into the kitchen and sure enough, she heard the juicing machine crank up. That was practically her only use to him now, to buy large quantities of fruit and vegetables for him to juice. There was hardly any washing to do and she wasn't allowed into any of the bedrooms. She would place his mail on the work surface each morning, which mostly he would ignore and then she would forward it to Michael. For some reason though, that morning, Tom did open his mail and Naisi heard him sobbing.

Tom slumped on a stool with his glass of juice. On the granite was the letter he had just read. He recalled his conversations with Beth about it: how they had argued at the time and how insistent she had been. And now she had been proved right of course. There it was in black and white. Only, she wasn't right, Tom raged to himself. She wasn't right at all; Beth was flat wrong. Tom snapped open his eyes and glared at the offending letter. This wasn't what he wanted at all. He ripped at the letter angrily, biting it and spewing pieces into the air. He leapt from his stool and grabbed at the jug of juice, hurling it at his Venetian glass screen, the central feature of their beautiful kitchen. The screen shattered, as did the jug, and shards of coloured glass and juice cascaded everywhere as he began to hurl heavy glass goblets at the floor, cracking the marble tiles and adding to the carnage. Naisi cowered in the hallway, peeping through the crack in the door, as Tom sobbed and yelled.

Chapter 11

Lotfus House was like so many preparatory schools: a large country house that had become too big to remain a residence and had either been donated or acquired cheaply for education. The pupils from Loftus went on to the public schools famous throughout the world and their illustrious alumni boasted the odd cabinet minister, famous actor and a smattering of distinguished medics and QCs. This Tuesday afternoon, pick-up was like any other: a procession of unnecessarily large vehicles driven by attractive mummies, snaking through the tree-lined avenue to the playground that was used as an impromptu car park. It was a pick-up that was ordinary in every sense but for the fact that, today, Tom Harper was also waiting to pick up his children.

Tom stared hard at the school door from where the children would emerge. He had run the seven miles to the school without giving much thought to how he would get his twins home. They certainly couldn't walk but it didn't matter; he'd figure it out. Perhaps one of the mums would give them all a lift. He was aware of attention being trained on him but he wasn't quite sure why. It appears people were avoiding his gaze or averting their eyes and even pretending to be engaged in conversations with each other. Indeed, all the mums now seemed to be in little huddles of rushed and earnest conversation. One particularly startled younger mum looked terrified as she grabbed at her mobile phone, and another ran off towards the school office. Tom observed it all with some curiosity. Something was going on but whatever it was, he didn't want to get involved.

Mothers continued to steal glances at Tom, who was barely recognisable, emaciated and wearing wet jogging trousers with a formal shirt, complete with cuff links.

'I'm picking up the boys today. Beth's busy.' He felt the need to call out towards a mum who had chanced a quick glance in his direction. Given how nervous she looked, he approached her tentatively.

'It's Toby, isn't it? Your lad's Toby?' he asked, as an image of a little blonde scrum-half popped into his head.

'Yes,' the woman managed.

'How is he? All right?' Tom asked, completely oblivious to the panic that he was causing.

'Yes, he's fine,' she barely croaked.

Being a small school, Loftus thrived on its parental involvement. The Harper boys had been popular pupils and equally, Beth had made some great friends amongst the other parents, and the accident had been a profound loss for them all and for the school. Many of the people present had been at the funeral and ordinarily would have been delighted to see Tom again, but none of them could have imagined that it would be in such circumstances.

Whoever had rushed to alert the headmaster had been too late. The old blue door flung open and a cheery Mrs Hall stood ahead of a bunch of excited children. She had taught each of the Harper children including Daniel who had now left and she knew the family well. She sensed immediately that something was awry and her sixth sense forced her to look to her left to the scruffy, gaunt man waiting expectantly. She did a cartoon-like double take when she finally registered who it was. Tom recognised her immediately and was now smiling and waving. Mrs Hall instantly understood the horror of the situation and she tried to hold the children back, but it wasn't possible. Children could see their mums or their au pairs and pushed passed her, clutching their book bags in front of them and art work destined for the recycling. Mostly, the school pick–up was a social gathering, a chance to catch up and to organise the calendar, but today no one wanted to linger for a chat and children were quickly gathered in and taken off to their cars. Tom kept his gaze firmly on the blue door, keen to see his twins the moment they emerged. They would be expecting their mum and no doubt, would be surprised and delighted to see him. The children were trickling out less frequently now and Tom was amused that his boys should be last. Probably kicking a ball about somewhere.

Mrs Hall looked around but could see no sign of the headmaster. She felt that she needed to do something and took a short step forward, smiling kindly at Tom.

'Mr Harper, hello...'

Tom smiled back.

'And, how are you?' She felt hopeless.

Tom looked at her and didn't answer. He looked over her shoulder at the blue door again – still no sign of his boys. Mrs Hall was now upon him and was beckoning him to accompany her, the way people do when they have something private to say. Tom resisted and the teacher glanced back. Where the hell was her boss? She was a tiny woman, less than five feet perhaps, and Tom looked down at her with a worried expression.

'Is everything alright?' he asked, making it clear that he wasn't moving. 'Is anything wrong?'

'It's just. We didn't expect you...'

'Oh...' Tom looked relieved. 'No, well, Beth normally does the pick-up but she's got something on today. I don't know what exactly; she didn't say...' His voice trailed off as he saw the alarm and fear registering on the teacher's face again. She kept glancing back at the school, as if looking for some help. A man was now running towards them, flanked by two other teachers. He looked familiar but Tom couldn't place him. It was the headmaster. Mr Monk was in his fifties, a kindly man with a portly frame and balding head, reflected in his surname. After thirty years of being a headmaster there wasn't much he hadn't seen, but this was certainly a first for him.

'Mr Harper. Hello. If you wouldn't mind coming inside with me for a moment?'

Mr Monk took Tom's hand by way of shaking it, but also to manoeuvre him aside. Tom resisted firmly. He recognised him now as the headmaster, but he couldn't remember his name. Something to do with religion, he thought; Mr Priest possibly, but he didn't want to risk it.

'What the hell is going on here?' he asked.

'If you could just come with me?'

'Where are my boys?' he demanded, and looked to break out from the cordon the two teachers had created around him. The mum he had spoken to earlier was dragging her boys towards the car park. Tom looked at her little blonde boy.

'Hello, you're Toby, aren't you?'

The little boy nodded and Tom felt worried for him because he could see that the child was crying. He was indeed the scrum-half in Luke's team.

'You're a friend of Luke's?'

Toby managed a confused nod.

'I'm sorry, Tom,' the mum said as she clutched her two boys close to her.

'Mr Harper, please?' Mr Monk now sounded much more insistent and Tom felt his upper arm being gripped as a young man in a tracksuit emerged from the school with another man in overalls, most likely the caretaker.

'What the hell is going on?' Tom shouted. 'Get your hands off me!' He struggled to break free but four men now each had a firm hold and started to muscle the frantic parent back towards the school building.

'Where are my boys?' Tom shouted, his flailing fist connecting with something soft, which felt like a nose. 'Luke!' he began calling about the place, as tearful parents scurried for cover. The ambulance was on its way and the head wondered if the police might be needed as the PE teacher took another whack to the face.

'Get off me! What the fuck is going on? I'm a parent at this fucking school!'

Despite being the lowest-ranking member of staff present, the caretaker was the strongest and more accustomed to such situations. With both arms around Tom's waist, he picked him up off the ground and hoisted him up over his shoulder into a fireman's lift, ignoring the fists and blows being rained onto his back by an ever-weakening Tom, and marched purposefully towards the main school building.

'Mr Monk, have we called for an ambulance?'

'Yes, yes.'

'Good, because he's collapsed.'

Suddenly, Tom had stopped shouting and resisting and his body had gone limp, resting on the caretaker's shoulder. His eyes had rolled back into his head and saliva was drooling from his bearded mouth. The caretaker hurried his pace and with much relief, in the distance, they could hear a siren. Although Tom regained consciousness briefly, it was only long enough to mutter the names of his children before passing out again just as the paramedics arrived.

It was the telephone call that Nell had been dreading and half-expecting as she sped towards the hospital, her mind racing ahead with all kinds of awful assumptions. She'd been too frantic to listen to what Mrs Hall had said on the phone. Tom had collapsed and was being taken to hospital. But what was he doing at the school? She was mad with herself for not seeing the signs, which could hardly have been more obvious, and she pressed hard on her accelerator, racking up points and fines as the greedy cameras flashed at her as if she was on the red carpet. Within minutes, she arrived at the hospital and tore into the ward.

'I'm here to see Tom Harper. I'm his sister, Nell.'

A young man dressed in greens ushered her to walk with him.

'What? What is it?' she demanded to know.

'It's OK. He's fine. I'm Dr Fernandez.'

'Where is he? What's happened?'

Dr Fernandez moved into an empty cubicle and motioned for Nell to join him.

'Everything's fine. Please…'

The doctor pulled the curtain across for privacy but by now Nell was frantic.

'Oh God! What is it? Please.'

'Tom's fine. He's sleeping now. But we've had to sedate him.'

'Why? What happened?'

Dr Fernandez smiled and tried to reassure her. 'It's just as a precaution, but when he came around, he was in a very agitated state and delusional…'

Nell looked out beyond the curtain, wondering where he might be.

'What do you mean, delusional?'

'Well, we don't know yet, not exactly, until we can speak to him and make some assessments, but my best guess is that Tom is suffering from acute shock.'

Nell nodded her head and blew out hard. 'He lost his family,' she began.

The doctor nodded. 'The headmaster from the school is here and I've also spoken with his doctor, Dr Collier. He's on his way here now.' He smiled again. He had a kind manner and was well suited to his profession. He looked young for a man of such responsibility.

'Can I see him please?'

'He's asleep, but yes, of course.'

Nell held Tom's hand and watched him finally sleeping peacefully, albeit with the help of the sedative being administered intravenously. And although she sobbed quietly, it was more with relief than anything else.

'Tom, this is the beginning,' she assured him as she held his hand, 'where you start to feel well again. A little bit better each day, not worse.'

There was a knock at the door and Nell turned around and smiled at Jeremy, who was barely visible through the vast bouquet he was holding to add to the other flowers that had arrived already.

'I can see I needn't have bought these,' he smiled, lightening the mood as they hugged each other warmly.

'Nice to see you, Jeremy.'

'Sure, you too! What a shock eh?' He said tearfully. 'How is he?'

'Fine, I think. They've sedated him.'

'Good. Well, they know best.' Jeremy laid the flowers down on the table. Tom was asleep and looked peaceful, so he turned his attention to Nell. 'And what about you? How are you?'

Evidently, she was not very well; she sighed heavily and Jeremy caught her in his arms as she started to sob.

'It's OK, Nell. He's going to be fine.'

As far as the doctors could establish with Naisi and Nell's assistance, Tom hadn't slept for more than two hours a day for over a year, and it was likely that he hadn't slept at all for weeks at a time.

As a result, his body and his mind, just couldn't function properly anymore. The doctors monitored him closely and after two days, they were satisfied that he had entered into what they referred to as a prolonged sleep and from which they were reluctant to awaken him. Nell had panicked when she first heard the term coma, and the medics quickly assured her that the word was misleading and that his sleep was now natural and independent of any medication. Adding that it was precisely what he needed.

Chapter 12

Tom's peaceful external appearance belied the frantic activity within his mind, his active brain uprooting memories that his conscious mind had long forgotten, like the time his dad had revealed to his mum the news of his cancer diagnosis. Almost like a third person, Tom was able to observe his parents and himself as an eighteen-month-old baby sitting in his high chair with a bowl of porridge and before him now, he could watch such a raw and tender scene play out. His young mum crying and being comforted by his dad. Evidently, they hadn't told Nell yet who was outside on her trike. His dad checked through the window where she was playing and out of earshot, and then he turned his attention to the high chair and his young son. He smiled kindly at young Tom as the baby raised his arms and chuckled, appealing to be picked up. And from here, Tom's mind flitted backwards and forwards to other seminal moments in his life: his graduation, Nell's wedding to Jonathan, seeing Beth for the first time, their wedding and the long-awaited birth of their first son, Daniel. And then back again to his childhood and a vivid September day that he had almost completely forgotten.

He was twelve years old, possibly thirteen, back at school on a particularly exciting morning for the children of St Edmund's Roman Catholic School in Bromsworth, a small town within the district of Birmingham. The school's new playground had finally been opened, a month late, and with the school field waterlogged and off limits, the pupils were beyond excited to finally be allowed on to the brand-new tarmac. Tom, in his second year, year eight in the new system, was a skinny and popular kid: a boy who lived for football and little else at the time.

It was a hot day and young Tom charged about the perfectly flat, newly lined surface. The playground was packed. At least four football games were taking place, each with an average of nine players per side. And even with eight makeshift goals and numerous other non-players just standing about, each player knew his own teammates, his opponents, the score and which ball was theirs – a masterly display of ordered chaos, like soldier ants on the rampage. Tom called an end to the game as their ball hit the fence, making a 4-4 draw and a fair result. He was wet through with sweat and he could feel the backs of his long trousers sticking to his thighs. Double science was going to be even more difficult now, but he was glad that he had saved his can of Lilt for the end of break. It was no longer cold but it didn't matter. However, as soon as he pulled the can from his bag, as if he had been waiting for him, Declan Connor appeared before him with his customary sneer and his cronies in tow. Connor didn't play football and he never bothered to buy himself a can of pop because it was much cheaper to just take somebody else's.

Connor was in the same year as Tom but was already on the cusp of manhood. He was a heavy kid and came from a notorious family; his elder brother had famously been expelled for punching the headmaster. This had happened before Tom's time at the school but the legend lived on. Everyone conceded ground and their belongings to Connor, including most of the boys in the years above. Connor beckoned for Tom's drink expectantly. Tom sighed heavily.

'Something wrong, Harper?'

Tom didn't answer and just stared at the ground.

'I like a nice wog drink.' A cruel reference to the Caribbean Lilt. Connor's crew cackled, including Marvin, a mixed-race kid who should have known better. The bully leaned in so that Tom could smell the glue and solvents on his breath. His mates were equally pockmarked around their mouths and one cleared his throat theatrically to demonstrate what was to come. This was Connor's party piece, his trade mark. It worked on sausages in the dinner hall and it worked particularly well with cans of drink, because no one wanted their can back once Connor had emptied his throat into it.

Tom looked at Connor's fleshy arm and grubby hand with his chewed-down nails and scabbed knuckles beckoning for his can.

'Come on then. Give it here.'

And young Tom felt a sudden wave of defiance. He opened

his can but instead of handing it over, he took a mouthful of drink and then returned the contents of his mouth back into the can. He looked up at Connor, whose eyes had widened with surprise. Neither of the boys moved for a moment and then Connor smashed the can out of Tom's hand. It hit the ground heavily and liquid fizzed out in all directions, the first blemish on the pristine tarmac. Instantly, Tom regretted his actions. It was a stupid thing to do. He hadn't even swallowed his only mouthful and now he was going to be beaten up for his trouble. Connor forced him back hard against the chicken wire fence, grabbing him by the lapels of his blazer and almost lifting him off the ground, his face twisted in rage.

'What the fuck was that, *Harper*?'

'But it's mine,' Tom whimpered.

'Yeah, so fuckin' what?'

'I'm sorry...'

The bell rang, signalling the end of lunchtime, but Tom knew it was likely to only delay his inevitable beating.

'You wanna be fuckin' sorry, 'cos after school today, I'm gonna kick the shit out of ya.'

'No, you're not.'

Both boys were equally surprised by such an interjection. Tom opened his eyes and Connor whipped his head around to see who had the temerity to interfere with his legitimate business. It was an enormous boy from the upper school who Tom didn't know by name, but Connor seemed more familiar with him and not at all intimidated.

'Fuck off, Lurch.'

Tom stared up at his big rescuer who, for whatever reason, was brave enough to become involved. Patrick Porter, known as Paddy had reached six foot by the time he was twelve and now, at sixteen, was already much bigger than all his teachers and he looked as if he still had some way to go. He was a happy looking kid with a permanent smile and he was only intimidating to people who didn't know him. He was certainly no fighter and no match at all for Connor and his like.

Connor snarled. 'You, still here? I told you to fuck off.'

But still the bigger boy refused to back away. Connor finally let go of Tom and the two boys squared up to each other. This time it was Connor who was forced to look up, but he didn't look worried. Finally breaking the stalemate, Paddy pushed Connor hard, forcing him backwards easily.

'Make you feel tough does it? Picking on little kids?' Paddy asked.

Connor shoved back instantly with both hands but made little impression on the boy at least three stone heavier and now Paddy even smiled a little.

'Not so easy now, is it? You'd better run along and fetch your Sean.'

Connor's eyes blazed at the mention of his older brother.

'Yeah, I fuckin' will.'

'Oh, really? Out of jail, is he?'

Connor bridled at the reference.

'Or you could always get your mum.'

'Just shut your fuckin' mouth or…' Connor's eyes glistened now. His mum was famed for fighting and rumour had it, she once knocked a man out cold because he had laughed at her rendition of the Bonnie Tyler staple on the karaoke machine. Connor twitched with rage. He looked like he might even cry.

'Just leave this kid alone. D'you understand?' Paddy went on. 'You're not going to touch him after school today or any day. You're gonna leave him alone.' He pushed Connor again for good measure as he moved backwards to signal that the incident was over. Connor looked angry but it seemed that his aggression had at least been pierced.

A teacher, Mr Pereira, whom Tom was fond of, quickly arrived at the scene.

'What's going on here?'

'Nothing, sir,' a series of boys mumbled.

'Connor, always you! What's happening?'

'Nothing's happening, sir. It's all fine, really,' the giant interrupted before Connor could open his mouth and make things inevitably worse.

'Then let's get back to class. Come on, back to class,' Mr Pereira shouted, trying to reclaim some authority back from Paddy Porter who towered above him. Connor skulked off with his entourage in tow, all of them careful not to draw attention to the fact that their hero had just been faced down. Tom was looking at the ground, hoping that the whole thing was over. He was cross with himself for causing the incident in the first place and he could sense that Paddy was staring at him. He forced himself to look up at the older boy and a moment passed between them. Tom nodded gently before averting his eyes, embarrassed at the whole episode. But the giant seemed satisfied. He nodded back at Tom and then turned to leave as Tom stared after him. He was incredibly grateful but conscious that he had not thanked him.

Chapter 13

After five days of sleep, the doctors decided that they needed to start reviving their patient. Understandably, Nell was anxious about what they were waking him up to, and his doctors couldn't give her any assurances as to how he would react. They did warn her however, that he wouldn't just wake up and hop out of bed asking for some toast. He would be exhausted and likely to take a considerable time to fully come around and recover.

Tom stirred momentarily and muttered a few indiscernible words before falling back into sleep again. This was progress according to the doctors but Nell wasn't convinced; her brother being the most energetic person she had ever encountered. The next morning, she held his hand again and waited patiently. He stirred and briefly opened his eyes and seemed to take in his unfamiliar and confusing surroundings. But then he focused his attention on his sister and he seemed to relax.

'Hi, Nell,' he whispered quietly.

Nell smiled broadly and didn't mind this time that he closed his eyes again. At least he wasn't blind and he still had some of his memory intact.

It took another day before Tom was finally able to hold a limited conversation. Nell pinched his hand as hard as she could. His eyelids were still very heavy but he kept them open a little longer each time. With the drip still connected to his left arm, he certainly wasn't at home and from the state of the dying flowers all around him, his stay in hospital must have been lengthy.

'Welcome back, Tom.'

'Yeah. From where?'

'From the deepest sleep, you've ever had. Six days!'

Her words rocked him a little and his eyelids drooped. Six days. How could he have slept for six days? He squeezed Nell's hand and tried to open his eyes again to reassure her, but he couldn't.

'He'll be fine in a day or so now.' A doctor had entered the room. 'He'll feel very groggy and tired, but he'll wake now more frequently and be able to communicate a little more each time.'

'Thank you. And when can he come home?'

The doctor shrugged. 'As soon as he feels able. And being home is the best place for him. So, let's see.'

Nell smiled and tried to appear positive.

The next morning, Tom was strong enough to raise his head and with the help of a pillow that Nell quickly stuffed underneath him, he could have his first brief conversation.

'Make that seven days,' Nell joked.

'Really? So how come I still feel so smashed then?' Tom crashed his heavy head back on to his pillow. He could see that the week had been hardest on Nell and he felt guilty.

'And, how are you?' he asked and she nodded as best she could.

'And the kids? How are the kids?'

For a moment, a look of horror flashed across Nell's face, until Tom squeezed her hand.

'Nell – your kids?' he almost laughed.

'Oh, Tom, I'm sorry.'

Tom half-smiled now. Sadly, he had his memory intact.

'They're great. We're actually staying at yours while Jonathan's away so I could visit and Naisi can help…'

A look of anxiety briefly entered his consciousness and Nell was quick to react.

'We're all in the annexe, Tom. None of the bedrooms have been touched.'

Tom smiled and was obviously relieved. 'Good, that's great. Naisi will love that.'

'She does. And the kids love her. The problem is, I think Jonathan does too.'

Tom chuckled and would have laughed if he had the energy, but for Nell, just to see the spark in his eye was encouragement enough.

'Ben scored a try yesterday, which he was going to dedicate to you, only the referee disallowed it. Forward pass.'

Again, Tom half-smiled as the doctor appeared at the door calling time on their little chat. Nell understood that she should leave him to rest. He wanted to ask her about the giant kid who they had been at their school with, but it could wait and he had yet to recall his name.

By Wednesday, Tom had recovered sufficiently and passed all the physical and mental tests. Fortunately, he had no recollection of his fateful visit to his boy's old school. The last thing he could remember was running along the towpath, which ends just before the school grounds begin, and no one felt the need to fill in this blank. Crucially, though, he could recall what had happened to his family and he even suggested himself that he needed to start recovering. This made the process of discharge and travelling home much easier for Nell, although she still worried about how he might react on seeing his house again and feeling its emptiness.

Naisi and Barbara, Tom's PA, fussed about the immaculate sitting room. Naisi spotted a stray hair and flicked it over the grate of the enormous fireplace. She had cleaned and tidied the house over and over waiting for Tom to come home and nothing was out of place, except for the irreplaceable Venetian glass partition that Tom had smashed. Jonathan hovered awkwardly, dreading what he would say to his brother-in-law, as his children whipped around the place and mostly ignored his various pleas to behave.

Tom sat silently in the back of his car. He felt nervous, knowing what was waiting for him at the house: the inevitable fuss and attention, and people avoiding his mental health – the elephant in the room. He couldn't recall much before his hospitalisation but he remembered shouting at Naisi and figured that he owed her an apology at least.

The heavy car entered the grounds of his house, drove past the three-car garage and around the turning circle, crunching the deep gravel as it came to a stop. The front door of the house was already open, a smiling Nell and Naisi the first people to come bounding out. He smiled back at them. Naisi looked instantly relieved when she saw him grinning, clean shaven and smartly dressed, just like he used to be before it all happened. He had even put on some weight and looked much better for it. He smiled warmly at her and opened his arms to beckon her towards him as soon as he got out of the car. She quickened her step and leapt into his arms and he hugged her warmly, picking her off her feet. Jonathan still hovered, wondering whether he might go with a man hug or just a handshake.

'I so glad you home, Tom,' Naisi whispered.

'I'm glad too. It must have been quiet for you?'

Naisi nodded as Tom put her down. She had assured Nell that she wouldn't cry and though her throat swelled, she worked hard to keep everything dry.

'Hey, Nell,' Tom said, extending his arms to his big sister.

'Welcome home.'

'Thanks. Thanks for everything,' he whispered before breaking off as Jonathan was upon him, flapping as usual. Still in two minds, he held out his right hand but his left also, making a complete hash of the whole thing, but it didn't matter.

Tom glanced around his immaculate house. The flowers, the newspaper and homemade cakes; only freshly baked bread and brewed coffee was needed to complete the house-for-sale feel. But despite such great attention to detail, the atmosphere was still strained. He felt tired and detached and really wanted to be alone. It didn't feel to him that there was very much to celebrate. He ran his foot along the gap in the marble, where the Venetian glass had been, as his memory of that day remained vague and fragmented. He couldn't recall what had sparked his fury but no doubt, it would come to him. He noted the brand-new television hanging on the wall across from the island. It was the same brand but it looked slightly bigger and doubtless offered an even sharper picture.

'You couldn't get the glass I see?' Tom smiled.

Nell shrugged. 'Do you know I actually tried?'

Tom was relieved that she hadn't tried too hard, given the effort it had taken Beth to acquire it the first time around. They both smiled thinly then Naisi came into the kitchen.

'Naisi, I'm so sorry for scaring you like I did,' Tom told her.

Naisi shook her head as if it were nothing.

'No, it must have been awful for you and I'm sorry.'

Naisi's tears rolled heavily down her face and Tom approached her and embraced her like a father would cuddle his daughter after a boyfriend had let her down.

'I promise Nell I no cry.'

'I know, but it's OK.'

'But when you say, the house must have been quiet –'

Tom understood immediately what she meant. It was the expression he had used moments ago, referring to his being away when in fact it was the absence of his children that really made the house so quiet.

'Naisi, I know, I know. And it's OK.'

Nell gestured to Barbara and to Jonathan that they should leave now, to let Tom be on his own. Jonathan was delighted; the strain of the whole thing was already too much and he hadn't said anything to Tom, just grunted a few sounds.

'Tom, Michael sends his apologies. He's in Brazil with Jeremy but you can call him on his mobile. In fact, he wants you to call him.'

Tom nodded but only out of politeness, because he wouldn't be calling Michael or anyone from the office. Not yet anyway. Nell looked a little disappointed. She had hoped that the mention of Brazil might spark his curiosity, but she didn't want to pursue it. All in good time, she reasoned, now that he was home and appeared to be recovering. What he needed was space and time, she told herself.

'Tom, we should all get going and give you some space.'

'And no more running,' Jonathan blurted out nervously, which made everyone laugh, including Tom. Jonathan was delighted.

Chapter 14

Having gone to bed after *Newsnight*, Tom was quietly relieved that he had managed to sleep through until 5.15 a.m., the time that he usually stirred for work. And, although he was already awake when his alarm sprang to life, he felt sure that he had slept. It wasn't perfect sleep. It was fitful with at least two visits to the toilet but crucially, he had managed to get back to sleep both times and he hadn't had any nightmares. He made himself a cup of tea. Naisi wasn't up yet and he was pleased for the quiet, sitting in his warm kitchen thinking not of his family for once but further back to his own childhood and his schooldays. His mind dwelt on the incident he had recalled in the hospital when the big boy had come to his rescue.

In the kitchen, he pulled on his running shoes and let himself out through the back door. It was a cold morning and the chill caught him, forcing him to run quickly out across the gravel and through the gates. Soon, he was running under the bridge where he had encountered the group of boys; but dressed appropriately this time, he did not attract any undue attention. He stopped just beyond the bridge and recalled the incident. It reminded him again of his playground encounter with another bully and how that time he had been rescued. Still, he tried to remember his rescuers name but he couldn't.

When he got home, Naisi was up and busying herself with not very much. He wondered how much longer she would stay. Being honest he would prefer it if she left. He liked being on his own and not being bothered by well-meaning people, but he didn't wish to hurt her feelings and certainly wouldn't suggest it. On his fridge hung a picture of Luke and Jack's school football team, which he brushed with his hand as he walked with his fruit juice into his office. He fired up his laptop and did a quick Google search for his old school, St Edmund's Roman Catholic School. The school's home page filled the screen, a picture of four boys from all four corners of the globe smiling out at him, and he noted that it was now a technical college, no less. Rather hopelessly, he searched the site for the old boy link or alumni section, which he eventually found and clicked on, unsure of what he was looking for. As expected, it wasn't a very detailed section and certainly didn't go as far back as his day. He looked at their sports record and gave a cursory glance at the school's lofty mission statement, but what he really wanted was a name – and he couldn't very well do a search for 'Lurch'. In his attic, Tom rooted through two cardboard boxes of his old possessions, which he had moved from house to house since his early twenties with a broken promise each time to finally sort through. Old team photos were no good because they hadn't been in the same year group, plus Tom didn't recall that the boy had been particularly athletic, although, he supposed he might have played in goal, but for his size and not his talent.

He called and asked Nell. She could remember the boy based on his size alone. 'The massive kid you mean. Bigger than the teachers, even?' But she too was struggling for a name – Peter perhaps or possibly Patrick? Inevitably, she wanted to know why but Tom was reluctant to explain because he didn't really know himself.

A couple of days later, sitting in his kitchen in the evening while watching nothing on television, something occurred to him. It was a nature programme and the male presenter was painting a watercolour of a bird, a blue tit, whilst it gorged itself on the garden feeder. As the painting took shape, a sudden memory jolted him: not the boy's name but that he liked to draw. The big boy at school had been an artist. He could draw boys' faces and he even had a nice little line in caricatures of teachers. Tom quickly climbed the stairs back to the attic and grabbed at a bunch of school magazines that he had already flicked through. Then he had scanned the class photos, concentrating mainly on the boys at the back of each group, but now he concentrated on the artwork that the magazine always carried in each edition. The first three magazines had plenty of drawings but none by boys that Tom could remember, and not by the boy he was after. He looked at the front cover of the fourth magazine – 1985–1986. He was running out of options. He flicked through the magazine and stopped at a cruel caricature of his old headmaster, Mr Dacey with exaggerated teeth and huge chin. It was comic but this was not why Tom was smiling. It was the artist's name that caught his eye – Patrick Porter. Nell had been right all along. His name was Patrick but he was known as Paddy. This was a childhood before political correctness has descended and even though, 'Paddy' normally denoted being stupid at the time, this hadn't seemed to bother this affable giant. Perhaps he really was stupid; Tom couldn't recall. It was just his kindness that he could remember.

Now that he had his name, Tom felt some need to establish just what his motives were for finding it. Only, he still wasn't sure. He assured himself that he had just wanted to remember him but now that he had, it made him even more curious. He wondered whatever became of him. Had he stopped growing he wondered? Tom remembered him fondly and looked elsewhere for things to distract him. But without the rigours of work or a family to attend to plus masses of time to fill, Paddy Porter kept nagging at Tom's vacant mind. He plugged the name into a crude Google search, which helpfully provided him with two million entries containing the words Patrick and Porter, most of which featured the life and works of an eminent nuclear physicist at the Massachusetts Institute of Technology. Tom was confident that this was not his man, which he confirmed when he read that the scientist had died in 1942. He idly flicked through a few more pages with no real hope of a hit before giving up on the haystack.

Tom hadn't been to his golf club, Stoke Park, since the accident. At first, he was simply in no state of mind nor had any desire to play, but ever since his hospitalisation he had avoided the club for the same reason he had avoided all places familiar to him. He didn't wish to have his family inevitably remembered, if not by actual words then with mournful looks. But this morning he had taken a call from his old playing partner, David, questioning whether he would like a quick hit, just the two of them, and the idea appealed.

David had been at the funeral and had visited him briefly in hospital, but he hadn't seen him since and was understandably a little bit nervous as he stood waiting in the car park. He sensed that Tom would probably like to head straight out on to the course, avoiding the club house or pro shop and sure enough, when Tom emerged from his Jaguar, he already had his golf shoes on. As Tom slung his clubs on his back and slammed his trunk, he was immediately caught by an elderly couple who had just finished their round. The lady looked particularly pained and put her hand on his arm and he smiled at her politely. David rushed over to rescue his stricken friend, but the same thing happened on the first tee with the lady four ball that had just teed off. They had seen Tom on his way over and they all stood and waited for him. They each wished him well and expressed their deepest condolences. Tom thanked each of them and wished them a good game, which would not be quick judging by the length of their drives. Tom and David both agreed to play just nine holes. He had nothing else to do all day, but nine would be enough.

There was no getting away from it. Wherever he went, people would feel compelled to emote with him. Human nature. Tom was the man and the tragic story that everyone recounted to their friends and anyone else who would listen.

Tom putted out for his par on the ninth, which was a good way to finish. David understood why he didn't fancy a pint and a sandwich, and left the chance to play again open.

Back in his car, Tom finally felt safe again, which was nothing to do with air bags or seat belts, but because he was alone. On the radio, he half-heartedly listened to a news item about a celebrity who had become embroiled in a sex scandal via one of those social media sites. Don't they ever learn? Tom thought to himself, and then another productive thought and possible avenue of enquiry occurred to him.

He rushed home and was pleased to find Naisi because she spent her life on Facebook and even said that she couldn't live without it. Tom had never been on any social media platform and surmised that he would need some help. Grateful to be of use, she obligingly joined his quest, her fingers racing across her MacBook, but nothing appeared for Patrick Porter. Similarly, Twitter was as unhelpful. There were plenty of Patrick Porters the world-over but Tom wasn't about to start jumping on aeroplanes on some wild goose chase. Still intrigued though, an old mate of his who had a passion for family trees suggested the good old-fashioned electoral role. In the Birmingham municipality, there were three Patrick Porters, but only one born in the mid-sixties and so Tom was confident that he had located his man. He was married to Mary and they had four children. His home address and even his home telephone number were listed, which Tom made a note of. He didn't know why because he certainly would not be calling him. And then suddenly, Tom stopped reading. He had listed 'retailer' as his profession. He was the proprietor of Porter's Fresh Fruit and Vegetables, a business on the Whitton Road, just along from his old school. And now Tom remembered. It was the fruit stall that his mum used to stop at on their walk home from school each evening. As well as the stall being useful, his mum had explained that it was important to support local shops and businesses otherwise they would all shut down. Sage advice and especially so without knowing of the internet days ahead.

Chapter 15

Five a.m. is an ungodly hour whatever the season, but it is particularly brutal in February and Paddy Porter still wasn't used to it after nearly thirty years of running his fruit and veg stall. At least in the summer months, a warm day might be in prospect. But in February there was no respite from the cold and even if the sun did eventually emerge, it never stayed for long enough to warm his feet up. Paddy still hadn't got the hang of the clocks moving either backwards an hour or forwards and it still took him by surprise every time. The winter move backwards was particularly spiteful and each year he would complain bitterly about the Scottish farmers who were responsible for robbing him of another hour in bed.

'And the Scots? They hate us as well you know!' he would moan to his wife, Mary each year.

Paddy chucked another box of apples on the pavement for his eldest son, Sean.

'Jesus, Dad! More apples?'

'Yeah. Fifty pence a pound.'

Sean scoffed, not just at his dad's refusal to use the metric system but because they already had more apples than they could sell. Sean was just eighteen and a reluctant helper on the family stall, especially in the winter. With a string of mediocre A-levels, Sean had decided against going to university and whilst he contemplated his future, Paddy was keen that he should start paying rent by working on the stall. Of course, as the eldest son and first heir to the Porter estate, Sean could reasonably expect to inherit the family business, but he had made it perfectly clear that he didn't want it, which Paddy thought was both commendable and hilarious.

Paddy chuckled as he trundled off back to his van, his enormous frame and bulk making light work of the heavy boxes. He had developed early in life: puberty had arrived at ten, which accounted for his colossal size at school, but from here he had got comparatively smaller as his peers caught up but few passed him. At six foot five and nineteen stone, Paddy was an enormous man and an equally enormous presence in his home town of Bromsworth.

Rather sheepishly this time, Paddy dropped another heavy box at Sean's feet without saying anything. Sean looked at him in disbelief.

'Fockin' hell, Dad.'

'Eh, language – fifty pence a pound.'

Sean tutted. 'The lot more like. We'll never shift this lot.'

'50 pence. And we'll deliver them 'n'all.'

'Yeah, where to? The dump?' Sean quipped.

Later that morning, at a speed ten miles an hour faster than Her Majesty would have approved of, Tom eased up the M40. Although driving at an illegal speed, his car still felt like it was being restrained, like a powerful dog itching to get off the lead. Perhaps Daniel was right after all, and his car was ridiculous. Bloody good fun to drive though, he thought as he flashed by another labouring truck. He assured himself of the path ahead and stabbed at the accelerator, watching the dial nudge effortlessly through ninety miles an hour, before settling back to a more acceptable, 'I'm so sorry officer' kind of speed. Not that there are any traffic police officers anymore, replaced by cameras who are more difficult to charm. Tom enjoyed driving but it was something he did less and less the more successful he became. He employed his driver, Jerry, for the convenience rather than the status. It allowed him time to work in the car, giving him an extra two hours a day, so freeing up his weekends to be with Beth and the kids, and it meant he never needed to worry about parking; the bane of more normal people's lives. Being dropped off and picked up from exactly where he needed to be was a luxury well worth paying for.

He hadn't told Nell about his impromptu visit to their old home town and more specifically to Porter's Fruit and Veg Emporium. She would think it was odd and no doubt would fret. He intended to be home the next day anyway, so she might not even know that he'd ever gone. It was just a fleeting visit, to soak up the old place and recall some of the events that might have shaped him. He didn't wish to sound melodramatic, but he didn't feel that he had a choice in the matter either. He felt compelled to make the trip. As though it was the right thing to do and he found himself becoming more excited the closer he got to home.

The blue motorway sign on the M40 appeared in the distance and got larger and larger before it quickly flashed by. According to the sign, Birmingham was only twenty-two miles away, but his sat-nav claimed that he still had twenty-eight miles to cover. He didn't need directions, but out of habit he plugged in the postcode of his old house, more for information and company than instructions. A navy-blue Bentley whipped past him in the outside lane at a furious speed making Tom wonder what its driver was late for: a plane, a meeting, or maybe even a suspicious wife? And suddenly Tom was grateful that he wasn't rushing to anything. He didn't have a plan to follow or a timeframe to stick to. He'd packed an overnight bag and that was it. His head was full of memories of the place that he wanted to revisit. He didn't know what to expect. It was just something he wanted to do and for now, this was enough.

The first thing that struck Tom as he turned into his old street, Hazel Close, was how narrow the road was and even more striking, how small its houses were, and not just in comparison to the house that he lived in now. Two up, two down, even for a family of four it must have been a squeeze for them and yet he couldn't remember feeling cramped at home. He eased the car along the street that was now choked with parked cars on both sides and didn't allow enough space to play football as he had done every evening as a child. He slowed the car and finally stopped outside number twenty-eight, the house where he was born and lived in until he was eighteen. Aside from its size, it wasn't how he remembered it at all. Their solid black door had been replaced with a frosted glass affair that made it look like the entrance to a large toilet and judging by the state of the front garden, it probably was. The tree his mum had planted after his dad passed was gone, and so too the two flower beds, now concreted over, presumably for a car to accompany the electric oven that was currently tucked under the bay window.

'Nice car, mister.'

A young boy appeared at his window, taking him by surprise. He was probably twelve or thirteen with a mischievous face and a thick Birmingham accent, which Tom had deliberately lost the moment he arrived at Exeter University.

'Thanks,' Tom said, unsure what else to say.

'Is it yours?'

Tom chuckled and didn't answer.

'How much were it?'

Tom shrugged; he genuinely didn't know.

'What? How come you don't know if it's yours?'

It was a reasonable question if a little impertinent and Tom didn't have a decent answer.

'Have you nicked it?'

Tom smiled. 'No, I haven't nicked it. It's mine.'

'What are you, a footballer?'

Tom smiled again: as flattering a question a man in his late forties could ever be asked. 'No.' Tom said and shook his head.

'How fast is it?' The boy leaned forward to get a look at the speedometer. 'Fuckin' hell! Two hundred and forty.'

'That's kilometres an hour, not miles.'

'Still, fast though, eh? What's that in miles?'

Tom was bewildered to be having such a conversation. 'I don't know. Too fast. Illegal.' He was growing a little impatient now. 'Anyway, look. I'm busy, so if –'

'You don't look busy.' The imp observed.

'Excuse me?'

'You don't look busy.'

It was a fair point.

'So, what's the fastest you've ever been then?' the boy continued, completely undeterred.

Tom sighed. 'I don't know.'

'Over a hundred though, right?' the boy asked.

'I guess…'

'Give us a ride, will ya?'

'What? No way!'

'Oh, go on! Why not?'

Tom shook his head. Where to start?

'Ah, come on! Please!'

'Absolutely not. No way. What has your mum told you about talking to strangers?'

'Why? You a paedo?'

Tom had had enough now and hit the window button just as he heard an adult's voice.

'Can I help you, pal?'

A gruff-looking man had wandered over, presumably the boy's father from the way he had his hand on his shoulder.

'I used to live here, that's all. Number twenty-eight.'

The man turned around slowly to pick out the house.

'Oh yeah. Paki family now. They're all right,' he said gruffly. 'Mind you, they could be bombers for all I know.'

Tom didn't reply; he didn't know how to.

'Dad, look, it's got two exhaust pipes.'

'You've done all right for yourself then,' the man said, almost accusingly. Tom shrugged and didn't say anything.

'What happened? You win the lottery?'

Both father and son looked at Tom jealously and he thought for a moment about his place in the world, his personal circumstances and the man's assumption.

'Yeah, I just got lucky.' Tom eased the car forward. 'My numbers just came up.'

Lucky old me, he muttered to himself once he was out of earshot. It had been an odd exchange: quite comic to start with, but inevitably it had a rather melancholic end. Everything he experienced and everyone he encountered reminded him of his family and what had happened to them. He had enjoyed seeing his old house again though, and the exchange with the kid had been progress also because it was an encounter with someone who didn't know his circumstances. The questions might have been a little impertinent but they didn't cover the incident that now defined his entire life and this at least felt liberating. Whatever awaited him in Bromsworth, it had been a good idea to make the trip.

Chapter 16

Even though Paddy was a popular fixture in Bromsworth, his popularity was a blunt instrument against the mite of the supermarket chains that now dominated his old market town. As well as the enormous superstore on the fringes of the town centre, Britain's chains were now fighting for the incidental shoppers within town by opening their local and metro stores everywhere they could. Paddy had complained to the Bromsworth Council but with hindsight, he realised that Mary had been right. Too little and too late. Mary had urged him to get angry and to galvanise support from the other local retailers, to organise a rally and start a petition to force the council to reconsider. But Paddy couldn't muster this kind of anger or energy and settled on making an irate phone call instead. Mary told him at least to make his feelings official by putting them in writing but Paddy hadn't written a letter for years, and he was too proud to ask anyone for help. His telephone call wasn't even answered, so he left a terse answerphone message with the council planning department, which did something for his conscience but absolutely nothing for his sales figures.

This morning was typically quiet. Just a handful of customers trickled by, most of whom Paddy had known for years.

'Any apples for you, Mavis, me love?'

'Not these ones, no.'

'Hey, lovely and soft, these apples.'

Mavis scoffed. 'Yeah, as soft as you are, Paddy. These wanted eating weeks ago.'

Paddy sighed and slipped an apple into Mavis's bag anyway.

'OK then, anything else, my love?'

'No, that's it thanks, Paddy love.'

'Two pounds flat then, please.'

Paddy took the money and helped put the bags into Mavis's

antique roller basket.

'Give my love to Arnie, will ya?'

'Eh?'

'Arnold. Give him my love.'

'Oh, him.'

Paddy chuckled. 'Tell him to get himself down the Nelson. I'll pick him up if it helps.'

'You'll have to get him dressed first,' Mavis scoffed as she shuffled off.

'You have reached your destination,' Tom's sat-nav announced proudly, but again he didn't need to be told as he drove along the Whitton Road towards Porter's Fruit and Veg stall. He remembered it vividly now, how his mum would buy some apples for a crumble that night and chat to the stallholder, presumably Paddy's dad. As he passed, he slowed his car enough to spot a huge man behind the counter of the beautifully tended stall. It had to be him. The stall wasn't in a market as such, but was a concession front amidst a small terrace of units with residential flats above. None of the other outlets looked to be functioning however, and some had been boarded up.

The flats above the shops were in a particularly dilapidated state. They appeared occupied but with net curtains so dirty, they might as well have been boarded up also. Tom noticed that the big man's eyes were drawn to his car. Immediately, he felt self-conscious and he quickened his speed. His sleek black Jaguar would be as conspicuous and no less of a talking point if it had been one of the wild panthers that are said to roam freely in Britain. Tom recalled the reaction of the father and son to his car and he wondered and started to fret.

It didn't take him long to locate a car-hire firm. He pulled into their large lot and parked up easily, reasoning that it would be easier to leave his car here than at his hotel. The car-hire firm didn't have a precedent for customers leaving their own cars but after a flurry of phone calls, it was agreed that Tom could leave his car while he hired a suitably modest Fiat. Tom secretly registered the mileage on his car before he handed over the keys, should they need to move it. The pretty desk clerk decided that most likely he was having an affair and that his wife was having him tailed by a private detective. He had an interesting face. Boyish good looks and certainly handsome enough to get himself a mistress. A little old for her, but so what and she batted her newly purchased eye lashes furiously to see if she might be added to his list, especially when she noted his local address as the sumptuous Hyatt in Birmingham.

In his Fiat, Tom adjusted his seat backwards and set off on his way again, feeling much less conspicuous now. He parked the car on Waldeck Road, a little down from Paddy's stall. It was a bitter day with a biting wind that hit him hard as he slammed his door and locked the car. As he approached the stall it was getting dark already and Paddy seemed delighted to see him – a customer at last.

'Thank God! Where have you been all me life?' Paddy smiled broadly, rather taking Tom by surprise. Surely it was a figure of speech and he couldn't remember Tom after such a long time?

'You've been waiting for me?' Tom asked.

Now it was Paddy's turn to look surprised. 'Well, no, not you specifically, like. Just waiting for a customer, you know.'

'Oh, right.'

Paddy was embarrassed. He hated it when his jokes didn't work and this bloke appeared well-to-do, which somehow made it worse. He seemed a little needy as well, as if he had wanted Paddy to be waiting for him, so he was quite possibly a homosexual, although he didn't look the type, but, then again, these days, it was so difficult to tell.

'So then, what can I get ya?' Paddy asked, needing to assert his authority to the situation.

'Er…'

'Tell me you want apples!'

'Er, yeah, apples, great.'

'Lovely.'

Tom smiled a little, giving Paddy the encouragement, he needed.

'Hey, you don't want a box, do you?'

'A box?'

'Yeah. For a tenner.'

'Er...'

'Do you have kids?'

Tom looked at the stallholder a moment before shaking his head. 'No. No kids.'

'No, well, lucky you. Too bloody expensive.'

'The most I'd need would be... say, ten?' Tom ventured.

'Call it a dozen, eh? Good lad. I'll charge you for ten, how's that? Anything else?'

'Bananas?' Tom was warming to his theme.

'Bananas. How many bunches?' Paddy laughed hard. 'I'm only joking. Will this do ya?'

Tom nodded and smiled as Paddy wrapped a bunch in a bag and popped them into a plastic carrier.

'Any mangoes?' Tom asked hopefully until Paddy looked at him in faux horror.

'No, OK then.' Tom responded quickly. 'Er, oranges?'

'Yep. We got oranges. Mangoes! You'll be wanting a Sharon fruit next?' Paddy bent down out of Tom's view. 'Fancy calling a fruit a Sharon...'

Tom proceeded to order much more fruit and vegetables than he could possibly eat but it was much easier than bringing up his real reason for visiting.

'And that's it, thank you.' Tom looked at the two bulging carrier bags.

'No, no, thank *you*. You're a bloody godsend. Best customer today by a mile. Hey, you're not moving in round here are ya?'

'No, no, just visiting.'

'Shame. OK then, so that's six pounds fifty please.' Paddy, quick as a flash, picked up on Tom's surprise. 'You can pay more if you like?'

Tom fumbled around in his wallet. He started to panic because although he had thought to change his car, he hadn't given any consideration to the sheaf of fifty-pound notes that filled his wallet. Desperate, he opened the change compartment hoping to find sufficient coinage. A couple of two-pound coins would be useful but typically, he was just short and Paddy began to shift awkwardly. Paddy was used to extending credit and running tabs, but this bloke didn't look short, plus he didn't even know him.

'If you're short, you can always owe me. It's not a problem,' Paddy lied.

Tom fumbled through his trouser pockets, hoping for a twenty or a tenner that he'd forgotten about but there was neither. Damn it because there was no way that Paddy had a card machine. Tom bashfully handed over a pristine fifty-pound note and winced when he saw the shock register on Paddy's face.

'Blimey. What the bloody hell is one of these?'

'I'm sorry. I haven't got anything smaller.'

'No, and there's nothing bigger either.'

Paddy was making a big play of the note, holding it up to the light and then for some reason, biting it also.

'If you can't change it –'

'No, no, it's no problem.' Paddy ducked below his counter again and began rooting through his cash drawer as Tom shifted from foot to foot, cross with himself, and even more so when Paddy re-emerged with a defeated look on his face.

'I'm sorry, but I need to pop over to the chippy.'

'No, no, please, don't worry.'

'No, no bother. I'll just be a minute.'

'Seriously. Look, why don't you just keep it? Keep the change.'

Paddy was aghast and Tom regretted his offer immediately.

'Ya what?'

'Er…'

'Don't be daft. Fifty quid for a bag of fruit? You can get a house round here for fifty quid.'

'Fine, well, I'm here for a day or so, so let's just run a tab, shall we?' Tom reasoned, trying to retrieve the situation. He knew though that he had failed because Paddy suddenly looked distrusting and guarded, his mischief and sense of fun had vanished.

'Are you being serious?' Paddy asked.

'Yeah, why not? All the fruit I can eat.'

'In the army are ya?' Paddy still wasn't convinced.

'I'm sorry?'

'Got an army to feed, have you?'

Tom blushed and didn't answer that he was on his own. Paddy looked at him curiously. All his instincts were telling him that he should refuse the offer, and his instincts were almost always correct. There was just something about the bloke that felt different. But he could certainly use the cash flow and so, against his better judgement, Paddy offered him his enormous rough and calloused hand. Tom felt embarrassed shaking it and squeezed back as best he could.

'So, who are you visiting then?'

'Oh, er…'

'Only, I know everyone round here, you know, having the stall 'n'all.'

Tom paused and looked Paddy directly in the eye, unnerving him a little more. It was a direct question and to Tom it felt like an opportunity.

'Actually, it's you that I've come to see.'

Paddy shut his eyes instantly. His instincts had been right all along.

'I knew it. I fockin' well knew it.'

'You *are* Patrick Porter?'

Paddy's eyes widened. 'Oh, Jesus!' he shouted. 'Patrick Porter!'

'What?'

'No one calls me Patrick. Ever. So, who are you? Come on, who? Jesus, are you from the tax?'

'No, no…' Tom tried to interject.

'No, well who then? Mr Fifty Pound Note. Who are you?'

'I'm Tom Harper.'

'I don't mean your shitting name. I mean what are you? Is this about me tax?'

Tom wasn't sure whether he was joking or not.

'No, I'm not the tax man.'

Paddy heard him but he still looked ruffled. 'Well, who then? Cos there's something not right here, I can just tell.'

'I'm Tom Harper.' Tom repeated but the name didn't register which was no surprise.

'We were at school together,' Tom added desperately and Paddy seemed to calm for a split second before quickly dismissing the claim.

'No, you weren't; not with that accent and those hands, you weren't.

Here, you can take your money back for starters.' Paddy slapped the note on a bunch of bananas from where it fell onto the wet floor. Tom retrieved the note. Since he had got out of hospital he had thought of little else than this encounter and now here he was, scaring the wits out of the poor guy. It certainly wasn't the start he had envisaged or why he had made the trip.

'Your tax aren't ya; I can just tell?'

'No. I am not the bloody tax man.' Tom shouted

'Well, then who the bloody hell are you?'

'I've told you. My name is Tom Harper. We were at school together, at St Edmund's just up the road here.'

Paddy's eyes narrowed as he processed this new and correct information, but that didn't mean much these days, he reflected, not with Google.

'Our head teacher was Father Young.'

Another tick but Paddy still wasn't happy and pointlessly began sorting out his display of unsalable apples to calm himself down.

'Well, I don't remember you.'

'No, well, I was a few years below you.'

'Right, so we weren't mates then?'

'No, not really.'

'Right. So, what do you want then?' Paddy barked bluntly, his attention now re-focussing on his earlier and equally worrying assumption that this bloke might be a homosexual. Paddy didn't like to use the word gay on the basis that they couldn't all be happy. Tom looked skyward. It wasn't an easy subject to broach and he had made it doubly difficult for himself now.

'Do you remember the time that we met? At school? It was just the one time.'

'I've already told ya; no.'

'No... right, well, there's just something I'd like to discuss with you, that's all.'

Paddy nodded impatiently. 'Right, well, go on then because I'm a busy man,' he said with as much conviction as he could muster.

Tom shifted awkwardly. 'Look, is there some place we can go? I'd like to buy you a drink?'

Paddy stiffened and looked Tom firmly in the eye. 'Look, you're not a poof are ya?'

Tom shook his head with dismay. 'No.'

'Only they love me, the gays. I don't know why. I think it's me size. You know, big lad.'

Tom didn't know, but he didn't say as much.'

'No. I am not a poof.' The word stuck in his throat because if he'd used it at work, he could expect a lawsuit.

'I was just a lad at your school. I was younger than you. Tom Harper. We were in the playground and something happened between us and a kid called Declan Connor.'

Paddy's eyes flickered with interest at Connor's name. 'Tom Harper...' he wondered aloud as some distant bell in his lazy memory began to toll. 'Harper...' And then he suddenly smiled. 'Were you that brainy kid? The one that got into university.'

Tom smiled. 'Yes. Exeter.'

'Yeah, that's right. Down in Cornwall. Bloody hell! You were the first lad from our school to go?'

Tom shrugged modestly.

'Not like nowadays, eh? They all get in now. Even my Sean's got a place and he's a few apples short of a decent fruit salad.'

'Er...'

'Yeah, I remember you now. Bloody hell! You were in the local paper and everything.'

Tom blushed some more and thought of the framed cutting that his mum had made, which he still had somewhere, probably in his attic. Paddy was now mightily relieved and offered Tom his heavy hand again.

'So, how's things then?' he asked

'Yeah, OK,' Tom lied.

'Obviously doing all right for yourself?' Paddy reasoned

correctly. 'At least you're not using your hands for a living.'

He was right of course and it made Tom half-smile as Paddy chuckled wildly.

'Jesus, for a while there, I thought you were tax.'

Tom smiled again and shook his head.

'There's something that I wanted to chat to you about. And don't worry, it's not your tax.'

'Good, because I do worry. Keeps me up all blinking night, them bastards.' Paddy answered.

'So, if we could meet then, you know, after you've closed up? Maybe go for a coffee somewhere?'

Paddy considered the prospect.

'On the tab if you like?' Tom suggested.

'Do you remember the Nelson?'

'Yeah, of course; it's where I first got served.'

'Right, well, it's still there – just. We can meet in there if you like, after me tea, say six thirty? You can have a coffee and I'll have a pint.'

'Great! Yeah, that'd be great. I'll see you then.'

'Any clues?' Paddy asked, seemingly forgetting Tom's mention of Connor.

Tom shook his head. It had been so long already; another hour or so wouldn't hurt. 'Let's save it for that pint.'

'OK, then.'

'Oh, and this is yours, remember?' Tom handed over the note once more.

Paddy smiled. Of course, he had remembered. 'Thank you.'

'No, thank you, Paddy. It's nice to meet you again. It's been a long time.'

Chapter 17

Tom sat in his hotel suite. There was nothing on television, he didn't want to read anything and the 'luxury' amenities provided by his hotel were not much of a distraction either. He just wanted to sit down and have a pint with Paddy Porter, but because this was some hours away, he busied himself with nothing in particular. His hotel room was already fully stocked with fruit, so he felt a little foolish for buying so much; much more than he could possibly eat. He bit into one of Paddy's apples and quickly emptied the contents into his hand before searching for the bin. He felt even sillier now. He grabbed his jacket. He couldn't hang around in the hotel with the CNN news loop any longer.

He'd picked up a copy of the local newspaper, *The Bromsworth Echo* and gave it a cursory glance, the front page featuring a picture of a smiling individual cutting a red ribbon somewhere or other. He registered the name – Councillor Lesley Irwin OBE, Head of Bromsworth Council – and didn't feel inclined to read on.

Lesley Irwin had been a public servant for over thirty-five years, the last fifteen as the leader of Bromsworth Council and at fifty-two; he was just a few years short of his well-earned retirement. Three years to secure himself a peerage, he joked to himself, except it wasn't really a joke. His OBE had been fun when he'd first received it, when it was new, but its novelty had worn thin by now. His name was still prefixed by 'mister' and he wondered if he might ever obtain the illustrious 'sir' that he craved. Sir Lesley Irwin certainly had a ring to it. Lesley was fundamentally a decent man, if a little vain, but he did have a weakness that had worn him down over the years and more recently, led him astray. Greed was Lesley's Achilles' heel and his recent partnership with local 'businessman' Daniel Green had easily exposed this area of weakness. Green was in his late forties and an unscrupulous operator in any number of different fields. A vulgar man, Daniel enjoyed the high life and always lived beyond his means, leading to his regular brushes with bankruptcy. He was bright and convincing and his next deal was always going to be the one. And maybe so this time, since it involved Councillor Irwin no less. It was a little oblique and protracted but his investors were solid for two million pounds, which Lesley assured him was more than enough. The two men had met at a property trade fair in Dubai some years ago and Lesley, a rather paranoid man, had been worried and suspicious ever since. If a connection was ever made between them, then not making the New Year's honours list would be the least of his worries.

Ahead of meeting Daniel Green, Lesley's dishonesty had been much more conservative and therefore manageable. Lesley had a thorough understanding of how public life operated and the levels of corruption that could be considered normal and even tolerated by their patrons, the great British public. And his dishonesty was only relative because it supplemented his paltry public salary. He worked hard for the people of Bromsworth and they would want him to do all right out of it. They kept voting for him after all – tacit approval then?

His dishonesty had followed the classic upward parabola, starting with his own expenses, which, naturally, he fiddled. But then, who doesn't fiddle their expenses? he assured himself. And even here, Lesley started off small: the odd meal or two, a hotel stay away with a girlfriend and a flight here or there. But as his confidence grew, so did his gumption and opportunities because he presided over a vast budget and private companies were effectively bidding for 'his' favour. Cash would have been lovely but was far too vulgar and clandestine. He wasn't a football manager after all. But construction companies could very easily mis-account for extra materials – a new digger here or there – which Lesley could liquidate abroad and with no ties back to him. As such, he reasoned that he didn't cost his voters anything at all, aside from the inconvenience of them having to suffer unnecessary mini roundabouts and traffic lights that had sprung up on his watch. He had all the figures in his head. He knew exactly what each project was worth to him personally, even down to his price per speed hump – which currently stood at four hundred pounds.

Lesley's style of council management had always been immersive but was now even more so as his collaboration with Green took shape. Now he had a passage to smooth out and tracks to cover. Far from winding down towards retirement, Lesley was working harder than ever, keeping over all the issues and keeping an eye on everyone around him. His wife hardly saw him which suited him fine. Lesley was so committed to this deal and feathering his retirement that he had put everything else on hold, including his divorce.

Tom hit his brakes hard. His wheels locked as his hire car skidded to a halt well within a safe distance of the car ahead, but he still felt the need to admonish himself. He had been driving erratically, distracted by the old landmarks of where he had grown up. After such a long time, it struck him how faint his memory of the place was. Either that or things had changed beyond all recognition and most likely a bit of both, he decided. Brand new shopping centres had been erected but enough time had elapsed already for them to look tired and in need of a revamp. The shops had all changed hands of course, except for the few high-street stalwarts. His local butcher was now a Chic-O-Land and the café where his mum had worked part-time had been transformed into a King Kebab. The park where he played football was still there, albeit smaller than he remembered, but the walls of graffiti remained. A pack of kids on bikes outside an amusement shop didn't bother to look at his Fiat and he congratulated himself on dumping his Jag. His cell phone rang and he was glad of the distraction but felt guilty when he looked at the display.

'Nell, I'm sorry. I meant to call.'

'Bloody hell, Tom! Where are you?' she asked angrily.

'I'm sorry. I'm in Bromsworth.'

'What? What are you doing there? I've been worried sick!'

She had every right to be angry and he rebuked himself for a second time, but this time for being thoughtless.

'Nell, I'm sorry.'

'Jesus, Tom! But you're OK?'

'Yes, I'm fine. I just wanted to come back to Brom. You know, see the old place.'

'Jeremy said something about you looking up an old-school mate?'

'Oh…' He had forgotten telling Jeremy such a thing. 'Yeah, well, he wasn't really a mate. Patrick Porter; do you remember him?'

'The big boy? The one you mentioned in hospital?'

'Yeah, that's him.'

Nell couldn't really think straight. Having been so worried, her mind was now flooded with an overwhelming sense of relief. 'What about him?' she asked angrily. 'I don't remember you two being friends?'

'No…er…'

'So why are you going to see him then?'

A fair question but not one he could answer, so Tom deliberated. He wondered how best to explain himself and decided that he couldn't. He didn't know himself yet and so he settled for just assuring Nell that he was OK and wasn't about to do anything stupid. In truth, he had never given any serious thought to committing suicide and the closest he did get, was when he requested a feral youth to take aim at his already broken heart. But whenever the option presented itself elsewhere, he quickly dismissed it. Despite the misery and pain, he always knew that he would carry on. It was what Beth and his boys would expect and thinking of his family reminded him that they were the reason he was back in Bromsworth.

'Look, Nell, I'll explain when I see you.'

Nell sighed. 'Fine. Which is when?' she asked and made no apology for sounding like his mum.

'I don't know. Tomorrow sometime. I'm staying here tonight, at the Hyatt in Birmingham.' His car approached a set of traffic lights on red. 'Hey, I'm at the lights at the end of the road from school. I'm about to turn right. If Suckling's is still there, I'll get you a bun.'

Nell reminisced and smiled to herself. Whatever he had in mind, it didn't sound like she needed to worry.

'A Belgian bun, please: the one with the icing.'

'Done.'

'You should have asked. I'd have come with you,' she added. That would have been nice but of course she had her kids to look after.

Tom waited for a gap in the traffic before making his turn and was instantly disappointed.

'Shit!'

'What? What is it?'

The tiny parade of shops was now an ugly block of flats festooned with 'To Let' signs.

'Suckling's is gone I'm afraid. I'll buy you an apartment instead.'

'No thank you very much. So, what's it like then, Bromsworth?'

Tom breathed out and shook his head. 'From what I've seen so far? Not great. Not as nice as I remember, anyway.' He drove past a particularly ugly office building. 'Actually, it's a bit grim.'

'Right, so come home. Because grim is the last thing you need.'

Tom thought about this for a moment before answering. 'Actually, maybe grim is exactly what I need right now. A little dose of reality.'

'Really?'

'Look, Nell, I'm back tomorrow. I'm going to meet with Paddy and then I'm back, I promise.'

'But you said you'd already met him.'

'No, I didn't.'

'Yes, you did, you said –'

'Nell!' By now, Tom had had enough of her inquisition.

She went quiet. No more questions.

'Can we do this tomorrow, please?'

'OK, fine.'

'Great. Thanks for ringing. I'll see you tomorrow,' he told her and rang off.

After his brief tour of Bromsworth town centre, Tom was pleased that the Nelson Pub had managed to remain exactly as he'd remembered it. It was long overdue for a complete refurbishment, but he was glad that it had waited for him. The pool table must have been replaced a couple of times but still occupied the same position, as did the bar, the toilets and the jukebox. A pretty bar lady half-smiled at him before he reached the bar.

'Pint of lager, please,' he said. In truth, he would have preferred a glass of wine but as a pint of lager had been his first ever drink in this very pub on his seventeenth birthday, it seemed appropriate now. Moreover, he reasoned that the red wine on offer was probably brutal.

'Kronenbourg OK?' the lady asked with a glass already hovering below the nozzle.

Tom nodded and paid then picked up the same edition of *The Bromsworth Echo* from the bar and carried his pint over to the corner table with a good view over the whole pub. He read briefly about what was making Councillor Lesley Irwin so happy, but then set the newspaper aside preferring instead the live pictures and stories that the pub had to offer of life in his home town. In his youth, he had spent many happy nights in the place. He recalled the hilarity amongst his friends when the condom machine had first been installed in the gents' toilets. He wondered if the same machine was still in place and if it was, he hoped that the contents had at least been replaced.

Paddy's loud laugh announced his arrival before he appeared in the pub with a couple of mates in tow. He said a general hello to the pub's interior in the way that Norm used to do in the brilliant sitcom, *Cheers* and then scanned the pub looking for Tom, who made to get up. Quickly, Paddy waved at him to sit back down again.

'What you having?' he shouted over.

'Er… a pint of Guinness,' Tom answered.

'Lorraine, my sweetheart, my usual and one pint of your very best Guinness. God love them; the Irish need all the help they can get.'

Lorraine chuckled as she set about her task. 'So, how's it going, Paddy?' she asked.

'What, since I saw you yesterday? Well, I'm afraid to say, about the same, or in other words, shit.'

Lorraine smiled as she plonked a pint of mild onto the rubber drip tray. 'Well, at least you're consistent.'

'Oh yes. That I am – consistently shite.'

Paddy glugged at his drink and winked at Lorraine.

'I'll bring the Guinness over.'

Tom stood up as Paddy approached his table and they shook hands again.

'Thanks for coming, and for the drink, when it comes.' Tom began, a little nervously.

'I didn't buy it. You did. The tab, remember?'

Lorraine placed his Guinness on the table and looked at Tom for a little bit too long.

'Yes, thank you, Lorraine. That'll be all.'

'Thanks.' Tom handed her his empty lager glass.

Paddy looked lovingly at her retreating back. 'That's the lovely Lorraine. Some of the lads have been banned from coming in here without their wives.'

'Not you though, I see,' Tom ventured.

'No, because my Mary trusts me and besides, all the women round here know that I'm strictly off limits.' Paddy chuckled at his little joke before his eyes widened with excitement. 'Hey, my Mary, she only bloody well remembers you!'

'No, really?'

'Yeah! I couldn't believe it.'

'What? The university thing?'

'Yeah, and that. Apparently, you were cute.'

'Oh...'

'But don't worry. I put her right. I told her that time hadn't been kind, you know.'

Tom blushed and rubbed at his chin instinctively.

'Hey, you might remember her,' Paddy announced, hopefully. 'She's younger than me. She'd have been in the year above you. Mary Ryan, she was.'

Tom fumbled; the name meant nothing to him and to save any embarrassment, Paddy decided to step in.

'No? Well, she's no oil painting, my Mary, but good legs though. Best pair of pins in Brom. I called her Steffi Graf there for a while.'

'Right, well, I'll look out for them.'

'Yeah, you do that, but remember she only has eyes for me, my Mary.'

'Of course.'

'Anyway, enough about me; I've been racking me brains and you're not in them. So, come on then, what is it? What did I do?'

Tom took a large slurp of his beer and quickly considered the lines he had rehearsed over and over.

'You remember Declan Connor?'

'Yeah, of course.'

'Right, so then - you remember what a bully he was.'

Paddy nodded for Tom to continue.

'Right, and one time, in the playground, he was bullying me and was about to kick my bloody head in…'

Tom paused hoping Paddy might join the dots.

'Yeah, go on.' Paddy beckoned.

'Until you stepped in.'

Paddy stared at him, more than a little surprised and Tom could almost hear the rusty workings of the man's brain. 'Did I?'

Tom shook his head. 'You don't remember?'

'No, not really, no.'

'No, neither did I until recently. And you don't remember it at all? You practically pushed him over and told him to leave me alone.'

Paddy breathed in deeply and shook his head. 'No, no memory of that at all.'

Tom laughed. 'You *are* Paddy Porter?'

'Yeah, but that doesn't sound like me because I wasn't much of a fighter.'

'It was definitely you all right.'

'Well, you must have caught me on a good day, because usually I wouldn't have got involved, not with Connor and his bloody family anyway.'

Tom nodded. 'And I was incredibly grateful that you did.'

'Oh, well – good.' Paddy looked at Tom, a little confused now. 'Is that it?' Paddy asked, making Tom feel awkward.

'Er… well. At the time, I didn't say anything, to you I mean.'

Paddy looked at him blankly.

'I didn't say anything to you,' Tom repeated, hoping that he wouldn't need to spell it out. But Paddy continued to stare.

'Like what?' Paddy finally asked flatly and very unhelpfully.

'Well, like, thank you...'

Paddy looked even more bemused now.

'...you know, because I was embarrassed. Although, to be honest, not as embarrassed as I am now.'

Paddy drained his drink and motioned to the bar with his two fingers in the air.

'And that's it?' Paddy asked. 'You've come back here now, to say thank you?'

Tom nodded. 'Well, kind of, and now I realise that you can't even remember it, I feel a bit bloody stupid.'

Paddy thought for a moment before rocking his head back and roaring with laughter.

'And please, tell me that I haven't been on your mind all these years.'

Tom laughed as well now which was a great relief.

'No, like I said, it all just popped back into my head recently.'

'What? Just like that? How come?'

Tom shrugged. He certainly wasn't going to elaborate. 'So, thank you then,' he stated formally, for the record as it were.

'You're very welcome. And I take it he left you alone?'

'Who?' Tom asked.

'Connor?'

Lorraine plonked two new pints on the table.

'Yeah, not a scratch on me.' Tom sipped at his new beer he suspected he wouldn't be able to finish even if he wasn't driving. 'And whatever happened to Declan? Do you know? Is he still around?'

Paddy looked up from his drink. 'Oh, yeah, but in the ground.'

Tom looked at him oddly.

'He's dead.'

'No.'

'Yeah. Must be ten year now. Got killed in prison.'

Lorraine arrived again and took care of the empties. Never had she waited tables so attentively.

'Oh, my God! That's awful.'

'Sure, but not such a surprise, eh? I mean, he was never going to be a doctor, was he?'

'No, I guess not. Still tragic, though. And I remember him being clever.'

'Yeah, well, not that clever. Not as clever as you, anyway.'

Tom half smiled. He was still shocked at the news – how he and a classmate's lives could have taken such different trajectories.

'Anyway, how were those apples?' Paddy asked, keen to change the subject.

Tom grimaced and Paddy tutted knowingly.

'Oh dear. I can see I'm going to struggle to get through that fifty quid.' Paddy roared again. 'But you're not getting it back. So, you best have another pint.'

Tom had barely touched his latest drink and was alarmed to see that Paddy was almost finished. His fat cheeks were flushed red already and his mischievous eyes wouldn't hear of any drinking abstinence. Tom knew not to argue.

A youngish man in his late-thirties glanced over from his position at the bar, seemingly irritated by the commotion that Paddy was making.

'Hey! Keep it down, will ya?' he called over aggressively.

Paddy glanced up, smiled broadly and kicked a stool out from under the table. 'Hey, McCray, get over here; someone here I want you to meet.'

The man came over and put his pint on the table to join them. He was a wiry, athletic-looking type, wearing a pair of tracksuit bottoms and training shoes. He was on the cusp of being too old for his trendy tufted hairstyle and had wisely removed the stud or ring from his eyebrow. He didn't have Paddy's easy manner and he considered Tom somewhat suspiciously.

'Joe, this is Tom Harper,' Paddy announced. 'Ring any bells?'

Joe stared at Tom and shrugged. Rather unfairly, Paddy tutted loudly.

'Come on! He was at school with you, but he'd have been a

prefect, when you joined, though. I'm assuming you were a prefect?' Paddy asked Tom mischievously and Tom nodded briefly and instantly decided not to add that he had been Head Prefect. But Joe was still none the wiser.

'Don't worry about it,' Tom started.

'I'm not.' Joe was terse and cool, but Paddy persisted like a dog with a bone.

'Yes, you do! Remember that brainy kid what got to university? He was in the papers and everything.'

Suddenly, Joe's eyes flickered a vague connection was made. 'Oh, yeah! I do remember, yeah.'

Paddy clapped his hands together. 'You see; I told ya.'

'I was in the first year,' Joe said. 'You were a big deal. Father Young called you our great hope.' Joe didn't sound entirely impressed. 'And my sister fancied you,' he added to which Paddy cackled and winced.

'Yeah, but Joe, in fairness, your sister fancies everyone. That's her bloody problem.'

Joe chuckled along. It was true enough but something only a man like Paddy could get away with announcing to a stranger.

'Hey, you're not single are ya?' Joe asked, although still managing to convey that he wasn't looking to do Tom a favour.

'Jesus, Joe!' Paddy shrieked.

'No? Fair enough,' Joe conceded.

'She's hardly a catch, your Morag. She's more baggage than Terminal Five.'

The two men shook hands as Joe continued to eye him. He had a distrusting manner and it was evident that he didn't entirely approve.

'So where do we live now then?' Joe asked, presuming it wasn't local anymore. Not with Tom's accent.

'Er, London. Or just outside, actually.'

Joe sniffed; just as he thought.

'London, eh? Fancy,' Paddy joked, trying to lighten the mood. But Joe didn't laugh.

'Yeah, good for you. Maybe Father Young was right, eh?'

Tom was keen to avoid any talk of his career and circumstances. So far, people not knowing anything about him was one of the great attractions of the place.

'And what do you do then, in London?' Joe asked bluntly, hoping Tom would reveal that he was a banker or something else heinous so they could send him on his way.

'Not a city boy, are you? Only you have that look. He does, doesn't he? You see 'em on the news?' Joe laughed to veil his insult.

'No, sorry Joe, I'm not a banker,' Tom answered coolly, fixing him with a firm stare to show that he wasn't intimidated by him.

'So, what then? What do you do?' Joe asked quickly, still sensing that he was onto something.

'I'm in sales. For a shipping company. Nothing terribly exciting, I'm afraid.'

Paddy now grabbed his opportunity to intervene. 'More exciting than my sodding job anyway, that's for sure.'

Everyone could laugh at this and agree, and Joe finally eased off, happy with what he considered to be his little moral victory.

'And what brings you back then?' Joe asked, but by now, Paddy had had enough and put his large foot down.

'Bloody hell, Joe! I didn't know you were a bloody journalist; let the man have his drink.'

Tom was grateful but he continued to be wary of him. Something bothered him about Joe: he mulled his name over in his mind and noted his athleticism again. He had the look of a PE teacher. Tom recalled how Paddy had referred to him earlier and then it occurred to him. 'Hey, you're not Joe McCray, are you?' Tom asked.

Joe softened immediately and Paddy sighed heavily.

'Bloody hell,' Paddy breathed. 'This is how we should have started.'

Tom looked over to the bar and the large sack that Joe had left leaning against a pillar. It was full of footballs.

'The footballer?' Tom said, much to Joe's obvious delight. Joe had caused quite a stir in the school when he had arrived as a youngster. He was already signed by Birmingham City and as a twelve-year-old, was quickly selected to play in school teams much older than his year group.

Wearily, Paddy got up from his chair. 'Seriously, don't get him started on what might have been or we'll be here all bloody night.'

'Shut up, Paddy,' Joe snapped affectionately.

'No, but I wish you would. I'll get 'em in. What you having, Joe? Apart from a box of Kleenex.'

'Paddy, no. I'll get these,' Tom protested, as much because he didn't want any more alcohol, but Paddy rebuffed him with a hand gesture.

'No, no! You sit here and listen to Roy of the Rovers. You're the only one in here who hasn't heard it.'

By the time, Joe had explained how his heady days playing for England Schoolboys hadn't been matched by a career in the professional game, Tom had drunk five pints and their group of three had swollen by three more, two of whom had also been to St Edmund's, although Tom couldn't recall either of them. Joe had left school to play for City but they released him at eighteen and then, playing for Crewe in the old Fourth Division, he had damaged his knee, effectively ending his career.

'Same injury as Gazza's,' he explained.

'Yeah, only Gazza's knee was worth fixing,' Paddy joked to the group's delight. It was probably a joke that Paddy had used many times before but no one seemed to mind. It was welcome levity because Joe's lost career in football was still very much an open sore.

'So, then I got into the coaching side of things, you know, try and put something back. I'm over at St. Ed's and I'm trying to establish a football club locally, you know, maybe run a couple of teams.'

Tom nodded enthusiastically. 'That's great. A friend of mine did that, you know, set up a team.'

Instantly, Joe's original cynicism returned. 'Oh, yeah? Where?' he asked quickly, too quickly for Tom to come up with a plausible lie and he faltered immediately.

'Er… Brazil, actually,' Tom answered, feeling a little flash and foolish.

'Oh, good, yeah, because Brazil really needs help with their football,' Joe muttered.

Tom could have made an irrefutable case that it did – that the club was in a favela on the outskirts of Sao Paulo, where Naisi's family still lived and where life expectancy hadn't hit the fifties yet – but he could see that it wouldn't help his cause very much. Paddy had also had enough.

'What is it with rich people helping people abroad?' Joe spat.

'Who said he was rich?' Tom responded.

'Yeah, right. Because how many ordinary people set up football teams abroad?'

Joe snapped quickly.

Tom was now a little unnerved. Joe was bright and as quick as he had been with a ball at his feet.

Paddy shook his head at his incorrigible and angry friend.

'Right, that's it! If you two can't get along, then I'm off. I've got a marriage to keep going and a stall to open in the middle of the bloody night, thanks to the jocks. Got them apples to shift, eh, Tom?' He eased himself off his stool.

Joe got up also. 'That's me n'all.' Despite their pleasant nostalgic football chat, Joe wasn't ready to be left alone with the old-school boy and his nice voice.

Five minutes later, Tom exited the local minicab office into the freezing night. A car twenty yards ahead of him flashed its lights, engine running – so at least it would be warm. He hurried over and jumped into the back seat, but regretted it immediately. He didn't know what make of car it was but it was a far cry from his Jaguar or even his rental Fiat, now coated in frost in the Nelson's car park. The mini cab spluttered into the traffic. Its suspension was shot and its brakes howled, but the car's safety features were the least of Tom's concerns: like the cab office, the car was filthy and reeked of every liquid that an off licence and a human body can combine to produce. The driver had obviously long given up trying to clean it up either, preferring to meet the noxious fumes with a pungent smell of his own – garum masala and body odour versus alcohol, tobacco and vomit. Tom realised that he must have mellowed since the accident because he would never have got into such a car before. But now, not wishing to cause offence, he literally sank into the dampness of the back seat and prayed that they wouldn't hit traffic.

He had never been so happy to arrive back at his hotel and literally leapt from the car before it had even come to a full and safe stop. He checked his phone: three new messages – Nell, obviously; Jeremy, just checking in; and Michael suggesting a meeting about nothing. So, everything was the same.

Chapter 18

Just after 7.00 a.m., having had a reasonable night's sleep, Tom made his way to the breakfast lounge with a copy of the *Financial Times* and a thumping headache. He sat at his cluttered table with enough space for either food or his newspaper, but not both. He put the paper aside and settled into a plate of fruit. The limp wet bacon on offer sat under large lamps and looked as though it had been cooked on a radiator. Selecting the most well-done bits, he separated off the rind and made himself a sandwich, quietly hopeful and excited at the day that lay ahead. He was going to visit his old school and some of his other haunts before swinging by to say goodbye to Paddy and heading home for the inevitable dressing down from Nell. He couldn't remember the last time he had sat in a pub with a bunch of guys, drinking pint after pint. A very long time if his thumping head was anything to go by.

Tom turned left at the lights into Addison Road and faced his old school, the two buildings, old and new, on either side of the road. He was struck by how shabby even the new building now looked. He remembered when it had been opened by the bishop in brilliant sunshine, and how everyone had been so proud – a vision in shining glass and brilliant aluminium, both of which had long since lost their sheen. What was also apparent was the expansion of the school: same footprint, double the number of pupils. The buildings had grown like Lego, with new prefabricated classrooms bolted onto existing buildings with no regard for aesthetics. A brand-new sign in royal blue announced to passing traffic in gold lettering that this was St Edmund's Catholic Comprehensive School, Headmistress, S.A. Frost, MA (Oxon). Tom studied the sign. It appeared a lot grander than the school it represented.

From her office on the third floor of the new building, Sarah Frost watched the man in the street studying her school and its sign.

He was well dressed and quite possibly attractive, but it was too far away to tell. No matter; he was a welcome distraction from her phone call with an irate parent whose daughter she had suspended for violent conduct towards a teacher. The mother was now on the phone proclaiming her daughter's innocence and threatening violence of her own if she wasn't reinstated.

'And I've already explained, Mrs Courtney –'

'It's Miss,' the woman hissed down the line.

Sarah leant back on her heavily laden desk full of pressing paperwork. 'Miss Courtney –'

'It ain't fair. People pick on my Shania; that's the problem,' the parent continued to rant. There was no point in arguing with what was obviously such a stupid statement because no fellow pupil in their right mind, or teacher for that matter, would ever pick on the terrifying Shania Courtney.

'And, what am I going to do with her all day at home?'

Sarah didn't answer, presuming this was not actually a question; only, it was, sadly.

'Cos, you're the school. It's your job to look after her, not mine; that's what you get paid for.'

Sarah looked at her watch. She was fast running out of patience. 'As I've already explained, it's now in the hands of the police and the local authority, and they will decide whether Shania is charged or not, not me.'

'Yeah, but, you can call it off, can't ya? Cos, it weren't Shania's fault. It was that bitch teacher picking on her!' And round we go again.

By now, Sarah had had enough. 'Then I suggest you write them a letter. And please copy me as well. Now, I really must get on. Thank you. Goodbye.' She put the phone down and pinched the bridge of her nose, imagining Miss Courtney hurling her own phone against the wall. 'If you can write, that is,' she muttered to herself.

Sarah was supposed to record all incidents of threatening or abusive behaviour, but if she complied there wouldn't be any time left to run her school. She pulled out a desk diary and, opening it at the current date, was about to make an entry when the light on her phone console lit up again – another incoming call; another irate parent?

She pressed the button on the phone.

'Yes, Jane.'

'Sorry, Sarah. It's Mr Hammond from the council concerning the request for the replacement water fountain.'

'Yes, and?'

'Apparently, the application form is incorrectly filled in.'

Sarah rolled her eyes.

'And that journalist from *The Echo* called again.'

'No, tell him, no.'

Tom walked along the side of the 'new' building until he reached his old playground, which came as another disappointment to him; he remembered how wonderful it had appeared to him when it had first opened with its newly painted basketball courts, gleaming black tarmac and silver chicken wire fences. The surface was now badly in need of fresh tarmac. The white lines had all but faded and competed with cracks to mark out any impromptu football pitches. And it was literally smaller as well because it now housed two Portacabins, presumably makeshift classrooms. But the oak tree remained. Listed, perhaps? Tom smiled to himself. Stuck away in the corner, the old tree was a welcome site. A little more gnarled perhaps and thicker even, it stood proudly and no doubt, still provided cover for all sorts of clandestine activities – smoking, snogging and fighting of course. The playground before him was a tiny piece of land and yet had given him so much joy and happy memories to rekindle and play with now. Hours of playing football in the knowledge that girls were watching and no doubt keeping tabs. Not all happy memories either, though certainly still formative. A little along from the tree, Tom stared at the spot where he had encountered Paddy Porter and Declan Connor, now deceased. He recalled the incident in meticulous detail and his circumstances in which this memory had resurfaced. He remained there for a moment to consider the three boys and what lay ahead for each of them. Paddy certainly got the longest straw and Tom half-smiled to himself. Connor, the poor sod was probably always doomed and then he thought of himself in the third person and what lay ahead. The frightened little boy that Tom saw in his mind would have an extraordinary life ahead of him until one ill-fated moment. And his memory then settled inevitably on images of Beth and his boys. Happy memories for the most part but images from the hospital and the funeral were always close at hand. Everything that he encountered reminded him of his family and images flooded his mind and which he could do nothing about. Traffic lights; Luke would try to guess when they would change. Marmalade; Daniel liked his coarse cut and typically was the only one. A post-it note; the guessing game they would play every year at Christmas and so it went on to Bromsworth itself, because it was his family's absence that had led him here. Tom took a moment to reflect before dragging himself off from the school gates to walk down Addison Road, along the side of the playground and towards the school field.

This had been his favourite walk as a child, and he could feel himself getting excited now. It rekindled the feeling he had felt as a kid, carrying his sports bag for a football match against another school, or even just a match amongst themselves. Tom had played left-back, even though he wasn't left-footed, but he was clever enough to realise that it was a position that almost guaranteed his place in the team. Most boys wanted to be upfront or at worst, in the midfield and there was always a shortage of left-footers. A memory of his that hadn't faded was the wet Wednesday afternoon when his school had played in the final of the West Midlands Schools Cup. The pitch had been sodden and barely playable and was lined with hundreds of cheering pupils. Although they lost, it remains to this day one of Tom's most exciting memories. Even Father Young, their headmaster, normally a man of great reserve, had stood amongst the crowd, screaming and shouting with the rest of them. Tom quickened his step as he reached the last house before the corner that gave onto the field; by now he was almost running. And when he arrived, he could barely believe his eyes – the field had gone. It was now a construction site. Yellow machines busied themselves about the place as a concrete truck poured cement into a huge hole in the ground, foundation piles stretching up high into the sky. A sign had been erected to proclaim the good news that Regus Developments were proud to be building thirty-eight luxury, one-, two- and three-bedroom apartments on the site. The sales board showed a gleaming picture of the completed flats, featuring an attractive lady enjoying a glass of wine who presumably came with any apartment purchase.

Chapter 19

The young man serving at the stall had to be Paddy's son. Although there was some physical resemblance, it was his height that really sealed it. The boy caught Tom's eye.

'Can I help you?'

'Er, yeah, is Paddy around?' Tom asked.

'No,' the boy answered bluntly. He was probably eighteen but he still looked like a child and being Paddy's son, he couldn't really manage a menacing glare.

'Right... well, I'm a friend of your dad's, so...'

The boy looked doubtful. Tom didn't look anything like his dad's friends.

'Well then, you can get him on his mobile, can't you, if you're a friend of his.'

It was a good point and Tom didn't have his mobile number of course. Tom picked off a banana and nodded his head for a price.

'Twenty pence.'

Tom fished in his pocket and didn't bother mentioning the tab. He only had a fifty pence piece and gestured that he didn't need any change.

'Are you at St Edmunds?' Tom asked, figuring now that he was owed at least one question and answer.

'Was,' the boy snapped and stood a little taller in search of his actual age. He had his dad's height but none of his charm.

'Yeah, so was I. No, really; a long time ago now,' Tom added as he recognised the surprise on his face. Call it the 'Joe' look. 'I was just there now at the school...'

'Yeah, and.'

'I was wondering what's happened to the field?' he asked, a little pointlessly because, wasn't it obvious?

'They've been after it for years and they finally got it.'

'Right, thanks,' Tom said, although he hadn't been very helpful at all.

He visited *The Bromsworth Echo* website and managed to find plenty of information on the sale of the school field and, going back even further, he even found the story covering the murder of Declan Connor. The headlines ran *Local Man Murdered in Prison*; *Gangland Prison Murder* and, finally, *Local Criminal Laid to Rest*, with a picture of a hearse festooned in flowers around a central wreath making the word 'DAD'. Tom stared at the photo of the adult Declan. He hadn't changed much. He was missing a couple of teeth, had a few more scars and his snarl and defiance had remained. And he too was a dad; Tom wondered about his kids and how they might be faring. Probably not very well was his guess, but much better than his own children of course. The pathway was different but the destination was always the same.

By evening, Tom still hadn't picked up his Jaguar nor checked out of his hotel. He had now resolved to stay until the next day and was mindful that he hadn't called Nell yet. Sitting in the Nelson, he was feeling more uncomfortable with each passing half-hour. He felt lonely and vulnerable. Paddy wasn't expecting him and he might not show up at all and what then? Tom didn't know. Unable to put it off any longer, he put a call in to Nell, hoping to get her voicemail.

'Hi, Tom. Are you home?' She was delighted to hear from him, but less impressed once she found out where he was. 'Just leave your mobile on,' she said sulkily as their call ended.

He'd been in the pub for almost forty-five minutes and was nearing the end of his second pint with still no sign of Paddy. He would need to get another drink shortly and as his stomach growled, he wondered whether eating alone was an option. Shortly afterwards, he thanked Lorraine as she laid a 'homemade' steak pie and 'fresh garden vegetables' in front of him along with a half of Guinness. Tom considered his plate and pushed the pie gently with his fork. The vegetables had never been golden and the pie was limp and forlorn. More bush-tucker trial than 'delicious homemade grub' as the pub blackboard promised. He was hungry but he wasn't dying. He tried a small mouthful of the pie and one thing was certain: it was only 'homemade; if Lorraine lived in a factory that wrapped reconstituted meat in wet cardboard and still there was no sign of bloody Paddy. He'd eaten all he was going to eat which would normally be embarrassing but as he wouldn't be returning to the pub again, any awkwardness was preferable to labouring through it. Exceeding the limit, he couldn't drive home now, so he resolved to try and catch Paddy in the morning before heading back to London. His trip back to his childhood had been mixed but it had been worth it. Paddy had been the highlight and he was glad he had made the effort and he fretted a little about what he was returning home to.

He folded his paper napkin over the offending dinner and was about to leave, when he heard Paddy's unmistakable laugh and the door was flung open. Paddy was with Joe and a few others and he spotted Tom instantly and beamed at him, bounding over with his arm outstretched. They were all smartly dressed, like they'd been to a wedding. Some young lads playing pool were pleased to see Joe and stopped their game to flutter around him, which suited Tom and Paddy just fine.

'Bloody hell man! You still here?' Paddy bellowed.

Tom shrugged, a little embarrassed. 'Yeah, I just couldn't leave.'

Paddy chuckled. 'I know; it's like that, this place.'

Tom smiled broadly.

'Hiya, Lorraine, love. The usual please. Tom?' he asked, stabbing a fat finger as his glass. Tom shook his head but it made no difference and the same finger now wagged the 'same again' gesture.

'How were the races, Paddy?' Lorraine asked.

Paddy scoffed.

'Are you up?'

'Are we bollocks! Daylight robbery. They charge you to get in and then they have the shirt off your back.'

Lorraine smiled. It was another of Paddy's lines that he had used before, probably every year after their annual excursion to the races at York.

'Which would have been a result for you, Paddy, with that suit on,' she quipped, which Paddy's mates all enjoyed.

'Paddy is going for the "just got out of prison" look,' Joe added to everyone's amusement, including Paddy.

Benny, a small fat man with fading ginger hair, smiled up at Tom. 'Paddy got fleeced; lost the lot,' he announced with rather too much glee.

'It's bloody fixed, I swear it.'

'And your Mary's gonna do her nut.'

'No, she won't,' Paddy said confidently and then paused for dramatic effect. 'Not if she doesn't find out.'

Everyone followed Paddy's lead and roared with laughter.

'And besides, my Mary, she's doing all right. She already backed a winner when she married me.'

More laughter but with hoots of derision also, and then Paddy noticed Tom's plate of untouched food.

'Bloody hell, man! Is that a plate of food? Tom, what are you doing? No one eats in the Nelson. Not even the dog.'

Marge, Lorraine's aunt, wandered over to collect the barely touched plate. 'You're a cheeky sod, Paddy Porter. Hello, love,' she said to Tom. 'I won't charge you for the pie. I'm changing my suppliers.'

'Suppliers?' Paddy bellowed. 'I thought they were *homemade?*'

'Shut up, you.'

'Round of drinks, please, Marge,' Paddy called after her. 'And bring crisps as well. Lot of crisps; there's a man here who hasn't eaten.'

'I came by the stall today, but you were...' Tom petered out lamely.

'Bloody hell! I only met him yesterday and he's checking up on me already!'

'Yeah, I wanted to talk about school, that's all.'

'Oh right! Did you get over then?'

'Yeah, I did which is what I wanted to talk to you about. You as well, Joe,' Tom said, looking at Joe.

'Why? Did I save you as well?' Joe laughed scornfully.

Tom looked at Paddy for an explanation but he just smiled.

Paddy gestured. 'Hey, there are no secrets in Brom I'm afraid.'

'Not with you anyway.' Tom smiled.

'So, what do you think of Ed's then? Changed, eh?'

'Well the playing field certainly has.'

The jovial atmosphere evaporated immediately. Paddy sighed heavily. Not the bloody field again. Joe's mood darkened immediately, which irked Paddy.

'Well? What happened then?' Tom asked, rather pointlessly.

'What does it look like?' Paddy answered. 'You're supposed to be a businessman!'

'Meaning?'

'Meaning, money is what happened. Apparently, there's more money in flats than there is in school football. Do you not read newspapers?'

'It's a fucking disgrace, is what it is,' Joe seethed.

'Yeah, OK, Joe. Calm down.' Paddy looked at Tom. 'See what you've done? We were having a nice day up until a moment ago. And despite our losses.'

Tom ignored him. 'But you tried to stop it?'

Paddy looked to the ceiling. 'No, actually, we all thought it was a great idea. It's just what we need round here, luxury flats. Of course, we tried to bloody well stop it!'

'Got a petition going,' Joe said, 'but it didn't do any good. What does it matter what we think anyway?'

'Exactly,' Paddy agreed.

'We all wrote letters to the council, didn't we, Paddy?' Joe added to which Paddy nodded but couldn't conceal his guilt.

'They got almost three million quid for it and –'

Quickly, Paddy raised his index finger as an appeal. 'Joe. Not this again. Come on, please…'

Joe went quiet and slurped at his drink and ripped open another bag of crisps.

'So where do we play football now then?' Tom asked.

'Blimey, look at him, "we".'

'Come on, where?' Tom persisted.

'Why? What do you care?' Joe asked spitefully.

Tom ignored him and looked at Paddy for an answer.

'They do a ground share with a school over in Brawnston.'

Brawnston was a borough right across the busy city and was hardly convenient. 'Which is shit, but what can we do?'

'Maybe your friend could help,' Joe chipped in. 'The one who set up the team in Brazil?'

Again, Tom ignored him and Joe got up and took himself off in the direction of the toilet.

'Something I've done?' Tom asked gesturing over to Joe.

'No. Don't mind him; he has anger 'issues'. He just takes a while, that's all.'

Tom nodded doubtfully. Not that he cared very much.

'Joe's not in a great place right now. Missus left him. Ran off with a salesman. Lives down South now with his little lad.'

Tom nodded. 'Okay. That's tough.'

'Yeah, but he's all right, Joe. He's good for the kids round here. They admire him, you know. He's still a magnificent player. And he's got a big heart which he –'

'Yeah, wears on his sleeve, right? I can see it,' Tom finished for him. Paddy smiled, pleased that Tom wasn't too offended by his attitude.

'What does he do?' Tom asked.

'Joe? I suppose, he's a youth worker. Both full- and extra time n'all. Which is something to be angry about, right? The state of the youth round here...'

Tom nodded and took his word for it.

'You're lucky that you're not a dad yourself,' Paddy went on. 'Joe works with the current crop of Declan Connors and they're bloody worse.'

Tom tried to imagine. He and Paddy had already spoken about the kids at St.Eds.

'That kid you told me about the other night?' Tom asked. 'Louis, was it?'

'No, Lewis?'

'Yeah, Lewis, the footballer. Like Joe was.'

Paddy shook his head. 'Bloody hell! Do not bring him up with Joe.'

'Why's that?'

'Because Lewis is Joe's big project. His big hope, more like and let's just say that Joe is very protective of him.'

Tom took a sip of his unwanted pint and looked at Paddy enquiringly.

'I think Joe sees a lot of himself in young Lewis.'

'What, the talent you mean?'

'To a point. Don't get me wrong, Joe was brilliant alright. But this kid, Lewis – he's off the charts. Way better than Joe was. Strong, fast. Quick feet. Joe figures he could play Premiership, England, the lot, until Villa let him go.'

'How come?' Tom asked although he suspected he already knew.

'Blimey, where to start? But fighting mainly. You name it, Lewis is in to it. He's got a tough home life and he's messed up. And Joe can't fix it, no matter how hard he tries.'

Joe reappeared from the toilets and stopped to feed the cigarette machine. Paddy wisely changed the subject.

'So, you can imagine how Joe's going to react when he finds out about these new flats on his field? Me and Mary are bloody terrified…'

Tom shook his head. 'What? Finds what out?'

Paddy shifted a little, barely able to contain himself. 'That, me and Mary, we've only gone and bought one of the penthouses.' He roared with laughter just as Joe sat back down.

'What's so funny?' Joe asked, but neither Tom nor Paddy wanted to explain, adding to Joe's irritation.

'Right, fine, then. Stay here and laugh like little schoolgirls. I'm off.'

Paddy watched Joe leave. 'He has jealousy issues as well.'

'Whatever,' Tom said. He hadn't come to Bromsworth to widen his circle of friends and Joe didn't interest him anyway. Paddy finished up his drink. 'Right, that's me as well. I'm away home.'

'OK then, Paddy.' Tom began. 'It was lovely to meet you again. I really enjoyed it.'

'Yeah, thanks.'

'I'm heading south in the morning, so good luck and thanks

again.'

They shook hands warmly.

'You staying over tonight then?' Paddy asked.

'Yeah. Can't drive now.'

'Hey, then, why not come over to mine?' Paddy suggested, rather taking Tom by surprise.

'To where? Your house?'

'Yeah. Meet my Mary and the kids.'

'What, now?' Tom asked, incredulous, shaking his head for good measure.

'Yeah, why not?'

'No, no, really…'

'Come on. My Mary would love to meet you, and the kids will still be up if we're quick.'

'No, Paddy, really, I can't…'

'Why? What else are you doing tonight?'

Tom dithered. The truth was that he didn't want to say goodbye just yet.

'Right then, that's settled, get your coat.'

Chapter 20

Paddy's house was just a few hundred yards away: a thirties semi that Tom must have walked past every day on his walk to and from school without realising who had lived there. The front door led directly into the tidy little lounge where Mary was ironing a mountain of clothes and Paddy's kids were sprawled on a huge sofa that was too large for the room, playing a computer game on an equally oversized television.

'Kids these day, eh? Billy, when I was your age, I wasn't playing silly games. I was watching telly.' The young boy didn't laugh or even react. Another of Paddy's stock lines perhaps?

'Hello, love.' Paddy leant over to kiss his wife.

'How'd you get on?' she asked suspiciously, referring to his race day before even acknowledging that they had a visitor.

'Yeah, good. Up fifty quid.'

Mary looked doubtful and would probably have turned his pockets out if he had been alone and Tom now suspected why Paddy had really invited him home.

'Hey look, I've brought you a treat.' Paddy pulled a reluctant Tom forward. Tom offered his hand rather apologetically to Paddy's tiny but formidable-looking wife. She was a plain lady, but she had a kindly face and standing behind her mountain of ironing, he couldn't yet verify Paddy's comparison to Steffi Graf's famous legs.

'Hello. Tom Harper.' Tom smiled warmly and instantly Mary softened. 'I'm sorry to intrude on you like this, but Paddy insisted.'

'Yeah, he does that – especially when he has something to hide.' Paddy laughed defensively.

'Anyway, you're very welcome,' Mary said, smiling up at him, her face shining now.

'Thank you.'

'Find yourself a seat, if you can. Would you like a brew?'

'Er... yes, please.'

A sense of awkwardness hung in the air as Tom looked around at the busy little lounge and the completely normal family. Suddenly, he wished that he was back at his hotel and on his own.

Paddy smiled broadly. 'I told you, didn't I?' he exclaimed.

'Told me what?' Mary answered.

'That he'd lost his looks.'

Mary snorted at him. 'Just ignore him, love. We all do.'

Tom smiled and considered the three boys on the sofa. The middle one had two toes emerging from his ragged sock and a dirty shirt with a ripped breast pocket. He didn't know what ages they were but a similar age to his boys. A little older perhaps; he was never a good judge and had learnt to not make guesses. The biggest boy, perhaps twelve, had obviously been playing football and was caked in mud. He had a mischievous face, and on his looks alone was obviously a handful to manage. But they made a very happy scene and Tom felt a pang of jealousy at what they had together. It all felt so utterly normal which punctured his own circumstances and how cruel they were.

'Hi there, lads,' Tom said, but they didn't respond apart from a glance in his direction.

'No, they won't answer. These three are totally wild. They can still only grunt. The big one, that's Billy. Beneath that shirt, he's still covered in hair. Couldn't walk when we found him.'

The kids grunted on cue, as if playing along.

'Lads, this is Tom. He was at your school and guess what? He can read. Billy's just taken delivery of his first set of hormones and they're freaking him out.'

Billy sneered at his dad.

'And this is Liam. Liam's eight. And this little fella is my Paddy. He's our mistake.'

'Dad.' The young child screamed in delight.

Paddy grabbed the smallest boy, his huge hands almost surrounding the boy's rib cage, and squeezed him gently, making him squeal with delight. 'Paddy's four.'

'No. I'm not. I'm five.'

'No, you're not. I've told you already, I'm not letting you grow up.'

The tiny boy squealed in protest until Paddy placed him back down.

'Paddy's five. He's my favourite.'

'Paddy!' Mary rebuked her husband even though her boys knew that he was joking.

'And there's Sean as well. You've met him already. He's out somewhere. Probably lost, like the rest of his generation.'

Tom smiled at the scene.

'Wow, four boys!'

'Yeah, a house full of willies,' Paddy quipped. 'Or, as Mary says, four willies and one great big –'

'Paddy! That's enough,' Mary interjected again. 'Sit down, Tom, love, will you?'

Taking a seat on the sofa came as something of a relief to Tom; the ceiling being so low, even for him, so God knows how Paddy managed. As an adolescent, it must have been a close thing whether Paddy would literally outgrow the house and even though he had stopped just in time, with four kids, the house was far too small for the Porter family. It was a freezing night and an electric fire belted out as much heat as it could manage to supplement the efforts of the single storage heater underneath the window. But no matter what the temperature gauge read, the atmosphere of the room felt warm to Tom. An array of family photos occupied almost every surface, with Paddy and Mary's wedding taking pride of place on the mantelpiece. In the photo, Paddy had more hair and enormous side-burns but essentially, he looked the same – a large head, ripening nose and fixed grin with his arm proudly around his new bride.

'Tom, love, are you staying over tonight?' Mary asked so nonchalantly that Tom wondered if he had heard her correctly.

'I'm sorry?'

'Tonight? Are you staying over?'

Tom couldn't believe the question. Judging by the size of the lounge and the number of Porter children, there was little chance that they had a guest bedroom.

'Er... no. No, I'm not.'

'Why? It's no trouble,' Mary continued, as she heaved the pile of laundry up in both her arms, almost covering her face.

'No, honestly…'

'Go on, man. Stay over. It's no trouble,' Paddy added.

'You're very welcome. That sofa you're on becomes a bed.' Mary added.

'Yeah. Got it, half price. Can you believe it?' Paddy quipped.

Tom squirmed a little more. He didn't have his wash things or a change of clothes. And he didn't do sleepovers anymore, especially not with people he hardly knew. And he hated himself for thinking about such inconsequential things as clean bedding.

'Go on. We'll get a curry delivered. You must be starving.'

'Hey! I've cooked.' Mary protested.

'Exactly.'

'Bloody cheek!'

'Yeah, but Mary, you haven't saved a dinner for Tom, have you?'

'I'll get some clean linen.' And that was it. It was settled.

Tom smiled, amazed and grateful for their hospitality.

'Good lad. I'll get the menus. Scrub the brew. Two beers please, love.'

'Thanks, Paddy. It's very kind of you.'

'No, it's no bother. Only, there is a downside though, that I should have mentioned.'

'Oh?' Tom looked a little worried.

'I can now give our Sean tomorrow morning off 'cos he's worked on the stall all day already. And I'm up at five, setting up, and you're helping. Is that OK?'

'Done.'

'Good lad.'

Tom ate more naan bread than he should have done and he certainly didn't want any more beer, as Paddy plonked another can in front of him, which helpfully he had already opened. Mary came in to say goodnight and pointlessly reminded Paddy that he had to be up early in the morning and that he shouldn't be too late to bed. Like, he didn't know? As the evening wore on, they finished reminiscing about school and they got on to Paddy's losses at the races, which Paddy was reluctant to elaborate on. He was very guarded about his finances, generally, and needed convincing all over again that Tom didn't have some ulterior motive.

'Aren't you a bit paranoid about the tax man?' Tom asked.

'No, not really. They're bloody hounding me.'

Tom seemed surprised. 'But why? I mean, given what you say about the stall?'

Paddy quickly clapped his hands together. 'Exactly! Thank you! That's what I've been telling her upstairs. I'm earning buggar all. But they keep on sending me letters and forms and more letters…'

Tom could sense Paddy's acute anxiety. It made him realise just how cosseted his own life was from the real day-to-day worries. He had a battery of professionals charged with handling such mundane necessities and he had the means to pay for whatever bills he faced.

'And these letters?'

Paddy sighed heavily. 'Look, if you don't mind, I'd rather not talk about it, OK. I just prefer to forget about them.'

Tom grimaced, understanding that ignoring Her Majesty and her demands was the very worst option to take.

'Right, I just wonder if I might be able to help, that's all.'

Paddy looked at Tom oddly. 'And why would you want to do that?'

It was a reasonable question.

'I don't know; because I can.'

Paddy shook his head.

'Paddy, you can't ignore the revenue, not an option I'm afraid.'

'No?'

'They don't just forget things and they definitely don't just go away either.'

Paddy scowled. Of course, he knew this already and he looked genuinely frightened about what might happen. His eyes darted to a cupboard and he clenched his jaw, still deliberating.

'I could just give you some advice, that's all.' Tom added helpfully.

'Fine, then.' Paddy stood up quickly, opened the cupboard door and began rooting around inside. He pulled out a large cardboard box and plonked it on the table. It was stuffed full of papers, from which he retrieved a bunch of letters in their familiar brown envelopes with HM Revenue emblazoned across the front. Most of them remained unopened.

'Interesting filing system,' Tom suggested as he fingered through them.

'Yeah, well, I don't do organised.'

Tom continued through the box. With Paddy's permission, he opened various envelopes; demands, threats and latterly, notices of fines. He picked up a letter at random and gave it a cursory read before he spotted the date and discarded it. He looked at Paddy ruefully. 'Anything more recent?'

'I don't know. It's all in there.'

Paddy sat silently, like a schoolboy caught in a defaced toilet with a spray can in his bag. Tom finally tracked down the most recent letter, opened it and scanned it quickly. The red ink emblazoned across the top rather gave its content away. It certainly wasn't a rebate. Tom gave it a cursory read and pondered Paddy's situation. He was certainly in need of something more than just the 'thank you' that he had already delivered. And attending to the taxman was a logical and pressing need. After all, Tom was a qualified accountant, if a little out of practice.

'Do you have an accountant?' Tom asked.

Paddy's shoulders slumped a little more. 'Do I have an accountant?'

Tom gestured for an answer.

'Oh yeah, of course, I do. I have a big London firm. We play golf together once a month, you know, to review things and discuss strategies.'

Tom chuckled. Angus had just mailed him suggesting a round at Sunningdale with Michael followed by lunch for this very purpose. He hadn't responded yet and now felt that he would have to decline.

'OK - so now you have an accountant?'

Paddy shook his head, confused. 'Who?'

'Me.'

Paddy looked a little worried again.

'Paddy, please, just let me look at your books.'

He sighed heavily. 'Me books?'

'Yes, and I don't mean your Dan Browns.'

Paddy didn't get the joke.

'Your accounts, Paddy?'

Paddy looked sheepish and after a long pause, he was up and into his cupboard again. 'It's cash mostly.'

'Right, but you still record it though, right? Or at least, some of it?'

Paddy didn't reply, which was answer enough. He reappeared with another box, the same size as the previous one and just as disordered, packed with loose bits of paper.

Tom did some preliminary digging around. It was overwhelming. Paddy hadn't been to confession since his wedding day and in the intervening years, his financial sins had amounted to mountainous proportions and too great to absolve immediately. With a little more gentle prodding though, Tom did establish that Paddy had re-mortgaged his house to meet his debts and currently had at least five separate loans, one of which he had taken out to pay off his last revenue bill. He couldn't say for certain, but all the signs indicated that Paddy was already technically bankrupt. Official confirmation of this was probably in one of the unopened letters and where it could stay for now. He didn't want to ruin Paddy's sense of hope for his future, a future he was now determined to secure. Smiling warmly, he told his new friend that he had nothing to worry about. And he meant it.

Later that night, as he lay on his makeshift bed, Tom stared up at the ugly ceiling that creaked with every movement of life from the floor above. He reflected on his couple of days back in Bromsworth. He should be back in London already but he was glad not to be. When he had arrived searching for Paddy, he never imagined staying at his house. But he was pleased that he had met him. He was grateful that his memory had freed up his encounter with Patrick Porter after such a long time and as uncomfortable as the sofa-bed was, he was quietly happy to be staying at his new friend's house. For the first time since the accident, outside the day of the funeral, Tom had a specific purpose for his day ahead and he was looking forward to it. It was just rudimentary accountancy, but no matter, he was excited at the prospect of helping his old 'friend'. The ceiling creaked again, more quietly this time; perhaps the footsteps of the youngest child making his way into his parents' bed, the way his Jack had done almost every night of his short life. Inevitably, his attention turned from Paddy's books to thoughts of Beth and his boys, just as it did every night before he tried to sleep. He wondered if they could see him now. He hoped that they could and that they would see that he was OK.

Chapter 21

In the morning, by the time Paddy emerged downstairs at just before 5.00 a.m., Tom was already sitting at the table in front of piles of letters and receipts, with more little piles spread around the floor and on every available surface in the lounge. He had made some progress but with years of chaos, there was much to do. In the van on their way to the wholesale market, Paddy had asked for a quick assessment and Tom had been quick to allay his concerns and he meant it, because if need be, he was going to simply write out a cheque.

At just after 5.30 a.m., Paddy pulled up outside Smithwick's Fresh Produce Wholesalers, a warehouse the size of an aircraft hangar, packed with every conceivable fruit and vegetable that the bountiful earth has to offer. Tom was staggered by the sheer quantity as he followed Paddy dutifully on his purchasing round. Paddy knew all the merchants well and exchanged banter or insults with them as he acquired his stock for the next three days.

'One hundred and eight pounds please, Paddy, love,' the cashier said through her plastic screen from within her tiny booth that looked so cosy with its little telly and mug of steaming tea. Paddy signed the docket without checking it and opened his wallet, his hand thumbing several credit cards, unsure which one to use.

Paddy always took breakfast in a cafe along from the wholesalers on the other side of Birmingham and like the Nelson, it seemed to be another much-needed extension to his tiny home. He introduced Tom in a general and suitably embarrassing manner.

'Everybody, this is Tom. Tom's on work experience with me for a week. He's special needs.'

People in the cafe laughed. 'He will be if he learns anything from you.'

'Nice one, Barry. Two breakfasts, please, Daphne, love. All the trimmings. Heavy on the grease; it's bloody freezing out there.'

Back in the van and on their way to the stall at just after 6.30 a.m., Tom was still bombarding Paddy with questions. It was a long time since he had felt as energised and excited, despite his almost complete lack of sleep.

'Bloody hell! You're not thinking of opening a stall are ya?'

'No, it's just –'

'Good, 'cos you can have mine. Or you can make me an offer, at least?'

Tom chuckled at this. 'Er Paddy, I've seen your books, remember?'

'Yeah, fair enough. In fact, with that fifty quid you gave me, you probably own it already.'

For now, though, Tom didn't want to talk about Paddy's finances but wanted to discuss the more general nature of the fruit and veg business.

'But all that fruit this morning – that was all seconds?'

'No, not all of it, but a lot of it, yeah.'

'What like, off?'

'No, not off.' Paddy shrieked with faux horror. 'But nearing its date, for sure.'

'What, sell-by date?'

Paddy nodded as he waited for a bunch of kids to cross at a zebra crossing. 'See that. Not one of them say thank you. Not even a friggin' hand gesture.' He wound down his window and called through it, loudly, 'Thank you…!' He viewed them in his mirror and hoped that they got his point. One boy held up his middle finger – obviously not, then.

'So, about this produce then? The seconds?'

Tom pressed, keen to keep him on track.

Paddy raised an eyebrow. 'Look, all fruit, or most of it, is at one-point class A, but the longer it's been picked, the less valuable it is because there's less time to sell it. Simple really.'

'What? Like your apples?'

Paddy laughed. 'Yeah, and sometimes I get it wrong.'

'So, that stuff this morning is the same stuff in the supermarkets then?'

'Yeah, of course; an apple's an apple. They don't have special orchards – even Marks and Sparks.'

'No, of course not.'

'There's only one kind of mango. They don't have special mango trees,' Paddy added, warming to his theme. 'But a lot of that stuff there this morning isn't about date either; it's about oversupply. You'll see stickers on the fruit from different supermarkets. Because the big boys, they sell what they can and then send the rest back.'

'What? And you lot take up the slack?'

Paddy grinned. He was now enjoying being able to hold court. 'Yeah, but not all of it.'

'What? How do you mean?'

Paddy tutted.

'I take it you don't do much shopping yourself then?'

'Er…'

'Like, when did you last go into a greengrocer?'

Tom thought for a moment. He couldn't even recall.

'No, thought as much. Pretty soon, stalls like mine? Gone. It'll just be blinking supermarkets and Amazon. That little baldy fellah with the beady eyes.'

Tom still had more questions than answers.

'Right and what about the stuff that can't be resold. What happens to that?' Tom asked, fearing he already knew the answer.

Paddy tutted once more. It was another stupid question, on a par with his enquiry about the school field. And this was troubling, because Paddy was secretly hoping that this bloke could solve his tax crisis and he clearly wasn't that bright after all.

'It gets chucked out; what do you think happens to it?' he announced flatly.

Tom sat quietly for a moment. 'What, as in, chucked away?'

'Yeah, and if not by the trade then by the punters themselves. You know – the soft pears at the bottom of the fruit bowl or the mealy apples. I'd say that up to a fifth of what you saw there this morning will end up getting buried.'

Tom glared at him.

'I know, it's best not to think about it. That's what I do, anyway.'

Tom's mind was racing now, recalling one of Daniel's many lectures about the scandal of food waste.

'The perishables are the worst, especially soft fruits, you know, raspberries and the currants,' Paddy continued, 'which is doubly bad because they're all flown in from Africa mostly and with that little girl from Denmark, Greta...'

Tom's mind continued to whir. He looked at his watch. It wasn't yet 7.00 a.m., so he still had time.

'Paddy, stop the van, will you?'

'What? Why?'

'I need to do something. I have an idea.'

'Right, but you're supposed to be helping me set up. For your lodgings, remember?'

Tom smiled. 'I'll be along later. This afternoon, I promise. But it'll be worth it, believe me and I'll make it up to you. And I'll do tomorrow as well. How's that?'

Paddy stopped the van. 'What is it, then?'

Tom smiled. 'It'll be much better if I show you.'

Chapter 22

The morning on the stall was particularly slow, even slower than normal, as the cold and drizzle kept people indoors. Ordering their food online from Uber fucking Eats, Paddy imagined. He'd set out his stall and for what? Thirty-odd quid takings and it was nearly lunchtime. And lunchtimes weren't the rush they once were either, with people preferring a battered sausage to a cold apple, and who could blame them? He called Mary to see how she was, but more specifically to get her take on Tom, their blast from the past. He hadn't reappeared yet and Paddy wondered if he would ever see him again. Nothing about him really made sense and although he seemed genuine enough, there was something not quite right about him albeit he didn't know what. Joe certainly agreed, but to be fair, this was probably just Joe being Joe. Mary wasn't much help either, stating that he was very handsome but that he appeared to be lonely. Why else would he be back in his home town and tracking down a lad he had never even been friends with? Mary agreed that something was wrong. She didn't buy his story about just coming back to Brom to thank Paddy for the Declan Connor incident. So why then was he back? Paddy asked himself and he immediately started to fret. Because what could be possibly want? Paddy felt sure that it wasn't money, which was good because he didn't have any. And he didn't appear to be short of means. He was nicely dressed and had nice nails, or so Mary had noticed anyway. So, what, then? And now Paddy started to panic all over again. Perhaps he was a con man: one of those confidence tricksters who do all sorts of unspeakable things. And what the hell was he thinking of allowing a stranger access to his private finances? Perhaps he wouldn't return at all because he already had what he needed: bank account details, numbers, that kind of thing. Paddy took some deep breaths and tried to calm himself down, assuring himself that there was nothing in his bank accounts to steal anyway. But still he worried. He looked about his stall and for the first time, he was relieved that there wasn't a customer in sight.

Michael was pleased, if a little surprised, to take Tom's call and to hear that he was on his way in to see him for an impromptu early morning meeting. Tom had sounded excited and enthusiastic, so it had to be important. Michael was just pleased that he wanted to see him. Hastily, he reshuffled his diary and had a little time to prepare. He was hopeful but guarded also. He had proceeded with his plan to considerably curtail Tom's access to his own funds and when he initially explained the situation to him, Tom had barely reacted at all and hadn't mentioned it since. Michael didn't enjoy overseeing such an arrangement and the sooner things could revert to normal, the more comfortable he would feel. The way Tom had sounded on the phone was certainly encouraging, but such hopes quickly faded when Tom, at just after 10.00 a.m., explained that he wanted to establish a new business that he would call The Fruit Bowl. Michael stared at his most successful client, trying to get a handle on what he had just heard. For some inexplicable reason, Tom was wildly excited at the prospect, an enthusiasm that Michael felt unable to share. Michael shifted awkwardly. He didn't want to patronise a man he admired so much. But he was more accustomed to acting for Tom on his plans to acquire billion-dollar assets, and so this represented a considerable gear change down. Not to mention that it didn't sound very plausible and worse, it could easily be a financial black hole.

'And you're going to fund this yourself?' Michael began, allowing a degree of incredulity into his voice to flag up his worries.

'Yes, but only until I get it started. Just in the short term, to demonstrate its viability. And then we'll get all sorts of government grants and local funding – we could even go to Europe for a slice.'

'You do recall that we have left.'

Tom brushed his hands dismissively.

'Whatever, there'll be grants. Bound to be but even if there isn't, I don't care.'

With this, Michael's sense of alarm increased.

'Michael, just consider the facts here; this is food being thrown out, which is an anomaly, no? We're dying of obesity, carbon emissions from food miles and we end up burying the stuff.'

This was all very worthy but what Tom was proposing was a charity and not a business. It could eventually dwarf his previous philanthropic contributions and so Michael was now congratulating himself on moving to secure his wealth. If he hadn't, he might even have blown it all already and he assured himself that he certainly wouldn't be relaxing the current arrangement. He felt confident that he would have Nell's support also, whom he would call the moment Tom had left. Tom had finished his petition and had already sensed a lack of support.

'Tom, this all sounds very laudable but –'

Tom shook his head. 'Don't patronise me.'

Michael grimaced. It was difficult not to. 'Right, sorry. But it's just that I worry about the funding.'

'Why?' Tom asked.

'What do you mean, why? For God's sake, Tom! What if you don't get any funding?'

'But we will.'

Michael sighed. 'Oh, really? And do you remember at school, when we used to get free milk?'

'Yes, but this is different. This is food being thrown out.'

'Oh, come on, Tom. It has to be thrown out to keep the price up; supply and demand, you know that as well as I do.'

'It's food being buried,' Tom shouted and Michael clasped his hands together and took a moment.

'Tom, I'm not arguing that it's ideal or even agreeable. But, for instance, just how long are you prepared to give it? To fund this thing yourself?'

Tom shook his head. It was something he hadn't considered. One of the hallmarks of his business career was that Tom had always been a scrupulous planner, a pedant for information with contingencies at every juncture, and this new cavalier approach was riling Michael and making him nervous.

'Tom, please, be reasonable. You must have thought about it.

How long? Six months? A year? Two years?'

'I don't know and I don't care. As long as it takes.' Tom shouted. Something else he rarely did before.

Michael shook his head. 'Well, I do care I'm afraid. That's my job, to protect you. Government grants? Jesus, Tom! That could be decades. And at best it sounds like altruism and not business. It's a folly.'

Tom bristled at this. 'Don't call it that. It's not a folly.' He hadn't driven all the way to London to hear logic. 'So, I take it that I've failed then?'

'Failed what?' Michael asked.

'You know what I mean. Your little sanity test?'

Michael didn't answer and Tom stood up angrily. He didn't have time to fight his own bloody lawyer.

'I could always get another lawyer you know,' Tom hissed.

'Tom, please! Come on, sit down so that we can discuss this rationally.'

But Tom was furious. He had been so excited at the prospect of The Fruit Bowl; he didn't care a jot much how much it cost. He looked at his watch and made a quick calculation. He needed to go. He needed to get back on the motorway.

'So, Michael, just to be clear then; I still can't be trusted with my own money, is that right?'

Michael pinched his nose. Not the words he would have chosen, but the result was the same.

Tom headed for the door. 'But I take it I'm still good for your fees?'

'Actually, no,' Michael countered angrily. 'Since the decision was taken, my office hasn't billed you at all, which you would know if you took time to read my bloody emails.'

Tom didn't respond. He certainly wasn't going to thank him and he slammed the door after him.

On the way out of London, he needed to stop by his house. It felt cold and unlived in, despite the heating being left on. Naisi had left it clean and tidy but thankfully, she was out somewhere, probably at a language class. He visited each of the bedrooms in the house and spent a quiet moment with each member of his family, and then quickly descended the central staircase. He unplugged Beth's juicer and after a further cursory glance about the place, reset the alarm and pulled the front door shut behind him.

Chapter 23

Lunchtime on the stall hardly registered and slipped into the equally quiet afternoon. Joe had been by and added to Paddy's growing apprehension about their old school non-buddy. Tom still hadn't returned as he had promised he would, which by now Paddy was hoping was a good thing. Paddy had a good protective instinct, a nose for things that weren't quite right, occasions just like this. He'd probably scarpered once he realised that Paddy had bugger all worth stealing and with his fifty-quid tab, Paddy figured he was still up anyway. Never had Paddy felt so relieved for being poor and if need be, he would resort to violence if he ever showed up again. After all, it was violence that united them in the first place, so he could use it again to cut him adrift. Only, Paddy wasn't a violent man. He tensed his arm muscles and clenched his fists. There was a first time for everything and he figured he had more than enough to send Tom packing.

It was after just 4.00 p.m. when Tom finally arrived back at the stall, scaring the wits out of Paddy.

'Jesus Christ.' Paddy screamed, leaping in to the air and clutching his heart. 'You scared the living shit out of me!'

Tom looked at him oddly, bewildered by his reaction.

'What are you doing back here? I thought you'd naffed off,' Paddy barked, trying to regain his composure.

'What are you talking about? I said I was coming back.'

'You know what I mean.'

Tom wasn't sure that he did. 'Has something happened?'

'Yes, you've turned up again – out of the blue. And where have you been anyway?' Paddy continued, still flustered and nervous.

'I had to pop down to London.'

'Oh, fancy. And I've been rushed off me bloody feet all day.'

'Well, that's good, right?'

'And what do you want with me anyway?' Paddy finally snapped.
'What do you mean?'

Paddy studied him carefully. He appeared innocent enough, but then wasn't that the skill of the master fraudster?

'Look, I just need to know what it is that you want with me.'

'I've already told you.'

'Yes, I know what you've told me. Thanking me and all that, but it doesn't make any sense, not after all these years. Even my Mary thinks that's bollocks. So there has to be something else.'

Tom wasn't entirely surprised by this reasoning; his story, as it stood, was just an outline and it lacked any real substance.

'Mary's been on. She thinks it's odd. Thinks it's weird. So, does Joe. He thinks it's weird; we all do.'

Tom had spent the entire journey to and from London pondering this very problem and still he was resolved that the truth was not an option. It was a nugget that was too valuable to forego, the advantage of being with people who didn't know his circumstances?

'Well, Paddy, it is what it is. You remember me from school, right?'

Paddy nodded.

'And it really happened, right? I'm not making it up. Me, you and Declan.'

'Yeah, but –'

'No, that's it. And it might be weird but it's the truth. And it turns out that you're in the shit and I'd like to help. That's it. But if you don't trust me, then fine; I'll leave you alone.'

Paddy noticed that he was holding a large carrier bag. Actually, it was three carrier bags in one, so whatever it was, it was heavy.

'So, where've you been then?' Paddy asked, his attitude softening, because he certainly needed help and he desperately wanted Tom to be real. His face relented a little further which Tom seized on.

'Unplug that radio, will you? I want to show you something.'

Paddy recognised the machine as a juicer immediately, but he didn't say anything as Tom excitedly got himself ready. He cleared a space for the machine and grabbed at Paddy's old tea mug. He emptied the remnants of tea in to the gutter, plugged the machine in and gestured for Paddy to pass him some carrots and he duly obliged. Paddy's face fell as he watched in disbelief but still he didn't say anything. One thing was now certain; Tom was no saviour. He was just a madman.

'Thanks. And hand me a couple of apples please.'

Paddy looked on in disbelief as Tom excitedly fed the machine and watched a line of liquid fall into his stained mug. It felt cathartic to Tom but not to Paddy. He looked on at the idiot, beaming back at him like a child on Christmas morning.

'What do you think?' Tom asked.

Paddy's eyes narrowed. 'Er...'

'Good, huh?' Tom appealed.

'Juice!' Paddy asked, hoping that there might be something he had missed.

Tom nodded. 'Yes. Can you see what this could mean?'

Paddy flapped his open hands at Tom to demonstrate his bewilderment.

The mug was full now and Tom took a quick mouthful. It wasn't great. Certainly, not as good as the ones Beth made for his boys, but he hadn't chosen the fruit and the tea sediment wasn't helping either. But no matter; it was going to be successful. Tom had no doubts at all. He handed over the mug for Paddy to try.

'Jesus, what are you expecting from me here? An orgasm?'

'Just have a drink.'

Paddy downed the lot. But there was no epiphany and still Tom was grinning at him like an idiot.

'Paddy, can't you see how perfect this is?'

'Are you fockin serious? Fruit juice! Have you not heard of the man from Del Monte? He's already said yes.'

'Yes, I know,' Tom laughed, 'but that's not the market we're after. Look, all this fruit we're chucking out?'

'Oh, bloody hell! Not this again?'

'And what's the big food story now?' Tom asked urgently.

'Er...'

'Oh, come on Paddy; the food story all over the news. On the telly?'

'Er, celebrity chefs. That twat who swears.'

'No, obesity! The obesity crisis. And carbon footprint.'

'Yeah, OK. Fat people. What about 'em?'

'And especially fat...?'

Paddy shook his head. He hated quizzes and always panicked.

'Come on Paddy, fat what?'

'Er... chavs?' Paddy ventured.

'No, kids! Fat kids!' Tom shouted.

'Oh, right! yeah, fat kids.'

Tom took a breath. 'And where do kids eat every day?'

Paddy was rapidly tiring of the questions. 'I don't know, McDonald's?'

'Jesus, Paddy!'

'Well, where then? I don't know. Stop with the questions, will ya? Seeing as though you already have all the bloody answers.' Paddy whined.

'At school Paddy! Kids eat at school every day,' Tom gestured, hoping that it would all now click into place for him. But Paddy stared at him blankly.

'And what does your Mary do?' Tom exclaimed.

'Er... moan.'

'At work? At St Edmund's?'

'She's a dinner lady.'

'Exactly. Now, can't you see? It's bloody perfect.'

Chapter 24

It wasn't that Paddy disagreed with Tom about his concept. He could see the natural synergies, the captive market, the obvious need and that it could well be rolled out across the country making him a multi-millionaire, but Paddy was a man who liked things just so. He didn't like change, unless it was the spare change he found in an old pair of trousers. Actual change, real change, frightened him. And setting up a new business was change on a grand scale. Even though he could see that his old business was failing, and the terrible consequences withstanding, it was still marginally preferable to doing something new. Paddy liked his hatch battened down and super-glued for good measure, but Tom didn't appear deterred and he felt confident that he could prise it open.

Tom had rushed off again, leaving Paddy alone to dwell on his thoughts. So far, he felt that he was losing the argument and that he was being manoeuvred against his will, and he regretted now not being honest with the man. He should have mentioned the concerns he had about Tom's business acumen. He didn't know why; it was just another of his instincts again kicking in. And, secondly, Paddy was terrified of Sarah Frost, the new head of St Edmund's, who was going to be central to Tom's plans. He almost had a full-blown panic attack when Tom casually asked him to set up a meeting with her. The last time he had been in her office was because his son, Billy, had been caught lighting his fart in a biology lesson, and now he was coming to her with a bloody business proposition.

His mobile rang. It was Tom, which irked him immediately. They'd only just exchanged numbers and he was calling already. This was all way too quick. What next? A weekend away, bonding?

'Hello.'

'Have you made the appointment yet?'

Paddy let the phone down to his side and pinched the bridge

of his nose. Now it was beyond doubt; this bloke was deranged and Paddy wished that he had the guts to just tell him to fuck off and leave him alone.

'No, the stall's been manic since you left. You should leave more often.'

'OK, well, get on with it and ring me with a time. I can make any time. OK, gotta go.'

Paddy looked around the place and sighed heavily. He certainly wasn't about to call the school to make the appointment. He needed to speak to Mary first. She'd know what to do.

The next morning, after another late night of bookkeeping, Tom's hotel suite was covered in bits of paper and little piles of notes. It was a mini victory for Tom whenever he located a receipt or an invoice with a month for which he had already started a pile. But still, Paddy's two cardboard boxes remained crammed full of utter chaos. When he began, he had intended to simply process his books and be on his way, as his way of saying thank you, but since his epiphany with the fruit juice he had become distracted and no longer felt as inspired by ironing out Paddy's loose trading history. He could leave things as they were of course, and let things play out as he predicted they would. But he wasn't keen to have a business partner being declared bankrupt so early in their partnership, and so he realised that he would have to call for some assistance.

Jeremy had left a couple of phone and email messages for Tom and was conscious that they hadn't been returned, so he was delighted to finally receive Tom's phone call.

'Yeah, sorry, I got them, but I've been busy with all kinds of stuff,' Tom responded a little sheepishly.

'No, that's fine. Don't worry about it. So, tell me, how are you?' Jeremy asked.

'Yeah, OK. Certainly, better than I was anyway.'

'That's great, Tom. You certainly sound it.'

'Look, Jeremy, sorry to be short, but has Michael spoken to you?'

Jeremy took a beat. 'Actually, yes, he has...'

'Right, so he's explained the situation about my capital.'

Jeremy felt awkward. He hoped that Tom wasn't calling him for a loan or anything as crude because he had promised Michael he wouldn't help in such a way.

'He did mention it, yes.'

'Right, fine, and did he mention what I was up to?'

'Er... something about fruit.'

'OK, good. So, I could use some help?'

Jeremy winced. This was a request he would have to refuse, a situation he hated.

'Don't worry, I don't need any cash. I just need a set of brains.'

The relief in Jeremy's voice was palpable, not to mention the delight he would find in being able to assist him. His assurances to Michael didn't cover personnel.

'Yeah, just some number crunchers really – basic accounting, bit of research, maybe, that kind of thing.'

'Of course.'

'And normally, I'd been fine for the firm to invoice me, but...'

Jeremy cut in immediately to save his old friend any embarrassment.

'Tom, that will not be necessary. It's done and the firm can pick up the costs. Not a problem.' Tom took a moment. 'Thanks, Jeremy. I'm very grateful.'

'And we'll get their expenses as well. We can assign them over as work experience. How's that?'

'Sure, that would be great.'

'I'll send up Ryan McDonough. You know Ryan, right?'

'Er, actually, I had Elliot in mind,' Tom said.

Jeremy paused for a split second.

'Yep, okay, fine. We'll miss him of course – his brain, that is – but sure, Elliot it is. He's on his way. He's got two trainees shadowing him for a month, so you can have them as well. When do you want him?'

'How about tomorrow?' Tom answered and Jeremy smiled. Tom's customary impatience was returning, which was a good sign and Jeremy was delighted that he could call on him for his help.

Packing away his stock, Paddy was thinking of excuses to

explain why he hadn't yet made the appointment with Ms Frost, and settled on the idea that she was away at a conference somewhere. But it didn't matter anyway because when Tom reappeared, he explained that he had made the appointment himself and that they were seeing her tomorrow at 11.00 a.m. Immediately, Paddy's head swirled and he quickly berated Tom for proceeding behind his back, a situation made worse because Tom seemed to find his reaction rather amusing. There was nothing amusing about their situation at all. They were still arguing when he pushed open his front door and entered his house with a bag full of fruit and Tom in tow with his blinking juicer. Mary was waiting for him and evidently hadn't had a good day either. She folded her arms and stared up at her husband.

'Well?'

'Fruit juice,' Paddy answered, his voice full of bitter disappointment.

'Fruit juice?' Mary repeated.

'I know, so don't go booking any holidays.'

But Tom was undeterred, busying himself in the kitchen setting up the juicer. Paddy retrieved two glasses, pulled a face behind his back and twisted his finger in a circular motion at his temple.

'I saw that, Paddy,' Tom said quietly as he fed a carrot into the machine.

'Yeah, well?'

'Just get Billy will you, and little Paddy.'

Paddy protested. 'They don't like fruit; I've told you that already.'

'Exactly. That's the point. That's exactly why it's going to work.'

Paddy lined up three of his sons in height order, with Billy first. Tom handed him a glass.

'Well, go on then,' Paddy barked impatiently.

Billy took the smallest possible sip, making Paddy snap. 'Jesus, wept!'

'Paddy! Language!' Mary rebuked him.

'Well, for God's sake, Billy! What are you, a bird? Take a gulp, man.'

Billy swallowed a marginally bigger mouthful as everyone

waited for a response.

'Yeah.' He seemed to approve. 'That's all right, actually.'

Tom beamed and Paddy shook his head; it was typical of his kids to let him down. The meeting with the headmistress was going ahead as planned.

Chapter 25

It was called the Triangle for obvious reasons: a small field and recreational facility on a triangular strip of land, boxed in by the railway line on one side and a road on the other. It sported a fenced basketball court and a dirty looking prefab building housing a pool table, a few arcade games, toilet facilities and a few workshop rooms. Part of Joe's remit was managing the centre with a staff of six. Posters warning about drugs and pregnancy adorned the walls and seemed to have little effect on its patrons who were highly experienced and proficient in both areas. Joe was sitting with Chenise; she had agreed to take a reading course with a view to sitting her GCSEs a year later than her classmates, but it wasn't going to be easy now that her daughter had arrived, and Joe waited patiently while she tried to feed her.

A tall handsome boy with a baseball cap poked his head through the door. Lewis Adele was mixed race (Nigerian father and English mum) and was as talented as he was troubled. Six months ago, as the cliché goes, he'd had it all to look forward to. An apprentice at Aston Villa, he looked set to be offered full professional terms until an aggravated assault charge saw him back in court, ending both his playing and school career. A squandering of talent but nothing new of course and a situation compounded in Lewis's case by his seemingly uncontrollable anger. His attitude towards women didn't help his cause much either. As handsome as he was, Lewis didn't want for female attention, which was heightened by his football prowess and his prospect of joining the professional ranks. But the doe eyed girls came at a high cost, usually in the form of aggrieved boyfriends or protective fathers. Lewis wasn't the type to be intimidated or to back down and often became embroiled in violent altercations. One boyfriend shouted insults across a busy bar about Lewis's mum and Lewis promptly broke the kid's nose and in doing so, significantly dulled his bright future.

With Joe providing character statements and a guarantee for his future behaviour, Lewis narrowly missed a custodial sentence. He was given a community service order instead, with the other upside being that Joe was appointed as his managing officer. At the Triangle Centre, Joe was always relieved to see him. His curfew was supposed to be strictly observed and this morning, like most mornings, Lewis was late. Joe didn't mention it. He didn't want to start another day with another argument and besides, he was pleased to see him because he had news that he hoped would cheer him up.

'Hey, man. How's things?'

Lewis didn't reply and Joe didn't try again.

'OK, so I have a programme for you today that will take you your full four hours.'

Lewis scowled. 'I ain't unblocking no more toilets.'

Joe smiled as he shook his head. 'I've spoken to the courts and they've agreed to include football training into your hours, as long as it's with six kids or more and that I submit a full progress report.'

If this was good news then Lewis didn't let on. In fact, he barely even smiled, which bruised Joe, given the effort he had put into getting it approved. He had hoped that Lewis would be delighted and might even be moved to say thank you. But Lewis did neither. Angrily, Joe grabbed two coffee cups off the table and moved towards the kitchen area. Lewis was an exhausting and frustrating project. Not since Gazza had such a talent been wasted, Joe liked to say, and even though everyone laughed at such a claim, he actually meant it.

'On the basketball court? Not on the field?' Lewis called out, as a kind of concession. He was in no position to be stipulating conditions but if it made for a quiet life... And besides, the basketball court did make sense. The field was too wet and boggy, not to mention the fact that it was covered with dog shit.

'Yeah, fine, on the court,' Joe agreed and Lewis almost smiled. He looked over at the kids and slowly nodded his head.

'OK, I'll do it.'

Joe slammed the coffee cups into the sink. 'Yep, good of you,

Lewis. Thank you very much indeed. Really, thanks a fucking lot,' Joe snapped.

Lewis shook his head with incomprehension. What? He'd said, yes, hadn't he? The sooner he had completed his hundred hours, the better.

Chapter 26

As Tom ran along on the towpath in the early morning mist, he was aware that his excitement had been replaced with nervousness. He hadn't slept very well, revisiting vivid memories of his own boys and the part they were playing in his new plans. It had been fourteen months since the accident and although he wasn't lying to Jeremy when he explained that he was improving, he still had very bleak moments. At least once a day, he felt as though he might just burst into tears. That moment had occurred already today, as he ran along the canal and passed a nursery, deserted at this early hour, but no doubt it would be heaving by 9.00 a.m. as mums and dads dropped their kids off for the day. But it was quiet with no one around and so safe for a lone man to peer through the chicken-wire fence without risking being arrested and ending up on some list. The outdoor play area was neatly ordered with everything in place ready for the children to destroy it all over again. The whole area was enclosed, all cordoned off with locks on the gates and closed to the dangers of the outside world. And Tom thought of his own children and how safe he had thought they were and yet look what had happened. He gripped the fence hard and squeezed until it hurt. He could hear another runner approaching and so he needed to get going again. He quickly picked up from where he had left off, only he ran faster now, harder, all the way back to his hotel.

Tom and Paddy sat outside the headmistress's office, ready for their 11.00 a.m. meeting. It was already 11.20 a.m. and Paddy looked more nervous than ever, as if he was about to meet with Lord Sugar in the fake boardroom. They had agreed that Paddy was just a figurehead and that it was all Tom's idea and as such, that Tom should do all the talking. The headmistress's PA, Anne, was an efficient-looking, middle-aged woman. She removed her headset and looked up at Paddy.

'Mr Porter. Miss Frost will see you now.'

Quite right, Paddy thought to himself. She can see me, but that's all she can do, because I'm not saying a bloody word.

'Excellent, thank you.' Tom jumped out of his seat.

'This way, please.' The secretary opened her stable door and they passed through a narrow corridor with shiny linoleum, at the end of which was a heavy white utilitarian door with a frosted glass centre. Tom knocked.

'Come in.'

Tom pushed the door open and entered. It was a large airy room with views on two aspects, over the playground and to the front of the school. A large desk with a mountain of paperwork fought for territory with an elevated computer screen and a keyboard. In the middle of the room was a table surrounded by eight chairs and to one side was a coffee table flanked with two low sofas. Ms Frost turned away from her filing cabinet and welcomed the two men warmly.

'Hello, I'm Sarah Frost.'

They all shook hands and she gestured that they take a seat around the table. Sarah Frost wasn't what Tom had been expecting at all. From Paddy's various descriptions, he had prepared himself for a fire-breathing dragon and not such a young-looking woman and one, so attractive. In fact, her youth was the only thing Paddy had got right. She would have had to be in her mid-thirties at the very least to secure such a job but she could pass for much younger and her appearance completely wrong-footed Tom. It was also a glaring omission that Paddy had failed to mention her natural good looks. Thick dark hair cradled her delicate face and contrasted sharply with her large bright-green eyes. She displayed the small beginnings of a furrowed brow – the only blemish to her taut and sallow skin – and the remnants of a tan perhaps or just a lovely olive complexion? She smiled at them both. She had a beautiful smile and Tom ranked her up to very attractive and even beautiful. He also ranked Paddy down to an idiot and a walking liability.

'So, how are you, Mr Porter?'

'Fine, thank you,' Paddy answered in a stilted fashion.

Blind and stupid, Tom would like to have added.

'And, how's young Billy? Staying off the baked beans I hope?'

'Oh, that, yes, and we've downgraded him to chicken korma as well.'

Sarah smiled and Tom added 'sense of humour' to the list of Paddy's hopeless omissions regarding the headmistress. He certainly hadn't seen any fire yet.

'So? What can I do for you gentlemen?' she asked, needing to stick to her busy agenda for the day. And as agreed, Tom took the initiative and made a good job of summing up their proposal to provide a glass of fruit juice to each pupil, each day. True to form, Paddy didn't say a word. His only contributions were some discouraging sounds and facial expressions; lest she should think he was in on his colleague's daft idea.

Sarah listened intently as Tom spoke and she largely ignored Paddy. The proposal was interesting and novel, certainly not what she had been expecting and although she could see hurdles and obstacles, she was charmed by the concept or perhaps by the man trying to sell it. The men before her certainly made an unlikely union. Paddy was a loveable rogue who couldn't be trusted with anything, but by comparison, Tom was impressive. He was eloquent and credible and rather like his proposal, he came across as a little unreal. He held her gaze with his interesting but serious face and when he briefly looked away, she quickly accounted for his marriage finger.

'And how do you two know each other?' she asked, genuinely interested.

'We were at school together,' Tom answered.

'Really? You were at St Ed's?' Sarah couldn't keep the surprise from her voice. 'You don't fancy being a mentor here, do you?'

Tom dithered, unsure how to respond.

'No, too early. But think about it?' she added.

'Certainly, I will.'

'So, were you in the same year then?' she asked and Paddy suddenly bucked up and beamed at her question.

'No, Tom was a good few years below me, but you could be

163

forgiven for getting that wrong. I moisturise daily; that's the secret. I'm an Olay man myself.'

Sarah laughed. This was turning out to be a rather enjoyable meeting in an otherwise difficult day.

'And just to clarify things? You intend to fund the whole project?'

Quickly, Tom stepped back in. 'Yes, but just for the trial period because like I said, with all the benefits and advantages, we're confident of getting local funding.'

Sarah's sleek eyebrows arched immediately. She obviously didn't share Tom's confidence and he recalled Michael's response.

'OK, then. Well, thank you both very much. I think it's a rather wonderful idea if a little ambitious. But I would love to be proved wrong and if you are right, then who knows? With healthier kids, we might even start charging up the league tables.'

Tom smiled broadly at her. It was the first piece of positivity to his idea from anyone. 'I certainly hope so, and we'll certainly do our best anyway.' He stood up and shook her hand. She was small, five foot four, possibly less, and slightly built, but she had an obvious spirit and determination. Her face flashed with intelligence and hope, and Tom caught himself for a split moment because he realised that he wanted to impress her and didn't want to let her down. And this immediately made him feel uncomfortable.

'Lovely to meet you, Mr Harper.'

Tom was flustered now and needed to get out. He suddenly wanted to be alone so that he could think and remember his Beth. He could barely manage another word, leaving it for Paddy to formally end the meeting.

'Yes, and you. Thank you. We'll be in touch.'

Chapter 27

Contrary to expectations, Paddy had enjoyed the meeting enormously. Of course, Tom was pleased by her reception to the idea and her approval of the trial, but he was troubled for more personal reasons that he could not discuss with Paddy. And Paddy was not helping with matters much, as mischievous as he was. Never had he seen Miss Frost so amiable and at ease, and there could only be one explanation, which he revelled in explaining to Tom.

'Paddy, please, will you shut up?'

But there was little chance of this happening and Tom knew it.

'What do you mean, "I could have told you"?' Paddy smirked.

Tom shook his head.

'Told you what, exactly?' Paddy asked.

Tom breathed out heavily, feeling increasingly uncomfortable. He looked at Paddy as he started his van. 'You know what?'

'No. I don't. So, tell me.'

He looked across the car park, back towards the school. He was careful not to give Paddy the satisfaction of explaining that he found her attractive. 'You said that she was a ball crusher.'

Paddy laughed. 'Yeah, she is… normally, with people she doesn't fancy.'

Tom closed his eyes as images of Beth crashed about his consciousness.

'I said she was young looking. What else should I have mentioned?' Paddy asked.

'Oh, just forget it.'

'No, come on! What?' Paddy insisted.

'Oh, for fuck sake, Paddy. That she's beautiful!' Tom shouted, angry with his friend although he could never explain why. 'You might have mentioned that she's beautiful. That would have been a good heads-up. OK, happy now?'

Paddy nodded, delighted with himself, and Tom gave him a withering look.

'Yeah, well, I only have eyes for my Mary.'

Tom tutted. 'Lucky Mary.'

'Plus, she knows that I'm already spoken for. Off the market, as they say.'

Tom sighed heavily, hoping that this might be the last of it.

'Plus, she's spoken for anyway.'

'Fine,' Tom answered quickly, but not surprised although she hadn't been wearing a ring.

'A professional cricketer, no less.'

Tom shook his head. He wasn't interested in continuing the conversation and they drove along in silence for a moment or two, both men thinking about the same thing and inevitably, it was Paddy to speak first.

'And anyway…'

Tom rolled his eyes.

'…seeing as though you're so "cute", how come you're not married then?'

Tom demurred. It was a reasonable enough enquiry.

'Hey, I'm only asking,' Paddy protested.

'Well, don't.'

'Right, fine.'

Tom stewed over the question. It was bound to come sooner or later and it wasn't going to go away.

'If you must know, I was married, OK?'

Paddy looked across at Tom, a little doleful. 'Oh, I see. Divorced, eh?'

Tom didn't deny it and let it hang.

'Well, I'm sorry to hear that.'

Tom nodded, happy for Paddy to get it wrong.

'Terrible thing. But still, you're lucky that you didn't have any kids.'

Tom nodded. He dwelt for a moment on the idea that he was lucky. He didn't feel very lucky.

'Can't be many things worse than being a divorced dad with

kids?'

Tom didn't respond. He could think of something easily enough.

'And besides, if you want kids, you can have one of mine – any of them, apart from my little Paddy. He's staying with me.'

Chapter 28

Paddy was looking forward to telling Mary about his meeting, particularly the part about Ms Frost, Tom and their chemistry, but the moment he saw his wife's face, he realised that his story would have to wait. She looked frightened and Paddy instinctively feared that it was because of him. It usually was.

'What's up, love?' He kissed her quickly, searching her face for clues.

Mary fixed him with a cold and tired stare. 'Paddy Porter, are we still in trouble with the tax man?'

Her direct question winded him and he struggled to recover. 'No. Why?' he lied, convincing neither of them.

'Right, so it's all sorted, is it? Financially, we've got nothing to worry about?'

'Well…'

'Well, what, Paddy?'

'You know, things are tight alright, like they are for most people, but why do you ask? What's happened?'

Mary scowled at him. 'I'll tell you what's bloody happened. I've had a phone call.'

Paddy's face fell. Letters he could handle, or at least ignore, but a phone call… 'The bastards! They've got no right to phone here. What did they say? What did they want?'

Mary shook her head and looked as if she was about to cry. 'Well, you can ask them, can't you, because they're coming up to see us, from London.'

Paddy's eyes widened and he quickly sat down before his knees buckled. This was serious now. He had ignored their letters for nearly a year, but now they were coming after him. Paddy swallowed and tried to think straight.

'Jesus. They're coming here? To our house?'

'Yes, tomorrow morning. I've been baking cakes all sodding afternoon.' Mary grabbed the pad from beside the phone and read. 'An Elliot Stapleton and Ernest Young. Paddy, what the bloody hell is going on?'

'I don't know.'

'Where are your boxes of accounts? I've been looking for them. Where are they?'

Paddy looked up at his beloved wife, her face etched with worry.

'They're with him.'

'With who?' she demanded angrily.

'Who d'you think? Him. Tom.'

'Jesus Christ, Paddy! Mr Sodding Fruit Cake?'

'No, listen; everything is going to be OK,' Paddy whimpered, clutching at any straw he could grab at. 'This juice business might be a goer. Ms Frost likes it anyway.'

'Yeah, well, she would, wouldn't she? Because she's not paying for it, ya daft sod! He's giving the bloody stuff away, so she's bound to like it!'

Paddy rubbed his eyes but they were still blurred and he needed to think straight. Retrieving his boxes was the best start he could think of and he grabbed his coat and his car keys.

Tom looked at the flat-packed shed that had just been delivered to the school by the local branch of Wickes. The shop assistant had explained that it was simple enough to erect with just basic joinery skills but now he had it on site, he worried that his skills would be a little too basic. The instructions were pathetic. More like a challenge than a manual and offered him little hope. He fumbled with the heavy bag of hardware, cut open the cellophane and began pulling the sheets of wood apart and laying them on the ground to identify them. He established the floor easily enough, but was struggling to distinguish the sides from each other and the roof. Clearly, he would need assistance to hold the various panels in place and ideally, this person would know their Phillips from a flathead. Paddy was the obvious choice. He was the only person he knew well enough and after all, he was a partner in their fledgling business. With perfect timing, Paddy's van hurtled into the school car park, screeched to a stop and he came running over, mouthing angrily and waving something in the air.

'What the fock is this?' he gestured to the shed lying on the floor.

'What do you think it is? It's a shed. For the trial.'

Paddy scowled. 'You never said anything about a shed.'

'Er, did I need to?'

'Yes, you did.'

'Right, well, I'm sorry. But what if it rains?'

Paddy didn't have time to argue, and it wasn't the shed that was worrying him anyway; he couldn't give a toss about the shed because he had Her Majesty's Revenue coming for tea and scones.

'Ah, bollocks!' Paddy scowled. 'Do what you want! I need my boxes of accounts back. Where are they?'

Tom was a little surprised. 'But I haven't finished with them.'

'Yeah, you have. Where are they?'

'They're at the hotel. Why?'

'Because the fuckin' tax man is after me, that's why.'

'Paddy, we've already discussed this.'

'Yes, but now they're coming to see me,' he shouted angrily.

'Really? When?'

'Tomorrow. They phoned the bloody house; spoke to Mary. Can you believe that? Scared the living shite out of her.'

Tom was now more confused than ever. 'Who? Who's coming?'

'Two blokes. Does it matter who?' Paddy grabbed at his bit of paper. 'Elliot Stapleton and…'

Tom would have laughed but he was worried that Paddy might have thumped him if he did.

'No, no, Paddy, you've got it all wrong. I can explain.'

'What? What do you mean?' Paddy glared at him, waiting for his explanation.

'Elliot is not a tax inspector. He's an accountant who works for a firm called EY.'

'Yeah, and how do you know that?' Paddy shot at him and made Tom flounder.

'You know him?' Paddy seethed. 'Jesus Christ! How fockin' dare you!' Paddy screamed. 'My Mary almost had a heart attack and I think I've actually had one.' Paddy clutched at his chest for good measure.

Tom could see his reasoning and he too was cross with himself. Knowing Elliot as he did and how ruthlessly efficient he is, he should have anticipated that he might have contacted Paddy and he should have warned him at least.

'Paddy, I'm sorry. I meant to say something...'

'Oh, did you? Well, it's too late now, isn't it?' Paddy hissed.

'I just thought it would be better to have a professional accountant deal with your accounts, that's all. Elliot's much better than I am and I'm going to get busy with The Fruit Bowl.'

Paddy raised his hands in despair and glared at Tom. 'What is it with you, huh? Just who the hell are you? First, it's a thank you. Then it's my accounts. Now it's a new business. Just who the hell are you? My Guardian Angel or what?'

Tom pulled a hand through his hair. 'No, of course not.'

'Well, who then? And why? Why are you doing all this? And please, don't give me some bullshit story about just saying thank you, because you've done that already. You've done that, and now we're even.'

Tom's mind raced.

'And unless you're honest with me this time - about all of this, then it's all off – the juice, everything. It's over.'

Tom pulled at his face and blew out hard. He knew that he would eventually need to explain himself and he was gauging now how much he needed to reveal.

'Because there's something else; there has to be,' Paddy continued. 'People don't just turn up after thirty years like this.'

'No, you're right, they don't. You're right. There is something that I should have explained.'

Paddy looked vindicated and keen to learn more. 'Right, well, go on then. What is it?'

Tom took a deep breath. 'I haven't been totally honest with you.'

Paddy nodded. He enjoyed that rare feeling of being vindicated and motioned his hand in a circular action, gesturing for him to get on with it.

'But not about why I want to help you. All of that's true – the bullying thing…'

'Yeah, yeah, we've done all that.' Paddy was impatient now.

'And the intentions for the juice…'

'Right, fine! Let's get to the bit that you've left out?'

Tom took a moment.

'Well, that concerns how I can afford all of this. Do you remember when you asked me if I was loaded or not?'

Paddy nodded.

'And I said that I wasn't.'

'Yeah.'

Tom paused again, his answer sticking in his throat. 'Well, that wasn't strictly true.'

'Oh.' Paddy looked a little pensive. 'So, what then?'

Tom chuckled a little as he considered his current financial arrangements with Michael holding his purse strings.

'Are you rich, then? Like a millionaire?' Paddy asked.

Tom shrugged. 'Well, rich is a relative term, isn't it?'

Paddy looked at him blankly.

'I mean compared to the Arabs who own Manchester City, then no, I'm not rich, but compared to the guys that I was at school with... then yeah, I probably am.'

Paddy watched him carefully. 'I knew it. I bloody well knew it. There's just something about you!'

'And what's important is that I can afford to do all of this, for the time being at least. Including getting Elliot to help you because I can't have a bankrupt business partner now, can I?'

'No, but it's still not right though.'

'Why?' Tom tutted.

'Because I can't repay you.'

Tom nodded. He could see his reasoning and there was no easy way of explaining that he already had done so – not without revealing the complete truth about his presence in Bromsworth.

Suddenly, Paddy started to look about himself, turning his head this way and that.

'What are you doing?' Tom asked, slightly unnerved.

'Am I being filmed right now?'

'What are you talking about?' Tom asked, slightly perturbed.

'Cos this is like that TV show. I dunno if it's still on, *The Secret Millionaire.*'

Tom winced. He hadn't seen the television show but he could guess its premise and how it would fit the current TV zeitgeist.

'Paddy, listen to me. I know you're a proud man…'

Steady... Not that proud, Paddy thought to himself.

'But this…' Tom gestured with his open arms, 'all of this is something that I genuinely want to do. I need to do it and I can't do it without you.'

Paddy softened immediately.

'You know the school. People like you here; they trust you. You know the fruit business, the wholesalers…'

Paddy continued to nod; his chest puffing. He was enjoying Tom's little speech on so many different levels.

'Plus, Paddy, I don't want to do it on my own.' Tom paused a moment. 'I want to do it with you.'

'Yes, but it doesn't feel fair,' Paddy protested feebly. 'The business I can understand, well sort of, because it could work, but what if –'

Tom stopped him. 'Paddy, listen to me. Believe me, this is going to work. It has to. It absolutely has to. And when we get that funding, I can see Porter's Fruit Bowls being rolled out.'

Paddy's eyes widened as he dared to dream. Porter's Fruit Bowls!

'And Elliot is a brilliant accountant. The guy is a machine. He's a robot who will go to war for you and he'll win, freeing you up so that we can get on with this. So, the two things are the same.'

Paddy grinned. Sold to the giant with his life in a mess. He looked down at the panels of the unassembled shed. 'That panel is wrong.'

'Really? Which one?'

'That one. That's the back, not the side.'

Tom grinned. 'You see, I need you.'

'Why don't you leave this to me; it's more my area than yours. I can have it up for you over the weekend.'

'No, but I need it up tonight.'

'Why?' Paddy asked.

'For tomorrow's trial.'

'Tomorrow!' Paddy cried. 'You're doing the trial tomorrow?'

'Yeah, why not?'

'But she didn't say anything about tomorrow.'

Tom was unmoved. 'So? She didn't say anything. Just that she was happy to do a trial.'

'Yeah, but I thought in a week or so. Or maybe after half-term. But not tomorrow!'

'Why? What's the problem?'

'Because we only just saw her! Jesus! And suddenly, we're doing a trial.' Paddy shook his head. The bloke might be rich but he was unhinged. 'I still need my boxes back.'

An hour later, Tom sat opposite Elliot and his two assistants, Martha and Phoebe. Elliot sat bolt upright. Prematurely old, he was a small man and wiry thin, which accentuated his rather enormous, balding head. If he had his time again, Elliot would almost certainly be diagnosed with one of the new American-based social disorders, but at thirty-three, he had avoided such labels and was happy with the reality that he was just different. With his thin lips and unfashionably round glasses, Elliot was comfortable in his very uncool skin. He was brilliant at his job though and he loved nothing more than numbers.

'Everything OK?' Elliot asked Tom, sensing that something was wrong. He had been excited to get the opportunity to work personally for Tom Harper, but he was slightly nervous given the circumstances.

'Yes, but nothing insurmountable anyway.' Tom began. 'It's not your fault, but I wish you hadn't called Mr Porter's house before I had time to warn him.'

'Ah. Jeremy gave me –'

'Look, it's fine. He's just slightly on the paranoid side, that's all.'

'Yes, I spoke with his wife – Mary.' Elliot recalled the conversation and didn't need to look at his copious notes. 'And come to think about it, she sounded terrified and almost hung up on me at one point.'

Tom pushed two boxes towards him. They were both now in slightly better order but Elliot could complete the task in no time, crunching the numbers and coming up with a figure that could make everything go away. It's what he did. He had a forensic mind and just needed to be set a task, and no one was better.

'Apologies because this is way below your skill set. But it's important work and there will be other things here I am sure.'

Tom needed to get on and he stood up to conclude his meeting. His flat-pack shed was probably still lying on the ground.

'How's your carpentry?' Tom asked, confusing Elliot. 'No, I'm joking. Did Jeremy mention anything else?'

Elliot nodded. 'He mentioned this idea of yours about the fruit juice idea.'

'Did he?'

'The Fruit Dish.'

'Bowl. The Fruit Bowl.'

'Oh. Which I like, I really do.'

Tom smiled, grateful to hear any support for his brain wave.

'Yes, there are so many obvious synergies. I did some basic research and all the economics and health implications line up very firmly with your investment criteria.'

Tom smiled at the 'odd' young man before him.

'The latest government initiative to encourage kids to consume more fibre – they spent eight million pounds alone on the marketing. It failed by the way. And there are health tsars and five-a-day champions and commissioners all over the country,' Elliot continued without drawing breath. 'Martha is going to start preparing a report for us on this while Phoebe and I visit Mr Porter.'

Tom chuckled at this prospect. He was glad that Elliot had been available. He was exactly the advocate that Tom needed. He held up his hand because he needed to say something and Elliot stopped speaking immediately, although his mind continued to rush with ideas.

'Nobody here knows anything about what happened.'

Elliot understood completely and gestured as much.

'Thank you, Elliot. It's great to have you here.'

Chapter 29

Having been warned to expect resistance from the Porter family, Elliot would proceed cautiously, but there was little he could do about his appearance, and this alone was enough to worry Paddy. At practically half his size, he looked like a gnome or a wizard, and Paddy half-expected him to pull out a wand. As it was, he offered up a limp hand that barely registered any pressure in Paddy's paw as the two men shook hands. Elliot immediately looked for a space to get their meeting started; he didn't do small talk and he wanted to get on. The two men sat down and as ever, Paddy decided to kick things off with a joke, to break up the atmosphere a little.

'I hope you've brought a calculator with ya?'

Another of Elliot's defining characteristics was his total and complete lack of humour. Funny people can only be funny if they are in the company of people who know how to laugh. Elliot's analytical mind didn't have a humour department. He was unable to recognise or discern a humorous comment and so he stared at Paddy intently whose comment was no longer a joke but a ridiculous question.

'Yes, of course I have.'

Mary fussed about the place while her husband squirmed. 'Cup of tea? Coffee?' she asked.

'Something stronger?' Paddy added, making one more attempt at levity to lighten the mood, but it fell on similarly stony ground.

'No, nothing, thank you. I've already had a cup of coffee today.'

'Oh?'

'Shall we get on?' Elliot intoned.

Mary quickly grabbed the laundry off the table and Paddy swiped away the old copies of *The Sun*.

'I can make a start here, but I will need to take your books away with me and work elsewhere.'

Thank the Lord, Paddy thought.

'Right, I have what you gave Tom, which I've had a quick look through, but I'll need to see everything else – your full records.'

Mary put her laundry down and folded her arms. This should be something worth watching. Concerning all the financial tribulations that Paddy had caused her over the years, this was a rare occasion that she was enjoying.

'Right, fine,' Paddy said as if Elliot's request wasn't a problem at all. 'I'll just get that for you.'

He busied himself in his cupboard, pretending that there was some order to the mess and confusion therein and after what he considered to be an appropriate amount of time, he turned around and plonked three more boxes on the table, each stuffed with bits of paper in no order whatsoever. He studiously avoided his wife's glare.

'I don't do IKEA when it comes to organisation.'

But Elliot looked undeterred. In fact, he looked almost excited at the prospect of the job in hand.

'And this is everything?'

Paddy nodded.

'Income, costs, receipts, bank statements and correspondence?' Elliot asked again.

'Yep. That's your lot.'

Elliot shot a fierce glare at Paddy, making him sit up straight.

'Right, what I propose is that I sort through your records, to get a thorough understanding of your finances and then we can reconvene later to discuss matters in detail?'

Paddy nodded dutifully.

'I'll need to speak to the Revenue on your behalf.' From his briefcase, Elliot produced a typed letter on headed notepaper. 'This is a letter giving me your permission to act on your behalf. We'll scan and email them a copy this afternoon.'

Not from here you won't, Paddy thought, but duly nodded, seeming to approve of such a move. He searched for a pen, but there was no need; Elliot had it covered.

'Here's my card. I have your numbers.' Elliot was already standing now, ready to leave and get on with the job in hand. 'We'll reconvene once I've made some sense of it and have my conclusions and recommendations.' Elliot held out his damp hand as Paddy clambered upright also.

'Right, so see you again then. What, next month?' Paddy joked, not yet learning from his earlier failures at levity.

'I beg your pardon?' Elliot asked, looking up at his client.

'To get through all this, I was saying that it will take you ages…' Paddy petered out because a joke that requires an explanation never flies – ever.

'I was joking.' Paddy explained.

'Oh.' Elliot seemed unimpressed. 'I'll see you tomorrow morning, then.'

Paddy laughed. 'Yeah, right?'

'I beg your pardon.' Elliot asked.

'You're joking, right?'

Elliot wasn't and Paddy quickly stopped laughing. 'No, you're not joking.'

Elliot was keen to leave now. 'Tomorrow morning, then? Eight O Clock?'

'Sure. Or earlier if you like.' Paddy smiled. 'Tomorrow morning is actually remarkably clear for me.'

On his way back to the school, Tom called Nell and had a rather stilted conversation about squeezing fruit and why he wanted to stay in Bromsworth for a couple of days longer, or maybe even for the rest of the week; he couldn't say exactly how long and he failed to elaborate on his plans to satisfy her queries. Just like Michael had done, he could tell that she thought the idea was ridiculous. She also could tell that he wasn't being entirely forthcoming, that there was something else on his mind and she was disappointed that he couldn't share it with her. If not her, then who could he confide in? She worried to herself long after he had ended the call.

Tom constantly reflected on his meeting at the school and still felt troubled by his encounter with Sarah and the possible line in the sand that it posed. It was an added complication that he hadn't been expecting and as vulnerable as he felt, it worried him. It wasn't just that he found her attractive; it was because Paddy had noticed his attraction to her and this was completely new territory for him. Of course, in his travels and business life he had encountered many beautiful women but since meeting his wife, Sarah was the first woman that he had ever been attracted to and this made him miss Beth even more.

The consensus was that in time, he would inevitably start being attracted to other people and that this would represent a milestone, signifying his readiness to move on with his life. Only, it didn't feel like progress. It just made him even more sad and stricken because it heightened his feeling of detachment from Beth and his boys. It had been a mistake not telling Nell. She would have understood and she would have known what to say. He grabbed at his phone and scrolled down to her name, his thumb resting on the green button, pondering the call. She knew that something was awry anyway, he could tell and no doubt she would be worried. But on reflection he put the phone aside. It was just too raw and too personal.

Tom fixed a screw in place and stood back to review his progress so far. Two upright flanks had been loosely fixed to the end panel, but it didn't look particularly sturdy and again, he cursed the pathetic single sheet of instructions that came with the contraption. So, he was as relieved as he was surprised to see Joe approaching from the car park with two young colleagues in tow.

'Hey, Joe.'

Joe gave him a cursory nod, not yet ready to be actually friendly.

'I didn't expect to see you.'

'No, well… Paddy sent me. He said something about a trial.'

'Did he?' Tom's face lit up.

'This is Danny and this is Lewis. They're going to give me a hand.'

'Great. Thanks, lads.'

The boys shook Tom's hand awkwardly and barely looked at him. Tom was particularly intrigued by the second boy, Lewis. 'I've heard a lot about you, Lewis,' he said kindly.

'Yeah? Like what?' Lewis glared at Tom, rather unsettling him.

'You know, about your football.'

'Yeah, and what else?' Lewis asked suspiciously.

Tom shook his head but Lewis didn't look convinced and he looked like he didn't care much either. He just wanted to get the shed up, get signed off and be on his way. Tom nodded in passive agreement. They both wanted the same thing then?

'Right, so let's get started then.' Joe suggested with as much energy as he could muster. Tom noticed the tags over each boy's expensive-looking trainers, and hoped he didn't react so that either of them had seen.

'This panel is wrong for starters,' Joe began, assuming the position of site foreman and Tom was happy to defer. He shook his head at Paddy's earlier shed-erecting instructions. He should have known and it was un-nerving that his new business partner was a bloody idiot. Joe grabbed his automatic screwdriver and quickly started to dismantle what Tom had already completed, grinning as he did so. Tom said nothing, happy to allow him his little victory. He didn't care who erected it. He just wanted the damn thing up.

Chapter 30

A couple of hours after Joe's arrival, the shed was finally taking shape. Tom had largely been a spectator and had even gone off on a coffee and chocolate run, which the two boys seemed to appreciate, if not Joe. And after his poor start, he had managed to engage Lewis on football and the wages that players could now command. Understandably, Lewis was a strong advocate of the current wage structure even if it did bankrupt their employers and Tom didn't wish to argue. Joe kept a close eye on his protégé and seemed a little put out that Lewis appeared to be engaging with Tom.

'If I was a player back in the day, man, I'd be gutted, knowing what players make today. Players today, they don't have to ever work again, man.' Lewis nodded approvingly.

Tom just nodded, wondering what he meant by the 'old days'.

'Players like, who won the world cup, having to sell their medals, 'cos they're skint. That's wrong, man.'

On this, Tom agreed completely and almost patted the kid on his back. 'But those players, the '66 boys, they'll always have their memories.' Tom suggested.

Lewis looked at him oddly and the other boy, Danny, cackled.

'Yeah, sure. But I'd rather have me a Rolex and a Porsche.' Lewis cracked.

'Like, for real.' Danny agreed.

Tom creosoted the final panel and met with Lewis's brush coming from the opposite side. It was finally finished. Tom was delighted and took a step back to admire it.

'Wow, great job, lads. Thanks a lot. I'm very grateful.'

Lewis nodded approvingly. He was secretly pleased with himself and the results, and he enjoyed the feeling of being appreciated by a man like, Tom. To Lewis, he appeared to be an OK kind of guy, despite what people had said about him and especially Joe. He had an air about him that Lewis admired.

Joe shook one of the joists attached to the roof and looked doubtful. 'If we get a real downpour, this joint won't be much good to you.'

But this was the least of Tom's concerns. 'It'll do for now. Good enough for tomorrow at any rate. Hey, lads, if you want to help on the stall in the morning, you'd be very –'

But Joe quickly stopped him. 'Yeah, right! These two hardly came to school by law, so you've got no chance now.'

Lewis smiled ruefully and Tom agreed, holding his hands up.

'I'll need you to sign some paperwork for the lads,' Joe said, gathering his tools together.

'Yeah, of course,' Tom said a little too anxiously. 'Will you be in the Nelson later? I'll buy you a drink.'

'No,' Joe answered flatly. 'I'll give the paperwork to Paddy for you to sign,' Joe finished up bluntly as he wandered off.

When Paddy arrived back at the school, Tom was alone again, sorting out an extension lead from the kitchen area of the school building to his new shed, which Paddy cast a dubious eye over.

'Joe came, did he?'

'Yeah. Thanks for that. He brought that lad, Lewis along and a boy called Danny. They seem like nice lads.'

Paddy shrugged. Really? Just as Joe had done. Paddy gave the shed a hefty shove. 'Bloody hell, if this thing doesn't work, we're going to look like right idiots.'

Tom ignored him as Paddy began unloading his van.

'Did you get it all?' Tom asked as he peered into the van and Paddy reminded himself about the little pep talk he had given himself on his way back from the wholesaler. He had rehearsed what he was going to say and now was his perfect opportunity to express his growing doubts about their business venture.

'Er, yep, I got it all,' Paddy answered, cross with himself for failing miserably. But Tom seemed so enthusiastic and he didn't want to hurt him.

Tom clambered into the back of the van.

'Great! You got pineapples! We need tomorrow to be as sweet

as possible.'

'Yes, I know that; it was me who suggested them, remember?' Paddy moaned.

'OK, great, and you got the plastic cups?'

Paddy nodded again. He humped a bag of carrots onto his back and hopped over to the shed.

'Should probably think about re-usable plastic glasses.' Tom suggested. 'Single use stuff is a little self-defeating.'

Paddy rolled his eyes.

'Let's see if anyone comes back first, eh?'

Chapter 31

The next morning, back at his hotel, Tom was already in the shower when his mobile alarm sprang to life. Having stayed in Bromsworth for longer than intended and without a change of clothes, he had been out and bought himself a new wardrobe and was enjoying the feeling of pulling on new clothes. He patted himself down and looked at his reflection in the mirror as his mind returned to his family and his boys. Beth would be thrilled to see him making a Fruit Bowl this morning and his boys, too. But immediately he mind flitted to his new quasi boss, the school's Head and whether his family had seen this encounter also and how he was looking forward to seeing her again. He skipped breakfast, deciding to pick something up on the way. Later, at school, he would have a choice of fresh fruit juices anyway.

The school was quiet when he arrived just after 6.00 a.m. A light frost covered the grass area between the empty car park and the modern building. Only the caretaker was there to greet him: a grumpy man who seemed wary at the extra work that the stall might entail. Paddy would be along shortly and as much as he enjoyed his company, for now, Tom enjoyed his solitude. The work area looked impressive. Joe had doctored a window panel so that one end of the shed gave way to a long table with a waterproof melamine surface, and they had erected a permanent awning for good measure. Suddenly, Tom felt a little nervous. Two professional juicing machines sat screwed onto the surface ready for the work ahead. These were powerful, avaricious machines, capable of getting through mounds of fruit and they would need a steady stream of customers to keep them busy. All the expenses so far had gone on Tom's one remaining credit card without any issues, but for how long? And if he did exceed the limit, then at least things would be brought to a head. Michael wouldn't dare prevent him from funding this venture.

He spent the next half-hour preparing the produce until two large hoppers were full. Carrots were washed but not peeled. According to Daniel, the skin held the most nutrients and who was he to argue? Same with the apples. Pineapples were peeled and halved. Oranges halved. Celery and grapes were lightly washed. And finally, with a tremendous sense of excitement, Tom turned on the first machine, opened the chute and dropped in a carrot. With little fuss and hardly any noise, a thin line of orange liquid streamed into an empty jug and quickly stopped as the hungry machine, empty already, demanded something else to pulverise. Tom dropped in three apples in quick succession, followed by a handful of carrots, and watched the thicker line of juice emerge, chuckling hopefully to himself. Beth would definitely approve. When Paddy finally arrived, he was already onto his fourth large jug and rather typically, Paddy was downbeat.

'Jesus! How much are you making?'

Tom smiled as he poured out two full glasses from a jug and handed one to Paddy.

'Good health, Paddy. And I mean, literally, good health.'

Paddy took his glass and they both downed them in one.

'Wow! That's not bad.' Paddy licked his lips. 'Not bad at all.' He grabbed at the jug to pour himself another but Tom stopped him.

'No, no, we might need all of this.'

Paddy grimaced and almost shook his head.

'How was Elliot by the way?' Tom asked.

'Jesus, you could have warned me.'

Tom laughed. 'I did warn you; I said he was like a robot.'

'Yeah, you're not wrong – the bloody Terminator. But is he the good Arnie or the bad Arnie? That's what I'm panicking about. He's got me signing this and that. And I'm pretending to keep up, you know, seeing as though Mary's looking on. But I don't know what I've signed. He could own all me assets now for all I know.'

Tom looked doubtful.

'And once he's gone, my Mary tears a bloody strip off me. Furious she was. I was nearly on the sofa bed last night, so thanks for that.'

At just after 7.30 a.m., children started arriving at school and although general curiosity drew some of them to the stall, their reactions were underwhelming.

'Do you do anything fizzy?' a young girl asked, smiling broadly as if to show the teeth she was determined to ruin.

Paddy, up to his elbows in orange pith and carrot peelings, reacted badly. 'Does it look like we do Coke?'

'Well, I only drink fizzy drinks,' the girl replied.

Paddy was about to remonstrate with her when Tom came over and suggested he should go and unblock one of the machines. He wanted to speak to the girl.

'It's fresh fruit juice. That's all we do I'm afraid and it's free.'

Immediately, the girl turned her nose up. 'Nah! I don't like fruit. It makes my teeth go funny.'

Tom didn't bother to respond and watched her leave. It was already 8.00 a.m. and they still hadn't given out a single drink. Tom could feel Paddy's 'told-you-so' face without even looking at him.

A heavy-set boy wandered over and Paddy greeted him by name. 'Stuart Stokes, just the lad we need. Would you like a drink, made fresh here this morning?'

'What is it?'

'Fruit juice. They're free.'

'How come? What's wrong with it?'

'Cheeky git! There's nothing's wrong with it. Fresh fruit that is. Freshly squeezed.'

The boy looked at the setup briefly and nodded his fat face. 'Yeah, go on then.'

Paddy tutted, like the kid was doing him a favour, and he handed the boy a full glass, aware that Tom was watching. He was probably twelve, possibly a little older; it was difficult to tell, but Tom had him around his twins age. He watched the boy drain his drink. It was a poignant moment for him and it was a start at least. Stuart handed his glass over.

'Yeah, nice. How come they're free?'

'They're just free for now. This is just a trial,' Paddy answered.

'Yeah, so, you know, tell your friends, eh?' Tom suggested a little awkwardly just as the boy was leaving.

Paddy waited for him to be gone and out of earshot before he said, 'That was Stuart Stokes. He hasn't got any friends.'

'Oh.'

Paddy spotted a bunch of kids over Tom's shoulder. 'Ah, now, these are the kids that we need over here. Hey, Nathaniel! Come over here, will ya?'

A good-looking boy with a heavy on top afro, giggling with his mates, marched towards Paddy with his friends in tow. The way he was wearing his school uniform, he might as well not have bothered with it: trainers with white socks, a tie as wide as it was long and a 'Z' shaved into the side of his head.

'This is Nat Baker. Very cool kid. Good footballer,' Paddy whispered as the boy arrived. 'Nathaniel, how about a free drink?'

'Sure. What is it? Lager?' His mates laughed raucously.

'No, fruit juice, actually.'

Nathaniel baulked and his crew chuckled. 'Fruit juice! Nah, I don't drink juice, man.'

'No, why not?'

Nathaniel considered Tom suspiciously and gently kissed his teeth instead of answering. 'What's in it anyway?' He asked Paddy.

'All kinds of stuff: oranges, apples, carrots.'

'Carrots!' Another teeth kiss. 'I ain't drinking no carrots, fam, too risky – they might make my Fro turn ginger.'

From his crew's demented reaction, they obviously thought that this was wildly funny. 'Hey, Nat, if you went ginger, you'd be like that Wes Brown for United. D'you remember him?'

Nathaniel high-fived a couple of his acolytes and began to move off with his boys in tow.

'They're very good for you,' Tom called out after them, and immediately regretted it as the boy turned and looked at him oddly.

'And who are you? My dad?' Nathaniel hissed as they all pushed off and away and there were no other kids to take their place. The trial most definitely had not been a success. And Sarah hadn't shown up either, as she had promised. But this was probably a good thing now. Paddy unplugged the machine from the mains out of ceremony more than anything else. They still had jugs of juice left and they certainly would not be needing any more.

At just ahead of 9.00 a.m., the school bell rang and Sarah hurriedly arrived at the stall. She looked hassled and frustrated.

'Oh dear! I'm sorry I missed it all.'

'Don't worry; it was just day one,' Tom smiled warmly.

'So, how was it?'

Paddy averted his eyes and Tom managed a simple shrug.

'Er, yeah, OK, I think. You know; early days and all that.'

'Right, and were there queues?' Sarah asked.

Paddy heaved a sack of carrots away to his van.

'Well, it wasn't exactly Harrods in January.'

Paddy still hadn't said anything.

'Oh, well, I'm sorry I missed it anyway.'

'No, it's fine.'

'Crisis in the staffroom I'm afraid.' Sarah looked at the jugs, still brimming with juice, which told their own story. Paddy made his polite excuses and explained that he needed to get back to the stall to relieve Sean, which was true, but still he managed to give the impression that he thought he should leave them alone anyway, which was entirely unhelpful. Tom poured her a drink and himself one, too – anything to avoid throwing it away which rather defeated the whole purpose. Sarah thanked him and looked at the shed.

'I wasn't aware that we'd be getting a new building?'

'No, well…'

'Or that the trial would be so soon?'

Tom sighed. He felt a little foolish now. Sarah took a mouthful of her drink and she clearly approved.

'And I'm told that Danny Higgins was here, with Lewis Adele?'

Tom nodded, sensing that this might be an issue. 'Yes, they helped put the shed up. They were here with Joe.'

Sarah didn't seem very approving.

'Why? Is that a problem?'

She looked irritated now. 'Quite possibly, although I'm not a lawyer, but I imagine that they have both contravened their court orders.'

Tom felt even more foolish now. 'Wow! I'm sorry. I had no idea.'

Sarah looked across as the remnants of her charges disappeared into her school.

'I haven't really thought everything through, have I?' Tom suggested.

'Well, it's certainly been very quick.' she added.

'Yes. I'm sorry.'

'Any reason I should know about the enormous hurry?'

'No, not really,' Tom answered. He suspected that she was more upset with something else. 'No news on the local government grant then?' He joked. 'I take it you've applied already?' Tom added, breaking the strain and Sarah finally smiled.

'Oh yes, of course – spent all day yesterday on it. And guess what? They've come through already – and it's a yes.'

Tom laughed and raised his eyes skyward.

'So, same again tomorrow then?' Sarah asked.

'Yes, absolutely. If that's OK with you?'

Sarah nodded. 'I'll put it on the school intranet; see if we can't drum up some support that way.'

'Great. And you'll be here I hope?'

'You have my word, only I'm not squeezing anything.'

Sarah walked off and he watched after but only briefly, worried that someone might be observing him.

Chapter 32

At 8 a.m. sharp, sitting formally opposite Paddy and Mary, Elliot had said a quick hello and once again had refused all offers of drinks. He wanted to get on with a summary of his findings and would have dispensed with greetings and pleasantries altogether if convention allowed it. From his briefcase he produced a file, which he opened and then looked up at his hosts.

'OK then, shall we begin?' he asked rhetorically.

'Just give it to me straight. Am I going to jail?' Paddy joked, still having not yet learnt his earlier lesson. Elliot didn't even smile and looked offended by such an enquiry.

'I thought we should begin with a summary.'

'Sure.'

'This is your completed tax return, which I will need you to check and sign. But if I could briefly explain its main findings.'

Yeah, good luck, thought Paddy to himself.

'Based on your set of accounts, you've paid too much tax,' Elliot began and Paddy's ears pricked up immediately. 'Records show that you have paid £2,300 in tax for the last financial year, and that HMRC are claiming a further unpaid liability of £1,200 for this same period.'

But Paddy couldn't concentrate anymore, fixated as he was on the idea that he was owed money. It was a miracle.

'Are we agreed, at least in principle?' Elliot asked.

Paddy couldn't respond, so Mary interjected on his behalf.

'If you could just go over that bit again – the bit about Paddy being owed money?' Mary asked.

'Our calculations have it that your liability for this period equates to £900, but you have actually remitted £2,300, in line with their demand, which means that you are owed a rebate of £1,400 – which I suggest we apply for immediately. I will need you to check and sign.'

As officially as possible, Paddy scribbled his name on the document and stared at the little man in disbelief.

'They owe me money?' Paddy asked incredulously.

Elliot didn't repeat himself. It was ground he had already covered. Paddy barely managed to contain himself. He considered whether it was worth a quick look at Mary since he had been right all along and he did have everything under control after all. But he decided not to; he'd save it for when they were alone. Paddy stood up and held out his hand but Elliot didn't move. He clearly hadn't finished and Paddy sheepishly retook his seat.

'Obviously, The Fruit Bowl will be established as a limited company with you as a director?'

'Er…' Whatever, Paddy nodded, not listening anymore, desperate to get Mary alone.

'But have you considered incorporating your own business?'

It was a specific question that required a specific answer. A yes or a no, giving him a fifty per cent chance of being correct.

'Er… yes. Yes, I have,' Paddy answered.

Mary glared at him.

'But you haven't done it?' Elliot asked.

'No… not yet.'

'Why not?' Elliot asked.

'Well, you know, it's on my list.'

'Below what?' Elliot sounded incredulous.

'You never told me.' Mary added curtly.

'Yeah, I have. You just don't listen to business talk.'

'Business talk.' Mary scoffed.

'Yes, business talk. I have always planned to er… incumberate the business. Just never got around to it?'

Elliot considered his newest client closely. 'Right, well I suggest that we do this right away.' Elliot turned to Phoebe, his assistant, who hadn't said a word after her initial hello. 'Phoebe, if you could make a start on… incumberating Mr Porter's business.'

'Yes, of course.'

Elliot began to set down a series of documents on the table in front of Paddy.

'OK, good, so, leaving aside your tax situation for a moment, we come now to your personal finances and in particular, your loans.'

Paddy swallowed hard. Mary straightened her back and gave Paddy a quick glance. He was about to be flung back in with the lions.

'These are the loans that you currently have running, which I've cross-checked with the bank statements you still have.'

Paddy was very worried now.

'Are you aware of the interest rates that you are currently paying on these loans?'

'Yes,' Paddy lied.

Elliot seemed flustered and would have preferred to hear the truth.

'Then why are you paying them?'

'Er...'

'Why are you paying such exorbitant rates?'

Paddy didn't answer. How could he?

'This loan in particular. At interest rates and your current repayment plan, you are scheduled never to repay the capital.'

Mary groaned. This was more like the man she knew and loved.

'And this loan!' Elliot continued. 'You've already repaid more than you —'

Paddy squirmed. 'Yes, yes! Well, let's not get bogged down in detail. Let's just concentrate on getting them back on track. Isn't that what you do?'

Elliot allowed himself a rare smile. He liked the idea of being a fixer.

'Five individual loans but from just two different holding companies. This is a letter I've drafted stating that I have been appointed to act on your behalf. And this is a letter explaining that you are disputing the terms and conditions of their services. Sign here and here, and we will courier them today. This will put us officially into dispute and consequently, I suggest you immediately withhold any further payments.'

Paddy now looked worried. 'Yes, but won't they be cross about that?'

'I hope so.' Elliot said quickly.

'And can't they come after my house because on the adverts…?'

Elliot shook his head confidently. 'Technically, they can, but believe me, they won't.'

'Right, and why's that?'

'Because of me.'

Paddy stared at the odd little man sitting before him and he realised that he would need something more to assure him. He wouldn't have long to wait.

'Because they will not want our lawyers crawling over their grubby terms. Amazing what a keen mind, a few threats and headed note paper can do. These are letters to your bank, instructing the withholding of any further payments.'

Paddy liked what he heard and merrily signed away. Yeah, fuck these loan people!

'Now, your mortgage is also a scandalously bad deal, but I'll need your credit rating to improve before I can do anything about it. In the meantime, I've organised for an independent survey and valuation of this property so that we can prepare the necessary paperwork in readiness.'

Paddy was bewildered by the speed and organisation of it all. The idea of having his house surveyed and valued. Paddy looked around his tiny lounge that was badly in need of a lick of paint. 'I could give it a once over; the walls I mean. And get the coffee on? And Mary will bake some bread?'

Once again, Elliot didn't get any of the points that Paddy was making. He had already said that he didn't want coffee and he certainly didn't want any bread.

'Right, then, moving onto your utilities, telephone and various insurances.'

Elliot continued for another ten minutes, laying Paddy's finances bare and having him sign yet more documents. And then he was done. As quickly as he arrived, he leapt to his feet up and offered his limp hand. Bankruptcy staved.

'I'll be in touch.'

'Yeah, thanks.'

And then he was gone. Paddy shut the door after him and blew out hard.

'Well, what a nice chap he turned out to be,' he added as casually as he could.

Chapter 33

After his miserable first morning on the stand, Tom didn't have anything to do all day but wait for tomorrow to try again. He drove around the town a couple more times, trying to recall other memories, then parked up and found himself in Bromsworth Library just off the High Street, scrolling through microfiche copies of *The Bromsworth Echo*. He had located the edition again carrying the untimely death of his old adversary, Declan Connor, and then he fast-forwarded to the weeks when Lewis had basked in the dubious limelight of the *Echo*'s front page. *Soccer Star Shamed* was one of the many headlines that attested to his downfall and the picture of his hapless mug-shot was usually accompanied by images of him celebrating a goal in happier times. Joe was quoted in various pieces, stating that he hoped Lewis could get back to football and his winning ways and that he would personally supervise his community sentence. He was about to shut the machine down when something on the front page caught his eye. In a red box, in the top right-hand corner, was an appeal for any local interest stories with a Freephone number to call.

The following morning, Tom was first to arrive again and quickly began setting about his task. He felt anxious, having not slept much after taking a call from Michael, which hadn't gone well. Michael assured him that his current costs would be covered, but it didn't feel like much of a concession and he certainly was not relaxing the restrictions or the arrangement.

At just after 8.30 a.m., a small number of children had visited the stall: some repeats from yesterday, including Stuart Stokes, the loner, plus a few members of staff, but not the mass demand Tom had hoped for and no sign of the headmistress either. Then, Paddy caught his attention and gestured towards the school, whereupon Sarah was strolling towards the stall. Tom patted the backs of his trousers and suddenly felt self-conscious.

'Any better this morning?' she smiled. Her hair seemed fuller somehow and was loosely tied against her black slim-fitting cashmere jumper.

'Yes, a little. But no flood gates yet.'

Sarah smiled and looked around at the sparse number of children and said hello to each of them by name as Paddy handed her a full glass.

'Thank you, and what's in it, may I ask?'

Paddy shook his head. 'I'm sorry, but if we told you that, then we would have to kill you... So, apples, carrots, oranges of course...'

Sarah grinned at her most incorrigible parent and seemed to be enjoying her detour away from her office or staffroom. Holding the glass aloft, she took a quick mouthful and was happy to approve almost immediately.

'Oh, it's lovely. Very nice. Nicer than yesterday's. What's the secret ingredient?'

'Actually, we use whatever is available. Whatever was going to be thrown out,' Tom answered.

'Oh, great, now you're really selling it to me.'

Tom smiled fondly. He could sense that she was busy and needed to leave. Duty called and this was just a flying visit, but now he really wanted her to stay and if the car pulling into the car park was who he hoped it was, then he really needed her to stay. A scruffy man emerged from the driver's seat with bed hair and days of stubble. He glanced down at a sheet of paper and then headed towards the stall as an even scruffier man joined him with a camera bag slung over his shoulder. Perfect. It was them. The press had arrived.

Tom had the good sense to look contrite as he introduced Sarah to the journalist from the *Echo*. He was confident that she would have agreed to it anyway but in the haste of arranging the whole thing, he had calculated that it would be easier for everyone if the media were a surprise. Naturally, Paddy disapproved completely and told her so, as he handed over her second full glass of the morning.

'I don't remember you mentioning anything about the press,' Sarah said quietly.

Tom shook his head, as if it was a surprise to him also. Sarah had featured regularly in the *Echo* since taking on her post a year ago and the journalist didn't need to be introduced. Indeed, he knew Paddy as well. The photographer quickly set about moving the two of them into position.

'You're looking lovely again this morning, Ms Frost,' the photographer offered and Sarah managed a rather strained thank you.

'Have you given any thought to my –'

'No.' She answered.

'Sean, just take the shot.'

The photographer clicked away as Sarah held up a glass with an embarrassed-looking Paddy by her side. Any number of headlines could accompany the shot, but Beauty and the Beast was about the best. Sarah took a little sip as the camera clicked away and a brave child from the small crowd, called out, 'Down in one,' which quickly caught on and became a chorus. Sarah had little option but to oblige and looked at Tom ruefully, and an enormous cheer rang out when she drained her glass.

'Right, that's it then,' the journalist said. 'It'll be in sometime this week; depends on what else is going on, but our editor has a very soft spot for Ms Frost, so I'd say soon.'

Tom nodded, conscious that Sarah was about to leave.

'OK, thanks, guys.'

Paddy quickly busied himself, doling out further drinks to anyone who wanted one and by now, Sarah looked like she really did have to leave, for the toilet most likely. Tom had some explaining to do. He needed to thank her at least and probably apologise as well, but now was not the time and he watched after her on her way back to the school.

Chapter 34

Sarah assured herself that her brief look through the school records in search of a previous pupil was perfectly normal and that her interest was purely professional. It confirmed that Tom Harper had indeed been a pupil at the school from 1975 to 1982, and that he had achieved three A's at A-level and gone onto Exeter University to read History. By Sarah's calculation, that made him forty-five years old. But she conceded that her Google search for a 'Tom Harper' couldn't be explained away quite so easily. It made her feel uncomfortable about what she might find but, in the event, nothing emerged – nothing relevant anyway. There were plenty of Tom Harpers, millions in fact and even when she confined her search to the UK, there were still some twenty million pages for her to peruse – artists, writers, journalists, the odd sportsman and more ordinary 'Joes' – but nothing on the Tom Harper that she had met and she certainly didn't have the time to scroll through the world of Google. Facebook and the other social platforms were similarly unhelpful, which didn't really surprise her because he didn't strike her as the sort to have a web life. A knock at her door made her instinctively shut down the page, even though her screen couldn't be seen. It was Anne, her PA. Anne had accompanied her to St Ed's from her previous headship, which had been one of her stipulations taking on the role of turning around a school that was officially 'failing' and in need of a 'Super Head'. Super Head was a ridiculous moniker and Sarah hated it. What the school needed most was a set of parents who cared about their children, not a Super Head. When she arrived, truancy was rampant and exam results were languishing somewhere lower than even staff morale. But, according to her employers, Sarah was indeed, the solution. And, in this age so obsessed with quotas and talents, Sarah had much to offer. She was female, at thirty-seven she was young and therefore, she had to be progressive, and with a law degree from Oxford, she was the perfect example of the teaching profession attracting the very highest of flyers. But a year into her role, she was already exhausted. The Fruit Bowl and Tom were welcome distractions. Standing in her office doorway, Anne had a smirk on her face, so it had to be good news.

'Dish of the day is served.'

Sarah couldn't help but smile.

'For his school tour?' Anne continued.

Councillor Lesley Irwin pondered his private diary. The 27th April was heavily ringed in red. Not that he needed reminding what an important date it was; it had taken over a year of meticulous planning and would provide the final feathers for his retirement nest. The opportunity had presented itself only because Lesley had such a handle over all council activities, plus his creative vision and dishonesty of course. Like all cash-strapped and cut-threatened councils, Bromsworth had needed to liquidate assets wherever possible to help balance its books and land sales and other assets had featured prominently over the last four years. He pulled the sales details from his top drawer, which had been scrupulously drafted because procedures needed to be followed. A brown field site, it would never get residential planning, and the demand for commercial land being so slow, depressed its value even further. The sales brochure was hardly inspiring: a grimy aerial photograph with a red line demarking the borders.

Plot of land, known as Lot A, is being offered for sale by Bromsworth Council by sealed bids only with a deadline of 27th April. A reserve price has been set at £1.5m.

Central to Lesley's plans was recycling. As with all local councils, all things regeneration, particularly recycling, were hallowed ground and particularly ripe for exploitation. Green issues and people's conscience was a particularly profitable equation for people in the know. And Lesley Irwin knew that Bromsworth Council's recycling capacity would be exceeded within the next five years and that a further facility would be required. This site was perfect. It's owners leasing it to the council for said purposes would create handsome returns for many years to come.

Lesley grinned at his cunning and imagined his bountiful pay-out. He scribbled on his pad the name, Elliot Stapleton. He wasn't familiar with him but he would be soon. Lesley made it his business to be over everything and everyone with anything to do with his council. His future depended on it.

Elliot had put himself on Lesley's broad and paranoid radar because, at Tom's request, he had registered his name with the local council's planning department for land sales. This was outside Lesley's day-to-day jurisdiction but under his regime; it crossed his desk no matter. Head of Council planning was Tony Holloway. Lesley didn't care for Tony and the feeling was mutual. Tony didn't appreciate being summoned to see his council head, on a whim as he saw it.

'Elliot Stapleton? Do we know who he is?' Lesley asked impatiently, doing his best to appear not particularly interested.

'No, why? Should we? Lots of parties register interest in land. It's what we want, right?'

Lesley chose to ignore his impertinent tone. Instead, he asked a question of his own. 'He hasn't specified for what purpose?'

'No, he hasn't.' Tony answered flatly. 'Anything else?'

'But he works for EY, I see?' Lesley pressed.

Tony breathed out heavily, 'So?'

Lesley tightened at the thought of a big London suit moving on to his patch. Dipping a polished brogue in to the water and creating ripples. 'So, he's representing a client then?' Lesley fished.

Holloway shrugged. 'Lesley, I don't know. But I'll ask him. When he comes in. How's that?'

Holloway enjoyed imparting the news of the appointment that Elliot had made with him, knowing how it would irk the leader of the council.

'Good. That's excellent,' Lesley lied. 'And when is that?'

Holloway looked a little put out. 'I'd need to check. Thursday, maybe?'

'Right, well, do let me know, because I'd like to meet him too.'

Tony glared at his colleague. Really?

'Yes. Why not?'

Tony gestured with his hands. 'Just seems a little odd.' Tony answered. 'A little bit below your rank.'

'No, nonsense. As you know full well, I like to keep abreast of matters, especially when a London firm might wish to invest in my area. I would say that it is entirely on my level, wouldn't you?' Lesley intoned to indicate that their meeting was over.

Tom was studying the school's academic records board when Sarah emerged from her office.

'That was my idea,' Sarah smiled.

Tom nodded approvingly. 'Very good. Both aspirational and inspirational.'

Sarah scanned the most recent honours and winced a little; knowing that too many names hadn't even completed their first year at university, let alone graduated.

'I probably should have gone back a little further.' Sarah began. 'Apparently, there was a boy here in 1983 who went on to Exeter.'

Tom smiled. It wasn't lost on him that she had thought to check up on him and should he be flattered or worried? He wondered what other information about his life might be commonly available?

Tom wasn't surprised how little he could remember of the school itself. Schools are functional buildings, and St Edmund's had not been designed with character to make it memorable and it had been continually modified since his time anyway. Thankfully, the gym hadn't changed at all and remained just as he remembered. He affectionately clutched at one of the thick twisted ropes that he used to scramble up and down in record time for his year group. He could never do it now, which saddened him a little. A series of posters filled one wall: notices about solvent and drug abuse and various pictures of sports luminaries, presumably the idea being that they had once just been ordinary kids doing PE at school. Taking centre stage was a photograph of a boy playing for England schoolboys at the old Wembley Stadium with the date and his name printed below. Tom studied the picture of Joe with some affection, recalling what a wonderful player he had been. He noted that Joe looked angry in the photograph as he challenged his German counterpart. He smiled because he knew exactly how the young German player felt. Posters of Beckham, Zidane and Messi crowded around Joe's photograph, but Tom felt sure that it was Joe who was more accessible and inspiring to the current crop of St Edmund's wannabes.

'Another idea of yours?' Tom suggested.

'Hmm…' Sarah didn't sound particularly comforted by her collage of achievement.

'The school is very proud of Joe. But, unfortunately, Joe is less pleased with his old school.'

Tom nodded and assumed he knew why. 'The playing field?'

Sarah sighed. 'If only I'd known was what coming down the tracks, I wouldn't have taken this place on.'

'But it was on your watch, right?'

Sarah sighed and looked at him knowingly. 'Believe me, with over six hundred boys and their raging hormones, it wasn't on my wish list.'

'So, why did it happen then?' Tom repeated the question he had asked Paddy almost a week earlier. Just then the double doors exploded open and a rush of young boys burst into the gym followed by a male PE teacher. On spotting his boss, the teacher immediately pulled his joggers up and blew hard on his whistle.

'Right, clockwise – running – round the gym please…'

The mass of kids reluctantly stirred into action – hardly a hive of worker bees – with one fat kid deliberately running in the opposite direction with his arms flailing and his legs askew. As ever, some kids were keener than others and started to make headway around the gym, quickly lapping the kids who didn't do running and prefer games that only required their thumbs. One little scamp of a lad suddenly stopped running and stared up at Tom, making him feel uncomfortable. He vaguely recognised the child but he couldn't recall from where.

'How's that car of yours?'

Tom now made the connection and shifted awkwardly, not least because he recalled his last question had been whether he was a paedophile, and now here he was in his gym class.

'Mikey Burton, keep on running please,' the PE teacher shouted from across the gym.

The kid grinned. 'One hundred and sixty-six miles an hour! I Googled it,' he called out to Tom as he began running again.

Sarah looked at Tom, who tried to wear his best confused look. 'He must have me mixed up. I drive a Fiat.'

Another kid slowed down as he past. 'Thanks for the fruit juice, sir.'

Tom smiled, relieved to now be on firmer ground.

'So, how's it going then?' Sarah asked.

'Well, not as I hoped to be honest, but it's early days, right?'

'You tell me. It's your money.'

'Sure, but if we get some good press – which I'm very grateful to you about, by the way,' he added quickly.

'I don't recall being given a choice?'

'No, sorry about that. I did mean to ask.'

Sarah did not seem convinced. 'Mr Porter tells me that there's a reason for the odd name, The Fruit Bowl. He told me to ask you.'

'Did he? Good old Paddy…' Tom faltered, which Sarah misinterpreted as shyness or perhaps because the story might not be so riveting.

'I can always stop you,' she suggested as he continued to wriggle.

'What now?' Tom asked.

'Or when you're ready? You're usually in such a rush.'

'Yes, sorry about that.'

'Perhaps I should give you some time to prepare, you know, so that you can spice it up a little.'

Tom laughed out of relief more than anything else. 'Sure, that's a good idea. Maybe let me get a few more mornings out the way first.'

'Great, I look forward to it. But I would rather hear it over a coffee than a juice, if you don't mind?'

'Of course.'

'Great, then. I look forward to it.' Sarah smiled and offered Tom her hand.

'Thanks for the tour.'

'Sorry it wasn't more exciting.'

Tom watched her leave again, his mind racing. Had she asked him for a coffee? He wasn't sure but he hoped that she had and predictably he suddenly felt cold. He needed to speak to someone, but the only person he knew well enough in Bromsworth was Paddy. He needed to call Nell.

Chapter 35

On the pavement, just along from the school, a bunch of rough-looking kids pushed past Tom. They weren't wearing school uniform and he wondered whether they might be pupils at St Edmund's. The church adjoining the school hadn't changed at all. Churches don't tend to change much and even when they become flats or arts centres, the exteriors remain the same. St Edmund's, however, had managed to remain a place of worship, but with most likely a much smaller congregation than it had enjoyed in Tom's day. He stood on the steps, the same stone he had stood on some thirty years ago all dressed in white for his first Holy Communion, with his mum proudly taking photographs. He must still have the photo somewhere, if he cared to look. The mosque across the road hadn't been there when he was a child and no doubt enjoyed an abundant following – another sign of the times. He tried the front door and was surprised to find it open. He sat in a pew, where he would have sat as a boy many times and been bored to tears by any number of services. But now he appreciated the quiet and the serenity of the place and he liked the smell. As a child, he had been fascinated with the burning incense, not just the smell but the smoke. He had always prayed that, just once, an errant altar boy would really fire the thing up with charcoal so that the whole church would be filled with smoke, but his prayers were never answered. The smell of incense, however, hung in the air, the smoke having soaked into every fabric and soft furnishing in the place. The large heavy crucifix that had transfixed him as a child still hung against the back wall, high above the altar. It was a vividly real carving, not one of these anodyne representations of what might have happened. This was a carving of a man in absolute agony, his body twisted in pain and his face contorted, and it wasn't dissimilar to how Tom had so often felt since the accident. Now, he stared hard at the altar, lost in his memories of both his childhood and his family.

'Is there anything I can help you with?'

Tom spun round to where the voice had come from and saw a kindly old man dressed in a black cassock. The church might not have changed that much but it still hadn't aged as well as Father Franey whom Tom recognised instantly and judging by how well he looked, Tom realised that he must have been a very young man when he had taught him all those years ago.

'Father Franey?'

The priest looked surprised but also pleased to be remembered.

'Yes, that's right.' His Irish accent was now even softer.

'I was at St Ed's. You taught me.'

'I know. Tom Harper. You were one of my big success stories.'

Tom's eyes widened but the priest, sensing his surprise, quickly explained himself.

'Paddy told me you were back.'

'Oh,' Tom nodded. 'I can't believe you're still here!'

The priest chuckled. 'Oh, well, it's one of those jobs. And sure, what else would I do?'

Tom looked at his surroundings: an odd workplace for a man.

'And you, Tom? What brings you back? Paddy tells me something about him saving you and now you're back, saving him?'

Tom sighed. It was a nice way of putting it. 'Well, I wouldn't put it quite like that. More like saving each other.'

The priest considered Tom for a moment, his wise old face alert and enquiring, trying to establish as much as he could without prying.

'Well, Paddy Porter certainly needs saving all right – and mostly from himself.'

Tom laughed as best he could.

'And as well as finding Paddy? Is there something I can help you with?'

Tom took a moment. He considered the question and the kind old man and he felt conflicted. Unusually, Nell hadn't picked up when he had called and he didn't leave her a message. And while he felt a strong need to share his feelings with somebody, he still preferred that no one in Bromsworth knew his circumstances.

'No, Father. Thank you.'

'OK, that's fine, but just so you know, I'm here and I am very happy to listen when you're able.'

Tom noted his use of the word 'when' in a knowing sense of the word and he thought again of his needs and options. But he shook his head again. 'Thank you, Father, but unfortunately, what I need is the impossible I'm afraid. Even for the big fellah.'

The priest nodded slowly, his inquisitive eyes still studying Tom. 'And who is it you've lost?'

Tom's eyes widened and the priest was quick to assure him.

'Over the years, you get to read the signs.' Father Franey opened his hands, Tom relaxed a little and he suddenly felt a huge sense of relief.

'Sure, will we go and have a cup of tea?'

Tom's resistance dissolved instantly. A tear burst from his left eye and unable to speak, he just nodded.

Tóm sat with the priest and cried uncontrollably as he recounted his story and his feelings of despair. Father Franey didn't say much, just listened and seemed particularly interested in Tom's feelings of guilt.

'Tom, a lie to deceive is a very different proposition from a lie to protect. And what you're proposing to do here in Bromsworth is certainly nothing to be ashamed of. If anything, it's rather wonderful. And who better to help than a man like Paddy Porter? Not to mention the kids at Ed's.'

Tom shrugged. 'Well, it's like I said; I'm not actually doing it for Paddy. I'm doing it for myself.'

'Fine, but isn't the outcome the same?'

'Yes, I guess. Thank you, Father.'

The priest smiled. 'For what? Don't thank me. Sure, I've done nothing.'

'No, I wouldn't say that,' Tom protested.

Father Franey held his hands up and Tom pondered him a moment, intrigued by the priest's intuition. He hadn't mentioned anything about his means, although he could have guessed since Tom was funding the venture.

'And is there anything else troubling you?'

Tom almost laughed and blew out hard. 'Do you play the lottery?' he asked.

'No, should I?'

'Yes, because you seem to just know things.' Tom joked.

The priest pushed his tongue against his cheek and narrowed his eyes at Tom. 'Some people are just more open than others. And sometimes even very private people; things happen to them that are just so enormous that they emit their need for help.'

Tom's throat filled again as he considered just how apposite this sounded.

Tom nodded. 'Everything I feel is somehow connected to my family. I can't help it. Everything. My entire being and every experience is anchored to Beth and my boys.'

'Of course. They were your life and they are still.' The priest suggested.

'It's just...' Tom began again, 'that... when Paddy and I first took the idea to the school and...'

Father Franey now smiled broadly and thought he understood. 'Ah... and would this happen to involve the lovely Ms Frost?'

It was a great release for Tom. He laughed for the first time and Father Franey joined him.

'Isn't she the most beautiful little thing you've ever seen?' Father Franey chuckled.

Tom was a little shocked but the priest was quick to rebuke him.

'And what's that look for?' he said. 'I'm still a fellah, aren't I?'

'Yes, but –'

'But nothing. Sure, I wouldn't be normal. I took a vow of celibacy not blindness.'

Tom gawped at the priest. 'But I didn't say that I found her attractive,' Tom protested.

'No, you didn't.' he answered wryly and both men laughed. It was a fitting way to conclude what had been Tom's most successful therapy session to date. As he left the church he was about to ask Father Franey to remain silent, when the priest quietly rested his index finger against his pursed lips. He wouldn't tell a soul and he didn't need to be told.

Chapter 36

The piece on Porter's Fruit Bowls in the Thursday edition of *The Bromsworth Echo* was the highlight of a very disappointing first week for Tom and Paddy's fledgling business. The article carried a lovely picture of Sarah and Paddy, but clearly the pupils of the school were not *Echo* readers because it didn't stimulate the rush on Friday that they hoped for. Or Tom hoped for anyway. The trial could only really be described as a failure. Paddy was disappointed but Tom felt hurt and even angry by the lack of response. The stall was supposed to be in memory of his boys. It was for Beth and the idea of it failing was something he couldn't countenance. He resented that his stall had been ignored. However oblique and irrational, it felt as if his family was being shunned.

For Paddy, although vindicated, it certainly didn't feel like a victory and 'told-you-so' statements didn't occur to him. He was disappointed for Tom and for himself as well. Foolishly, he had allowed himself to be seduced by the idea, but he wasn't surprised that it hadn't worked. In his experience, such good fortune didn't fall so easily into his lap.

After their unavailing efforts on Friday morning, Paddy was ready to throw in the towel. In fact, he felt duty bound to do so because no matter how wealthy Tom might be, he was clearly wasting his money. Paddy stubbed his cigarette out by his van and strolled back to the stall, pondering how he should broach the subject. He decided it would be best if he was straight and honest, but catching Tom unawares and seeing the anguish on his face, he suddenly lost his confidence and conviction. The man looked wounded already and now was not the time.

'Thanks for all your help this week, Paddy.'

'Yeah, sure.'

'It hasn't been the week that I had in mind,' Tom stated glumly.

'No. And it's not a good sign when we can't even give it away.'

Fair point, which he would need to consider. It was apparent that customers wouldn't ever pay for their Fruit Bowls, which meant local funding would be the only viable way forward. Tom shook his head and imagined what Michael would say. Paddy watched him drain yet another glass of juice.

'And so, the question is Tom – how long are we going to do this for?' Paddy asked as gently as he could.

Tom finished his drink and just shrugged his shoulders. 'I don't know; as long as it takes.'

'Really? What, like, another week? A month?'

'Paddy, I don't know,' Tom snapped, shaking his head. 'As long as it takes.' He grabbed a bag of carrots and lifted them back into the storage bin.

'Right.' Paddy pulled at his stubble. 'But what if –'

Tom whirled around to face him. 'Paddy, I'm not giving up after a week. No way!'

'Fine, but we need to know for how long though?'

Tom didn't want to become embroiled in a date or a time. He was just going to make it work and he couldn't be expected to know how long it might take. Paddy set about clearing the stall. He too was angry now; cross at Tom's intransigence, but also because presumably he would be expected to waste his time on this doomed venture. He already had a failing business of his own and didn't need another one dragging him down. He didn't say anything further, but he didn't need to. His body language alone articulated that he thought the whole thing was a folly.

'Paddy, I could use some support here.'

'Tom, man, we can't give it away.'

'Right, fine, so what else are you going to do, eh?' Tom stabbed back at him. 'So, without this, what's your plan, Paddy? You tell me.'

Paddy didn't answer Tom's barbed question and he could see that the big man was wounded and he instantly regretted his question and his manner.

'No, you're right. I have no plans. Nothing…' Paddy shouted back, 'which makes me feel even more pathetic. Because I'm banking on this long-shot bullshit just like you.'

Both men considered each other a little wearily. All along Tom had wanted to avoid this very scenario, whereby Paddy felt reliant on him. Paddy might be a buffoon but he was no fool and beneath his brash exterior, was a fiercely proud man whose delicate self-esteem was an obvious weakness. And if anything, Tom felt more reliant on Paddy.

'Paddy, I'm sorry. I didn't mean that to sound like –'

'No, but its right, though isn't it? I'm relying on you. On a bloke I don't even know. We were at school together, but big deal. It was a long time ago.'

Tom shrugged. 'Relying on each other sounds better.'

'Yes, but why?'

'What do you mean?'

'You don't need to be doing this – juicing bloody manky fruit. You're rich, remember? You're not like me. So why are you doing it?'

Tom sighed. There was a perfect explanation of course. 'Because it's what I want to do. Isn't that enough?'

Paddy shook his head.

'And it's going to work,' Tom added.

Paddy shook his head. 'No, it's not. Not on this health angle anyway.'

'How do you mean?' Tom asked, intrigued now and a little hopeful.

'We've been in the newspaper, on the radio. We've got the headmistress on side – or at least you have – and still they aren't coming, and do you know why?'

Tom shook his head.

'Because juice isn't cool. Fruit juice is not cool. Pepsi is cool.'

'Paddy, we're not giving out Pepsi.'

'I know that. But that's the problem with juice.'

Tom was disappointed. He had been hoping for something a little more insightful and constructive. 'Right, and that's it? Fruit juice isn't cool?'

'Yeah. Kids don't do anything these days unless it's cool. But you wouldn't know that because you aren't a dad.'

Tom didn't correct him. 'Right, so what do we do then? Chill it?' Tom joked angrily, but Paddy didn't laugh.

'Because, Paddy, is that just a statement of fact, like a fait accompli, or does it come with any possible solutions? Because solutions are what I could use right now!'

'Hey, don't start shouting at me,' Paddy defended. 'This was all your idea, not mine. You came to me, remember? And yes, I do have a solution actually.'

'Well, then, great. Cos I'm all ears.'

'Fine.' Paddy nodded.

'Well, go on then,' Tom shouted.

'We have to make The Fruit Bowl cool.'

Tom opened his eyes wide. There had to be something more and Paddy duly nodded.

'And we do that by getting the boys to the stall.'

'Right…'

Tom let the idea swirl around his thoughts for a moment or two.

'And?' Tom beckoned.

'You get the boys here, then you get the girls. Its basic biology – the birds and the bees.'

'Yes, Paddy. Thank you. I know…'

'And you get the boys here by making the stall cool. Stall and cool. They almost rhyme which is a good omen'

Tom slapped his haunches in frustration. 'Jesus, Paddy, will you start making sense?'

'And we make it cool by having someone working on the stall who the boys admire – not a naff old dad like me and some bloke who looks like he's never worked a day in his life.'

Tom's eyes flickered at his reasoning. Of course, Paddy was right. It made perfect sense.

Paddy could sense his idea registering, which emboldened him to continue. 'And that person is Joe. The boys love him. If Joe was on the stall, the boys here would want to support it and if the boys come…'

Tom smiled broadly at his brilliant business partner. 'Paddy, it's just like I said.'

'What is?' Paddy asked.

'I couldn't do this without you.'

Paddy beamed at him. 'What, so you agree then?'

'Yes, of course. It's brilliant. So, you'll ask Joe then?' Tom asked.

'Me?' Paddy shrieked, now seeing an obvious hole in his theory.

'Yes, of course. I can't do it. He'll never say yes to me and he'll never say no to you.'

Tom was right on this and Paddy was now wishing that he had kept his mouth shut. Tom's eyes suddenly flickered again as something else occurred. 'Hey, I've got it!'

Paddy heaved his shoulders.

'As well as asking Joe, why don't we ask Lewis as well?'

Paddy gulped.

Chapter 37

Councillor Lesley Irwin studied the photograph in the *Echo* of Sarah Frost, the pretty Super Head standing next to Bromsworth's most popular giant, Paddy Porter. His assistant, Mark Hooper, had spotted the piece in the paper and brought it to Lesley's attention. It seemed like a harmless enough initiative, if a little unusual, but still Lesley wanted to find out the motivation behind it and the mechanics of the thing. And so, he made a few phone calls.

'And who's this chap, Harper, again?' Lesley fingered the copy with the single mention of Tom's name.

'According to the journalist, he's just an old schoolmate of Paddy Porter's.'

Lesley held up the photograph of Tom that the *Echo* had emailed over at Mark's request.

'He doesn't look like a mate of Paddy Porter's.'

'No, I thought that. Colin thinks he's from London, but wasn't sure.'

Just the mention of the capitol was enough to set off a small internal alarm in Lesley's psyche. He rubbed his chin and studied the photograph again.

'And they're giving these drinks away? For nothing?'

'Apparently.'

'And why would they do that?' Lesley asked rhetorically.

'For now, at least, but I think going forward, the idea is to get local funding.' His assistant continued and Lesley's curiosity grew. Local funding would mean bringing his council on board. So, whatever it was that they wanted, they would need Lesley's approval and patronage and his alarm quietly dimmed. As ever, he held all the cards and he was in control. Everything was fine.

Later that day, still basking in the brilliance of Paddy's staffing idea, a reinvigorated Tom knocked on Sarah's office door. She had requested to see him, which had further brightened his mood, until he saw her face that is.

A copy of the *Echo* was lying on her desk amidst the mountain of paperwork. She looked up but didn't smile. She looked hassled and aggravated. She pulled off her reading glasses and crashed them on her desk.

'Everything OK?' Tom asked.

'Not really, no.'

Friday evening was the night when the staffroom emptied quickest, but it didn't look as if Sarah was going home for a good few hours yet. Tom sat down a little sheepishly, the way he would have done as a child in trouble.

'Are you insured? The stall, I mean; is it insured?' Sarah asked bluntly.

'Er...'

'Because I've had my local authority on the phone shouting about insurance because there are machines and knives, I take it? To cut the fruit?'

Tom held his hands up. 'Sorry, I'll get onto it.'

Sarah sighed. 'I wasn't aware how much your trial was going to take over my life. The immediacy of the trial, the shed, the press... Look, I'm in the papers again.'

Right on cue, her mobile rang. 'Excuse me,' she said and brought it to her ear. 'Garth, hi. I'm in a meeting. I'll call you in ten minutes or so. Are we still...?' She stopped talking and as she listened, her mood darkened. 'Right, fine... Bye.' She ended her call in an ever-darkening mood. Tom didn't know where to look.

'I've had the council on. The Health & Safety executive. Are you CRB checked?'

Tom looked bewildered.

'Oh, Jesus!' she scribbled something in her pad. 'Child protection services, the parole office, the police...'

'Bloody hell! Why? It's only fruit juice.'

'Because. That's why? All these people have jobs to justify. You

217

had Lewis Adele here on school premises, which is a violation of his court order. There are proper channels to go through for things like this and your ignoring them has made me look like a maverick.'

Tom's eyes widened. 'Oh dear, I'm sorry.'

'Yes, so am I.' She grabbed at her pad again. 'Produce probity?' she read and fired at him like an arrow. 'Botulism hygiene? Listeria? Salmonella...'

Tom's day now lay in ruins. His idea had intended to be a force for good. And a memorial to his Beth. The last thing he wanted was to land a mass of red tape onto her desk. The whole trial had been too urgent and earnest. He had been foolhardy and Paddy had been right all along.

'Sarah, I am so sorry, really, I am. Look, I'll postpone the trial.'

'No, don't do that.'

'No, I have to. Until I get everything in place and agreed. I have a colleague up from London. He does bureaucracy and paperwork in his spare time and with his staff, he might even be able to help.'

Sarah looked at him, even more frustrated now. 'Colleague? From where?'

'From London, where I work.'

'What, just like that?'

Tom shrugged and did his best look of 'so what?'

'Oh, please, don't look so surprised.' Sarah responded.

Tom shifted in his seat.

'Because you've got everyone around here completely foxed.'

Tom didn't respond.

'You appear out of nowhere, take everyone by surprise and suddenly, it's all guns blazing. Why?'

Tom just shrugged. This question was going to keep cropping up. 'I don't know... I'm sorry.'

Sarah tutted. 'And stop apologising. You do it a lot and it doesn't suit you.' She had grown a little tired of his bouts of diffidence. 'And what did you want to see me for?' she asked quickly. 'Anne said that you called.'

'Oh...' His excitement about Paddy's staffing idea had understandably diminished by now, especially in the light of her call from the probation service. 'It was nothing, really.'

'No, go on. It might cheer me up.'

Tom doubted it. 'It's just that Paddy had this idea to make the stall more popular.'

'Right, go on?' This was at least encouraging for him because it appeared that she wanted it to work.

'Making it cool is Paddy's thing. By getting Joe to serve the drinks.'

Sarah pondered this for a moment. It made some sense at least. The kids admired Joe and she could see that it might help. Her nod was enough and emboldened Tom to press on.

'And he even suggested that Lewis might help out too.'

Immediately, Sarah's face altered and her antagonism returned.

'But if that's a problem, we can just go with Joe.'

Sarah just shrugged. She had had a brief conversation with Joe earlier in the day about Lewis. Joe explained how much Lewis had responded to the task of building the shed. And although this was encouraging, if she was honest with herself, it had also rankled because she had completely failed to engage the boy when he was under her charge.

'And have you asked Joe?' she asked, because it seemed that Joe would be a reluctant helper.

'Er, no. Not yet. That's Paddy's department.'

The only way that Lewis would be allowed to work on the stall would be with her permission, which she didn't bother to mention. She was doubtful that Joe would do it and even more sceptical about Lewis, but if he agreed and it was good for him, then she would be happy to sanction it. She rolled her eyes and half smiled to signify that he should continue with his plans.

'Thank you,' Tom said.

Sarah smiled for the first time. Her mobile bleeped again. She looked at her screen hopefully but it was not a conciliatory boyfriend, so she ignored it.

'And you still owe me that explanation, by the way.'

Tom looked resigned.

'The Fruit Bowl?' Sarah stated. 'It's an odd name and it doesn't make much sense.'

'What, now?' Tom asked regarding his explanation.

Sarah looked at her in-tray and shook her head.

'We should involve coffee and Anne's gone home now which means that I've only got instant.'

'Fine, let's save it then.' Tom suggested.

'How about tomorrow?' she asked, taking Tom by surprise. 'Or do you have plans already?'

'Er, no...'

'Well?'

'Sure, tomorrow is fine.'

'You don't sound too convinced.'

He smiled. 'No, I am, why not? I figure I owe you a coffee at the very least for all the problems I've caused you. I'll have the story highly polished, I promise.'

'Assuming, that is, that I can get through this paperwork,' she said, knowing that she would leave it if need be.

'Sure, just let me know.'

'There's a Thai café called The Ayuda on Mayflower Street. If we meet there, say, twelve?'

Elliot had spent three hours in the council records department studying its constitution and cross-referencing other precedents in dry legalese documents with the aid of explanatory manuals, which the council made available to its citizens. Elliot was the very first citizen to ever call upon such a facility and so it was no surprise that a metaphorical fog horn was sounding in Lesley's office. The dense legal speak and contract prose had slowed his progress but his nimble mind and determination were more than a match for the council's barriers to entry. He enjoyed the challenge. He relished the rigour and being thorough. He checked his conclusions one final time. Everything dotted and crossed. No leaks, he smiled and finally placed a call to Jeremy.

Jeremy was always going to keep Michael abreast of any developments with Tom and his excursion to the Midlands. After all, he had Tom's best interests at heart, as they all did. Michael hadn't been unduly concerned when Elliot was dispatched to assist him, especially since it was just to help an old friend complete his tax return. But the fruit business was worrying and he hit the roof when Elliot informed him of his tentative enquiries about plots of land. He barely managed to restrain himself from placing a direct phone call to Tom, to discuss a matter he wasn't supposed to know about. At least his client's funds were still safe and off limits. Something he congratulated himself on and not for the first time.

Early on Saturday morning, Elliot waited for Tom at a derelict piece of land that was owned by the council and up for sale. Tom's car pulled into the car park and he emerged in his jogging gear having already been for a run. Elliot greeted him and they made their way gingerly through the gate, careful as they crunched over the broken glass and other debris.

'Martha has done some research into the Health & Safety and hygiene hurdles and it isn't going to be a problem.'

If Tom was relieved, then he didn't show it, his attention focussed on the land he was now inspecting.

'And insurance. We now have full indemnity insurance. But I need your passport for your CRB check.'

Tom smiled, happy that Elliot was on his team.

Colloquially known as the Quadrant, the plot of land that appeared to be perfect on paper was much less so in reality: a derelict site complete with two burnt-out vehicles and rubber markings on the cracked and uneven concrete. A decrepit old building with boarded up windows and a door that had been forced open stood in the middle of an ugly, raised concrete slab. Tom pushed his head inside, not sure what he would find. Fortunately, it was empty, but the stench of decay was enough to keep him at bay. On the floor amongst the general debris, he could see ripped up pornographic magazines, cigarette butts, syringes and used condoms. The remnants of several fires and empty cans and bottles were scattered about, and, in the corner, he spotted a full nappy. He had seen enough and so had Elliot. Given Michael's reaction, Elliot was quietly relieved by the unsuitability of the site. Whatever Tom's plans were, he would not be buying this plot, which would be good news for him to share with London.

Tom didn't say much as he mooched about. Concentrating hard, moving debris with his feet and looking all around. He kicked an empty beer bottle and tried to imagine how the site could look.

'And this is the nearest site to the school?' he finally asked.

Elliot nodded, trying to hide his surprise.

'Walkable?' Tom added and a sense of concern gripped Elliot.

'Yes, but Tom, an application has been lodged for municipal planning on this site, so –'

Tom stopped him. 'Yes, I know, you said. But the auction is closed bids, right?'

Elliot nodded. They had already discussed this. It was why he had spent an entire morning in the council records department.

'Don't worry, Elliot. I'm not going mad.'

Tom gave him a small pat on the back, which was not very reassuring. He sensed his anxiety and reasoned that he knew why. No doubt, Michael was being kept informed of any developments and this would be particularly worrying for him. Indeed, Tom rather enjoyed the apoplexy it would undoubtedly cause.

'But I'll need the auction open.' Tom stated calmly.

'Right.' Elliot replied cautiously. Knowing Tom never participated in closed sales, he had already identified a possible window but he wouldn't volunteer it just yet.

'And price?' Tom asked.

'It has a reserve of £1.5 million.'

Tom chewed on his lip and looked at the site one last time.

Lesley congratulated himself for identifying a potential problem; there were advantages to presiding over a town where nothing very much happens and when two gentlemen appear from nowhere, one enquiring about plots of land and another trying to feed the poor, they tend to put noses out of joint and particularly, Lesley's. His contact at the *Echo* had long been in Lesley's favour, providing various pieces of information, and confirmation that he had seen Elliot Stapleton and Tom Harper together in the lounge at the Hyatt was all the connection that Lesley had needed. Until then, he had been completely bemused by the initiative known as The

Fruit Bowl, but now he had a reasonable idea of its actual motives and unsurprisingly, it was linked to profit and gain. People playing his game then and in his back yard. Lesley smiled. He loathed the arrogance of Londoners and he looked forward to giving these two a bloody nose.

Chapter 38

Back at his hotel, Tom fretted. He was anxious about everything – what to wear and what to expect – and he kept telling himself that it was just a coffee and nothing to be nervous about. In fact, was it coffee or lunch? He didn't really know; it hadn't been established. Coffee had been discussed but then she mentioned a restaurant, so he had settled on a light breakfast and nothing else. He allowed himself the luxury of a brand-new razor blade, a concession even for the rich, and marvelled as the blade got almost as close as it promised. On his way from the site inspection, he had quickly stopped off to buy some further clothes. He pulled off his new knitted top and scrunched it up a little to try and shake out some of its newness. He looked at himself in the mirror. The top looked smart and he worried about whether he looked like he was making too much of an effort.

Tom poked his head into Elliot's hotel conference room ahead of his leaving. It was a hive of activity and Elliot barely looked up, his eyes fixed on his screen as his fingers pounded his keyboard. Elliot hadn't long got off the phone to London and he wondered if either Jeremy or Michael had called Tom with their concerns. Perhaps so because he seemed a little tense, more so than during their site visit yesterday.

'Everything alright?' Elliot asked.

'Er…'

'You seem tense?'

'Do I? No, not really.'

'These Health & Safety criterion are pretty stringent but we're all over it. They won't be a problem.'

'Great. That's good to hear. Thanks.' Tom motioned a hello to Elliot's two colleagues who had barely looked up from their work.

'And I need to talk to you about this auction.' Elliot ventured.

'Sure, but not now. I've got erm...' Tom didn't finish because he didn't know what he had ahead. He didn't know what he was going to in his new clothes!

Elliot shook his head. 'Can I just flag this with you?'

'Sure, what is it?'

Elliot stood up. 'I've found a new mandate in the council's recent winning manifesto: a clause called "Open and Democratic Local Government". I suspect it was in response to something elsewhere, in Westminster even and –'

'Elliot...' Tom hurried him, not wanting to be late.

'OK, very simply, if a majority of the electorate deign that any council motion or transaction be conducted in public, then the will of the electorate shall prevail.'

'What, so like a referendum?' Tom asked, fretful at referenda weariness of the UK.

'God, no – far too complicated, not to mention out of our time frame.'

'So, what then?' Tom was almost out of the door now.

'Possibly, a simple petition, albeit a properly audited one.'

'Right, fine.'

'Problem being that we'll need over twenty thousand signatures and all within the next ten days!'

Tom reflected for a moment on this considerable hurdle.

'OK, we'll talk later.'

'Sure.' Elliot looked Tom up and down and he seemed to approve. 'You look very smart.'

'Do I?'

Sarah was already in the restaurant when Tom pushed his way through the front door. It was more café than restaurant, which he decided was a good thing. It wasn't a date after all; it was just a coffee and possibly a quick bite and a chat with a new work colleague. The place was airy and light with a spread of daily newspapers, and was predominantly busy with mums and daughters on their weekly shopping pilgrimage. A pretty Thai lady greeted him with her hands pressed together and her head bowed. Tom smiled and bent forward a little, unsure of the exact protocol.

The weather was mild, certainly the warmest day of the year so far, with promises of the warm spring weather in store for everyone. Sarah wore a simple sleeveless dress and flat pumps, and her hair tied back. She had little makeup on and a couple of bangles that Tom had not noticed her wear at work. It all looked effortless, like she had just thrown on the first things she'd found in her wardrobe. It made Tom feel even more self-conscious as they shook hands.

'Nice top. Is it new?'

Tom allowed himself a little smile. 'No, I just have a very good iron.' He looked at his mobile, more out of habit than anything else.

'Expecting a call?' Sarah asked.

'Yes, the BBC. I'm trying to get you on Radio 2.'

Sarah laughed as a waitress appeared at their table. 'We're going to eat, right?' she asked.

'Er, yeah, sure.' Tom was pleased.

'You do like Thai food, right?'

'Does anyone not like Thai food?'

'Great. They do this really good set lunch with jasmine tea.'

'Sure, that'd be great.'

'And it's very reasonable.'

Tom liked the idea that price was a factor. It was novel for him and felt real. He truly couldn't recall the last time that he had had to consider the price of a restaurant, not since his twenties when he and Beth were first dating. They used to visit a restaurant called Strawberry Fields and so that they could afford a pudding to share, they had to insist on tap water and always apologised for doing so. He and Beth had laughed at this fond memory ever since. He was surprised to see another Thai waitress approach with two glasses of orange juice and judging by the smile on her face and Sarah's, he realised that this was Sarah's little joke.

'Thanks, Lulu,' Sarah called out to the waitress who was still giggling as she made off.

'Very good,' Tom smiled.

Sarah took a sip. 'Nice. Not as good as yours, but I thought that it might set your story up rather nicely.'

'Thank you. You're too kind.' Tom smiled at the bright and funny woman sitting opposite him. He caught the eye of Lulu and asked if the kitchen might happen to have a grapefruit and a sharp knife, preferably a curved one with a serrated edge. Lulu had neither but explained that she could fetch a fruit from the local stall and insisted on doing so.

'I should really wait for the grapefruit, but I could make a start on the background at least.'

Sarah nodded and poured them both a glass of water.

'OK, are you ready to hear this? When I was a kid, like most parents, my dad wanted to get my sister and I eating more fruit, you know, other than just the odd apple.'

'Right, and what was he, a nutritionist?'

'No, an accounts clerk actually, but he was just way ahead of his time. Somehow, he just knew about vitamins and fibre. So, on his way home from work, he used to buy these grapefruits from the local market...'

'Not Porter's?'

'Do you know what? I think it might have been.'

Sarah smiled. 'Nice connection to Paddy then.'

'Yeah, I guess it is. Anyway, he would cut the grapefruit in half in the normal way, and my sister and I would simply refuse to eat them, point blank.'

'Yeah, I get that. Way too bitter?' Sarah suggested.

'Right. Awful things.' Tom agreed.

Sarah sympathised. 'Certainly, ambitious anyway because grapefruits are quite an acquired taste. More for adults, then.'

'Right.'

'My mum used to do them as starters for her dinner parties and even then, I could hear the adults groaning. Oh, you've done grapefruits - really, you shouldn't have.'

Tom chuckled. 'Yeah, I remember those. A half grapefruit to start, blimey. In my book, a starter absolutely must include garlic and preferably prawns.'

'Or mushrooms?'

Tom laughed and duly agreed. 'So, anyway, back to my dad. No matter how much sugar he added, we still wouldn't eat them. But he was a stubborn old boot and so he kept on bringing the bloody things home and then finally, he comes up with a cunning plan…'

'He's not Baldrick, is he?'

Tom ignored her joke and spotted Lulu on her way over with a large, very impressive-looking pink grapefruit.

'Ah, thank you very much. This is perfect.'

Lulu left a knife with him and he quickly set about catching up his story by cutting the fruit in half.

'OK, so this is a pink grapefruit, which we didn't have in my day obviously. I don't think they had been invented back then. But no matter, because my dad works out that we won't eat the fruit but that we will drink the juice.'

'What, so he juices them?' Sarah asked flatly. It was hardly revelatory.

'No, no, hang on. Not yet anyway. He took the grapefruit half and would cut out a small piece from the middle like this, just to make some space really and then, with his knife, instead of cutting the fruit into segments in the usual way, he would cut and stab at the flesh until it was a little bowl of juice and because he'd already added the sugar, which by now had dissolved, they were delicious and we loved them. And he called them fruit bowls, because the skin of the grapefruit half became a little bowl, full of juice. And that's it. The Fruit Bowl.'

Sarah watched him complete his own little bowl of juice in front of her. She enjoyed his obvious enthusiasm and his warmth for the memory.

'And then, because he was excited that we finally started eating fruit, he wanted to do other fruits as well: apples, melons, whatever, and so he progressed onto a juicing machine and we ended up with a jug full of juice each morning but the name stuck, The Fruit Bowl. And that's it.'

Tom looked at her for her verdict but he could already tell that she was enchanted.

'But that's a wonderful story.'

'Really, thank you.'

'I don't know what Paddy's talking about. It's not boring at all!'

'Good, I'm glad.'

'And he sounds like a lovely man, your dad.'

'Yeah, he was.'

'Oh, I'm…'

'No, don't be silly. He died ages ago, when I was…' Tom stopped himself. He was about to tell the truth and thereby undermine his elaborate lie but he managed to correct himself in time. 'He's been dead over a decade.'

'And what about your mum?'

Tom shook his head. 'Nope, afraid not; six years this summer.'

Sarah looked slightly shocked and saddened for him. Most of her friends had at least one parent still on the go and she didn't know anyone without either.

'And yours?' Tom asked, out of politeness more than interest.

'Er, yes, both still going strong,' Sarah answered. 'And still together – almost happily. I don't see them as much as they would like, which is their fault because they moved to Eastbourne. Can you believe it?'

'Oh dear. Have they joined a bowling club yet?'

'Not that I know of. Dad plays golf and mum does church stuff mostly.'

'Brothers? Sisters?'

Sarah shook her head. 'No, just me. Which was a shame, for them I mean, and for me as well I suppose. They must have tried for more but I never liked to ask.'

'No. So, it all came down to you then?'

Sarah chuckled. 'Did it ever? Piano lessons – grade six. The day I finally gave up, it was like they had been bereaved. Eleven-plus, grammar school, ballet lessons and I never did get the pony they promised me for my O-level results.'

'Sounds like they're very proud of their little girl.'

Sarah sighed a little too heavily. 'Yes, they still are. And a little too much for my liking. They worry about me.'

Tom laughed. 'About what?'

'Oh, you know – everything! My job is currently one of their major concerns. Mum reads the *Daily Mail* so she thinks I work in a juvenile prison.'

'There was that headmaster in London…'

'Oh, please, don't.' Sarah rolled her eyes. 'Dad used to be a teacher, a headmaster actually, and he didn't want me to follow him. He was very academic, so I was under some pressure in that area. But I did well. I worked hard, but if I'm honest, I was lucky because it came fairly easily.'

Tom chuckled. 'Get you!'

'No, but you know what I mean? I could just remember stuff.'

'Yeah, sort of. I think things came less easily to me.'

'It was a huge thing for him when I got into Oxford. I don't think I've ever seen him happier. He'd been there himself and he was absolutely thrilled.'

'What did you read?'

Sarah looked a little embarrassed. 'Law.'

'Oh, blimey!'

'Oh, shut up. Mum and Dad took me up there on the first day. We lived in Bristol. God, they were so proud. Looking back now, it was quite embarrassing. Dad had it all mapped out. He wanted me to be a barrister, a QC no less.'

'So, what happened?'

'Well, to start with, by the time I qualified as a solicitor, I realised that I hated being a lawyer.'

'Ah…'

'Yeah, exactly, and then when I mentioned teaching – well, I might as well have said beauty therapist, the way he reacted.'

Tom giggled along with her. 'But he's OK about it now, right? Now that you're a Super Head?'

Sarah winced at the term.

'It's a huge job. And a pretty lonely one, given how many colleagues I have.'

Tom nodded.

'But you enjoy it though?' Tom asked.

Sarah pulled a face. 'Yeah, mostly. I like the bigger picture, you know, the challenge of the job and the romance of it all, but actually the job itself? The day-to-day is pretty tough and difficult to enjoy.'

'Why, because of the kids?'

'Yeah, some of them. Some of them are a real challenge but so are some of my staff. But it's more the structure. The targets and the bureaucracy – oh my God! The red tape. And then there's the parents and my local authority. It's all completely overwhelming and to be honest, I'm not sure if I can do it.'

Tom didn't really know how to respond at her being so personal and candid.

When Lulu arrived with the bill, they had been chatting for well over an hour but it seemed much less to them both. Tom put a twenty-pound note on the table and firmly insisted that it was his pleasure and Sarah had the good sense to agree and thank him. Both had studiously avoided any more personal subjects. Outside the cafe, the street was busy, the sun was still out and Sarah slipped her sunglasses down over her eyes.

'So, what does the rest of the weekend have in store for you?' she asked, confident that her question wouldn't be misinterpreted.

'I'm working with Elliot this afternoon and evening.'

'Is he at the Hyatt as well?'

'Yep. For the time being at least.'

Sarah seemed impressed. There were much more affordable hotels in the area.

'And my sister has threatened to arrive for Sunday lunch.'

'Oh, lovely. Well, I'm off to watch a cricket match.'

Tom nodded knowingly. 'Right, yes, Paddy mentioned that you...' he tailed off awkwardly, 'have a friend who plays?'

'Did he?'

'Paddy said he's South African, so if he's any good, he'll be playing for England soon.'

Sarah didn't laugh at his joke and seemed perturbed at her 'status' being discussed.

'Well, have fun anyway.' Tom reached out and they shook hands warmly. Tom marched off down the street in the opposite direction.

He desperately wanted to turn around to watch her walking away but he managed not to, which was both a relief and a disappointment to Sarah, as she did turn to see him disappear into the Saturday shopping throng...

Chapter 39

Nell and Jonathan made a fuss of Tom and the kids were also delighted to see him. Tom suspected that they had changed their plans to accommodate his impromptu visit. It was a Sunday and the bikes lined up by the garage were enough to cause him a pang of guilt. Nell was interested enough in The Fruit Bowl and its potential, but more from the perspective that it was good for her brother's health than for the nation's. She had obviously been in contact with Michael, because she knew about his land speculating and she managed to transmit both her interest and disapproval at the same time. Perhaps, understandably, the kids at her old school not having a football pitch wouldn't keep her awake at night but her brother's loneliness did and she missed him terribly. He was now into his second week away and she was struggling to make sense of it all.

'Nell, I'm not moving to Bromsworth.'

'But then what are you doing?'

Jonathan re-entered the living room and Nell shot him a look that made him turn on his heel instantly.

'And is there anything else?' Nell asked, giving him as much scope as possible but still he shook his head.

'And what about this trial? Is it successful?'

Tom looked at her knowingly. 'No, not really, but you know what kids are like. They need everything to be cool, but I'm sure it will work in the long term?'

Nell's eyes widened at his choice of expression.

'Nell, you know what I mean. Paddy has an idea. There's a young lad called Lewis, a brilliant footballer who all the kids love...' Tom could see that Nell was struggling to hear about people she didn't know and didn't much care about. 'And Elliot Stapleton is up there helping me with a couple of trainees...' Tom tailed off.

'Well, it's all good because you sound happy – or happ*ier* at least.'

'Yeah, I am - I think.'

'Good. Will you stay tonight?' Nell asked hopefully. 'The kids would love it.' But he shook his head quickly.

'Nell, I can't. I'd love to, but tomorrow morning, I need to get the stall open, you know, keep the momentum going and all that.'

Nell nodded her head to say that she understood, even though she didn't and he hugged her warmly.

Chapter 40

Tom needn't have hurried back because the stall on Monday morning wasn't busy and not helped by the continual downpour the forecasters had predicted. A vicious wind blew through the shed and water breached the porous joints in the roof, adding to his misery. It was cold and he could see that a bowl of soup was needed and not a glass of cold fruit juice. It might be an idea if The Fruit Bowl confined itself to the summer term only and he cursed himself for starting a trial in March. At this rate, it was set to fail and they wouldn't be around to see if the bright summer mornings would act in its favour.

Fortunately, he'd called Paddy and told him not to bother joining him this morning. Paddy relayed the bad news that Joe wasn't interested in helping on the stall. It was no surprise and it wasn't that he was too busy. He just wasn't interested which put Lewis out of the frame as well. A drop of rain made its way through a join in the roof and with Exocet precision; found fell the gap in Tom's collar and ran down along his bare back, making him shiver. Joe had been right about the structure and Tom wondered if he could pay him to make the necessary waterproofing improvements. It could be usefully extended as well to create more space for when demand had increased and more staff were required. Pie in the sky, Paddy would have called this, but still, the idea briefly warmed him just as Anne arrived with a mug of coffee, sent out by Sarah. She hadn't wanted to deliver it herself and wondered if Tom would realise why. She hoped so. Tom was the talk of the staffroom and she didn't wish to fan the rumour flames.

Lesley sat with his business partner, Danny Green, in the bar at his golf club, looking out at the windswept course where a couple of ladies were finishing up on the eighteenth green. They were enough to put him in a bad mood even without the trauma of learning that

Elliot Stapleton had been in the council offices again, seemingly still interested in his plot of land.

'But why?' Danny asked: the golden question which neither of them could answer.

'Unless he's got the same idea as us,' Danny suggested.

'Don't be ridiculous.' Lesley stated firmly. 'No one outside the council could possibly plan for such a thing? They would need to know things about the council, its capacity…' Lesley stopped talking as a dark thought occurred to him.

'Unless someone has blabbed.' He looked at Danny accusingly.

Danny snorted at such a suggestion. 'Who, me? Don't be stupid. You're driving this, remember. Without you and your strings, that land is worthless.'

Lesley mulled this point for a moment. It was true enough and he enjoyed the reality. It was soothing and stroked his ego. It made him feel powerful and safe. But the question remained. What could possibly interest a land speculator in a plot with only municipal planning? It didn't make any sense and the altruism of the fruit business perplexed matters even more. Businesses seeking to operate within the public sector are usually mindful to keep the regulators on side, but not Porter's Fruit Bowls. They seemed not to bother with such protocol, which irked Lesley and heightened his suspicions. He didn't like their confidence either. And matters weren't helped since most of his council colleagues seemed to think that that Porter's Fruit Bowls was a bloody marvellous idea. And it was. Giving kids free juice drinks, some of whom had probably never seen a pineapple in their lives, let alone eaten one – what's not to fucking like? But why? That was what Lesley needed to find out. There was something he was missing. Had to be. People only give stuff away if there's an ulterior upside, something in it for them? But what though?

Later that day in his office, Lesley was still pondering this enigma when a thought occurred to him. He pondered it a moment, playing out different scenarios and outcomes. And then suddenly, it all became clear. It had to be right and he smiled broadly. It was certainly a protracted and risky play on their part but not unheard of: to establish good favour with an authority by doing something altruistic but with a view to allowing some other venture elsewhere?

They must have plans for the land and municipal planning can be misinterpreted or even reverted? Lesley's anxiety grew with the thought. Industrial units? Storage space? Car park? A warehouse? It didn't matter what and then his anxiety flipped to excitement, because maybe this was an opportunity for him? A chance to cut himself in to whatever they have planned? And to cut Danny Green, out perhaps? 'Be adaptable, Lesley. Keep all you're your options and all your doors open,' He muttered to himself.

If the fruit juice business was conceived to curry favour with his council, then there was a much quicker and more direct way of achieving such an outcome. Lesley smiled again. Whatever the ridiculously named Fruit Bowl was costing, Lesley was confident that he would be much cheaper and all they needed to do was ask. He had half a mind to set up a meeting to air such delicate matters, but of course, this would only weaken his bargaining position. Better then to wait for their inevitable approach – after all, they were in the squeezing business. Lesley laughed at his little pun. Things were going to work out, just fine.

Chapter 41

Tom stopped by Paddy's stall after his morning at the school.

'Hey, Tom, how'd it go?' Paddy asked. Tom thought about lying but he couldn't be bothered and just shook his head.

'Oh, well, the weather couldn't have helped,' Paddy offered kindly.

'Yeah, I guess,' Tom answered. 'Listen, Paddy, I was wondering…'

Paddy looked immediately troubled.

'What if I ask Joe myself?'

Paddy looked skyward. Dog with a bone, sprang to mind.

'I know you've already asked him and he's –'

'Tom, no! That is not a good idea,' Paddy interrupted, panicking slightly because he hadn't yet asked Joe and had just assumed that he would say no.

'Yes, but what if I paid him?'

'No, don't do that. Joe won't like that; you know what he's like about flashing the cash.'

Paddy fingered his mobile phone in his pocket, anxious to get an urgent call in to Joe as soon as Tom moved off.

'Where are you going now?' Paddy asked nervously.

'Back to the hotel, why?'

'No, no reason.'

'Maybe, you're right.' Tom said a little wearily.

'I am, definitely.' Paddy let go of his phone.

'Maybe if I run it by Lewis?'

'Jesus, man, are you out of your mind?' Paddy protested.

'What? Why not?'

'Because Joe won't like it.'

Tom scowled. He was getting more than a little bit fed up with Joe. His mobile rang. It was Elliot calling. He listened briefly before

238

handing the phone to Paddy.

'It's for you. It's Elliot. Why don't you answer your phone Paddy? Here - he needs to speak to you.'

Paddy took the phone with a look of dread, which worsened as he continued to listen. When he ended the call, he looked terrified.

'Jesus Christ! The council want to see me.'

'What about?' Tom asked.

'What do you think? The bloody Fruit Bowl, what else?'

Tom smiled. 'Don't worry about it; Elliot will go with you. He'll eat 'em alive.'

Later, when Tom arrived at the youth centre, Joe was taking a frantic call from Paddy which was interrupting one of Lewis's supervised football coaching sessions. Tom nodded at Joe as he sidled up to have a quiet word with Lewis, which Joe registered keenly and no doubt it hastened his conversation.

Lewis was suspicious and more than guarded in greeting Tom. He had a small cut over his right eye and Tom wanted to ask how it occurred, but managed not to – a football incident, hopefully?

'Hi, Lewis… Tom from the stall, you remember?'

Lewis reluctantly took Tom's outstretched hand.

'So, how's it going?' Tom asked hopefully.

Lewis looked at him oddly. 'What do you mean?'

'I don't know, just generally.'

Lewis didn't bother to answer and just looked about his surroundings. It was hardly Villa Park.

'I see that you're teaching the kids. You enjoy that?'

'No. I don't.'

Tom shifted awkwardly.

'Paddy tells me you might start playing again, you know, for a local side.'

Lewis said nothing, just stared and shook his head. Tom could understand his point. Whichever team it was, it would be a far cry from where he had been, but nonetheless, it was a start and a step in the right direction. Joe had moved another mountain for Lewis to make this happen, which he had yet to appreciate.

'Well, I'm sure if things go right…'

Lewis shook his head angrily. 'Listen, man. I don't care what you think. You get me?'

Tom took the hit. He wasn't sure if there was any point in trying to continue but he decided to make one more attempt. 'Why, because kids, like you –'

'Fuck you, man. "Like me". What do you know about me?'

Tom glanced over at Joe, not that he would be much support.

'And what do you want anyway?' Lewis asked. 'That's what people want to know.'

'Oh, is that right? Like who?' Tom asked.

'Just people. So, come on then. What do you want?'

Tom stared hard at Lewis as he considered how to respond. 'What I want son, is the same thing as you.' Tom put a heavy emphasis on 'son', which is not a word nor a title he would normally use. But Lewis's sense of self was a little over-blown and what he needed perhaps was to hear some ugly truths.

'Oh, really? Is, that right?'

'Yeah, I think so.' Tom answered a little angry now.

'Well come on then, what?' Lewis countered. What do I want, then?' He wasn't intimidated by Tom's seniority and he didn't flinch. Quickly, he had grown tired of being so demur and malleable.

'To be happy,' Tom answered quietly and it completely disarmed the angry child before him. Lewis thought for a moment but then quickly recovered and he laughed coldly.

'And are you? Are you happy then?' Lewis asked snidely.

'No. Actually I'm not. Or put it this way, I've been happier.'

Lewis chewed his lip before continuing.

'Yeah, cos, your stall sucks, right? I heard it's stinking the place out?'

Tom bristled. The stall was Beth's memorial and he hated the idea of people disparaging it. Joe hastily ended his call and made straight for Tom and Lewis.

'Right kids, come on, let's look lively,' Joe called out generally but to include Lewis also. 'What do you want?' he asked Tom curtly.

'Oh, hello, Joe. I'm fine thanks.' Tom replied sarcastically.

'Yeah, well, I've got things to do here…'

Tom interrupted him. 'I was just chatting with Lewis...'

'Yeah, I can see that. Only he's got things to be doing, so...'

'Right, well that's all three of us then.' Tom answered.

'Right - so come on then. What is it? Spit it out.' Joe flicked his hand and turned to leave but Tom hadn't finished yet. 'Actually Joe, it's you I needed to chat to.'

Joe spun around and took a step forward. Lewis looked on. Joe pointed at him and shot him a look. 'You, get over there and get on with your bloody session?'

Lewis tutted and sauntered off.

Tom clenched his jaw. 'Joe, is there something I've done?'

'What do you mean?' Joe asked with one eye on Lewis who was moving, but too slowly for his liking.

'To upset you?' Tom continued. 'Because if I have, then you might like to explain it to me?'

Joe fixed Tom with a defiant stare. This was the second time it felt like he was being told off and he didn't like it. 'Just leave Lewis alone. He's doesn't need people like you.'

'Oh, is that right?'

'Yeah, that's right. And while you're at it, you can leave Paddy alone as well.'

'Meaning what, exactly?'

But Joe didn't bother explaining and turned again, leaving Tom hanging.

'What is it? Are you jealous?' Tom called after him and instantly Joe stopped, turned and marched back.

'Jealous? Just who the fuck do you think you are?'

'You still haven't answered my question.' Tom replied defiantly.

'You listen to me. Just because Paddy could use a break or two, doesn't mean you can exploit him.'

'Oh? And is that what I'm doing?' Tom moved forward giving his answer even more force.

'Yeah, you are. Having him running around after you, like some little employee.'

'He's a partner, actually.'

'Oh, fuck off! Partner, my arse?'

241

'Now, hang on…'

'No, you hang on, pal. I don't know why, maybe you got bullied as a kid, who cares? Because you're the one doing the bullying now…'

A sudden look of anger flashed across Tom's face. 'I'm bullying Paddy?' He asked incredulously.

'Yeah, you are. Paddy doesn't want to be doing all this fruit juice shit - you do? Meeting with that little bitch over at the school and now the council.'

Tom flinched at the reference to Sarah as his invective continued.

'Paddy's a bag of nerves because of you. And now he's calling me up, asking me to get involved. And d'you know what I told him. You can shove it up your arse.'

Tom's eyes narrowed. 'I'm trying to help Paddy!'

'No, you're not.' Joe pointed in Tom's face, no doubt just how he'd done at hundreds of referees and opponents. 'You're helping yourself and you're using Paddy. And you're patronising the shit out of him as well, paying for this, paying for that, like you're some fucking big shot.'

Tom's fist shot out, more as a reflex than a premeditated punch. It was the first time he had ever consciously hit anybody in his life and it took him a moment to register that it had actually happened. He regretted it instantly and not just because it wouldn't have helped his cause at all. Joe was equally surprised and grabbed at his face, more out of shock than pain, moaning loudly like any true professional football player. Tom stole a quick look around; Lewis and the kids were staring and he wondered what he should do. Joe straightened and glared at Tom. A thin line of blood seeped through his closed fingers.

'Jesus, Joe, I'm sorry. I didn't mean to do that. Are you, all right?'

'The session is over kids. Go home,' Joe shouted and then he ran hard at Tom, pushing him backwards hard against the fence. But now Tom was back in control of his emotions and he raised his hands in submission.

'Joe, I'm sorry –'

'Just leave us all alone. Just fuck off altogether why don't you.'

Joe skulked back to the pavilion, leaving Lewis standing alone with Tom on the court. Tom looked at him for a moment, to try and engage with the boy, but Lewis was wary now of responding and turned away.

Chapter 42

Back on his own stall, Paddy was fretting badly and not because of Joe's broken nose. His impending meeting at the council was foremost on his mind, even more so than his lack of customers all morning. Right enough, trade was quiet, but it was still busier than the new stall he was manning at the school where they literally could not give the stuff away. And this rather brought home to Paddy how precarious his whole situation had become. None of it had been his idea and yet somehow it was his name in the title of the 'business' and on the front cover of yet another document that Elliot was preparing. Damn it, he thought. The blinking robot was running riot. How had he allowed this to happen? Mary had let him whinge on a little last evening but quickly got bored and told him to shut up.

'Think about what they're doing with your accounts, Paddy Porter?' She added dryly, which only made Paddy feel more beholden to Tom and even more miserable.

Elliot was looking forward to the meeting and in contrast, Jerry Danvers, the head of Environmental Services at the council, was not. He was under strict instructions from Councillor Lesley Irwin to put Mr Porter and his Fruit Bowl through the ringer. He didn't know why, he daren't ask and even more worrying, he didn't know how to. For this reason, Lesley had assigned Mari Evans, an ambitious attack-dog to accompany Jerry to the meeting, which was to take place in the Council State Room – something about a double booking for the boardroom, which Lesley had pre-arranged. The council building dated back to 1805 but had been substantially modernised and added to since. What remained of the original building was largely taken up by the central hall, now used for corporate functions and dinners and very occasionally, meetings when intimidation was required for the council to flex its muscle. Jerry sat down, arranged his pad and pens and waited for what felt more like a showdown than a meeting.

Paddy arrived at the council offices as agreed at 10.45 a.m., his mood not lightened by yet another lame morning on The Fruit Bowl. Naturally, Elliot was already waiting for him and had a large black briefcase parked beside him.

'Another shite morning,' Paddy announced, tapping his foot and looking at his serene-faced colleague.

Elliot didn't respond.

'So, what's this meeting about then?' he asked nervously, as if he had better and more important things to do with his time.

Elliot turned and looked at him briefly. 'Don't worry, Paddy.' Elliot said kindly.

'No, well, I do worry. I bloody well do. It's just something about me and officialdom...'

Elliot rested his hand on Paddy's enormous knee and gently squeezed. It was a rare display of emotion from the tiny brainbox. It was meant to be a reassuring squeeze but it had the opposite effect and quickly he removed it and they both sat there in a rather strained silence.

They were met at reception by a young lady who led them down a long-tiled corridor and while they walked, Paddy finally spoke up.

'Look, just because it's called Porter's Fruit Bowls and I'm Paddy Porter, that doesn't mean that you can't take the lead in there today.'

Elliot didn't bother to thank him.

'I mean, don't get me wrong, I'll be there, if you need me. I've promised Tom. It's just that I don't mind if you want to, you know...'

'Paddy, please…' Elliot appealed and Paddy stopped talking.

'Don't worry, Paddy. I'm all over this.' It was an odd use of language for Elliot. An Americanism that jarred a little. Elliot couldn't wait to get in there and get started. Fully concentrated, he was about to go over the wall, armed to the teeth and raring to go.

'Here we are.' The lady from the council clutched at the brass door handle and pushed the enormous oak door open. 'Mr Patrick Porter and Mr Elliot Stapleton.'

Sitting in a line behind a heavy central oak table in the middle of the grand room with oil paintings adorning the walls were six council officials. A huge fireplace dominated one end of the room and surely, a moose's head must have hung over it at some point. While Paddy visibly shrank and crumpled, Elliot kept his gaze forward, staring at each official in the eye and in turn. The start of any meeting is the most important and when Elliot was at his most concentrated. The introductions were cursory and pointless for Paddy, because he forgot each of their names and job titles instantly. But Elliot didn't. He placed each person in a separate memory store, complete with their job title and function and which he would call upon later. It was one of his party pieces and it never failed to impress and intimidate.

Elliot said nothing as team Danvers launched their assault, led mostly by a cold and detached Mari Evans who was suitably compelling, setting out her council's official position. Elliot was unmoved and sat impassively, soaking up each blow and each veiled criticism. Paddy, in contrast, was convinced by her argument and could see the council's position entirely. He just hadn't considered that there could be so many implications to something as simple as fruit juice. Health & Safety, insurance, fire hazards? Many of these he understood but he wasn't sure of the term *due diligence*, which had cropped up a few times.

'…and so, you will not be surprised by our decision given how stretched the council is in providing the services we are already committed to,' Mari ended. She had taken about twenty minutes or so to deliver the verdict that had been completely predictable – that The Fruit Bowl could only proceed with the council's support and that official support was currently pending and conditional? What was less clear was that this support rested on the retirement plans of the council boss, Lesley Irwin.

Mari was pleased and a little surprised that there had been no interruptions during her well-prepared speech and she now expected a quiet surrender. Elliot, though, had other plans. He smiled a little and held his hands together, with his fingers interlocked and his two index fingers straight and resting on his lips. It was his turn now. Show-time and he enjoyed making them wait for a little longer.

'Well, first, can I say thank you very much for inviting Mr Porter and I to see you today. It's been most interesting listening to the points that you've made and also very constructive and helpful.'

Mari's eyes narrowed, sensing that this was not an acquiescent opening.

'Because I think that we can all agree on one thing: The Fruit Bowl is good news for the children of St Edmund's School and for this reason alone, all of us here this morning have a vested interest to see it succeed.'

It was a smart statement because who could disagree with giving malnourished kids vitamins and fibre.

'So, really what we have here - is a series of obstacles that we must overcome?'

Another awkward nod from Mari. Elliot allowed himself another half-smile in anticipation as he bent down to retrieve a file from his briefcase. Paddy didn't know where to look as Elliot placed a fat folder on the table and pushed it very precisely towards Jerry

Danvers.

'I do apologise, but we weren't expecting so many of you. In fact, we were only expecting Mr Danvers, so I only have one copy just now, but rest assured, I can provide copies to each of you this afternoon if you so wish.'

Jerry mumbled something about photocopiers, sharing and trees before Elliot continued.

'Mr Danvers, this first report is really just a market report and operations document on the establishment and the running of Porter's Fruit Bowls: its market, supply chain, logistics, ethics and execution. Our certificates of insurance, of course, and our hygiene criteria and policy, in line and compliant with the Ministry of Food, Agriculture and Fisheries guidelines – so we aren't expecting any issues or problems on this front at all. We quite agree that the health of the children is paramount and indeed, this is the very focus and motivation of our entire operation and purpose. But perhaps, just as important, if I could draw your attention to Appendix C, which highlights the benefits and synergies between the local authorities and our schools.'

This wasn't going how Lesley Irwin had expected and his assistant, Mark Hooper, swallowed hard. Jerry fingered the impressive document, which ran to perhaps fifty pages in full colour, complete with graphs and pie charts. It looked like a postgraduate dissertation after three years of research and Elliot and his team had knocked it out in little over a week.

'But obviously, much more on this later,' Elliot added casually to which Jerry smiled and Mari blanched. Elliot retrieved another slimmer document from his file. 'Please forgive the business speak, but this is a simple but comprehensive SWOT analysis, considering the pupils, staff, the regulatory body and crucially, the supply chain, wholesalers, growers and importers.' Elliot pushed it towards Mark

Hooper this time. Elliot had calculated that none of the reports would be read in any great detail: they were all highly repetitive and reliant on bland management consultant speak that could be applied to any company and industry in theory, but probably none in actual practice. But even if they did read them, the language was so pompous and the theory so bland, he was confident that they would suffice. Elliot had waited five years for his MBA to be of any real use to him and he was sensing his moment had arrived.

'In this report is a particularly enlightening essay on the development of education in Chile, which is directly attributable to the fruit industry and I believe that Bromsworth have a close association with a charitable foundation in Chile. Anyway, Mr Hooper, if you could have a read, I would be grateful to have your input.'

Mark Hooper nodded feebly. It was Elliot's second name check and it raised an eyebrow or two. He hadn't even got on to job titles yet.

'There is also a breakdown and analysis of county councils in the UK, with its pupil population to school's ratio. We envisage that The Fruit Bowl could even be rolled out nationwide within the next few years, with Bromsworth as the progressive council setting the all-important precedent. And this no doubt, would reflect well on this council and its leader, Councillor Irwin.'

Third name check, and he wasn't even present. Elliot produced another file.

'Ah… This is much more salient.' Elliot looked at the people in front him. 'Mr Lyons, if I can give this to you, since you're the liaison officer?'

'Yes, thank you.' A startled Richard Lyons had just uttered his first words of the meeting.

'This is a report commissioned by the Royal College of Food

Nutritionists on health implications of diet and fibre on physiology. It pays particular attention to fruit and vegetables and its effect on health and the causal social ramifications, going forward five, ten and twenty years hence. Nothing new here, the principal conclusion being the avoidance of obesity, its health benefits and the linking of learning and academic prowess to diet.'

Richard thumbed the report and nodded as officially as he could manage as Elliot produced yet another file from his TARDIS of a briefcase and turned his attention to Mari Evans. Paddy sensed a confrontation and shifted awkwardly.

'Mrs Evans. As you said earlier, "the council wishes it could do many things, but everything has a cost and everything has to be paid for and audited." I quite understand and completely agree. So, if I could draw your attention to this, The European Directive on Waste Management and the Use of Resources, to maximise efficiencies and minimise waste. This isn't the whole report obviously, just the salient points relevant to us here today.' Another file. 'Busy as you all are no doubt, to save you some time, this is a summary of its findings with corresponding recommendations for good practice and, most exciting of all, is the happy conclusion that Porter's Fruit Bowls meets all the necessary criteria to qualify for a full European grant, which can be up to eighty per cent of all costs.'

'Only we've left Europe.' Mari managed to splutter.

'We have indeed. But given most of this fruit is imported from Southern Europe, such grants favour their farmers and as such all trading partners are eligible to apply. Turkey is a recipient for example and for Lychees of all things.'

Paddy was nodding vigorously now at everything and anything that Elliot was saying.

'Now, clearly, any application for such a grant needs to be made in conjunction with a municipal authority and knowing how onerous such applications can be, and the time constraints and pressures on your staff that you've already alluded to, we propose that we should conduct all the necessary due diligence on behalf of the council...'

Paddy nodded again and agreed loudly. He might as well have said, *Here, Here*. Due diligence was given another airing which he still didn't understand but by now, he was fully on-side and he didn't care.

'...and our lawyers will complete all the required paperwork for any submission, subject to council approval, of course, and furthermore make any petitions in Brussels as and when required.'

Mari managed a strained smile.

'And finally,' – the coup de grace and last file – 'a summary of all our findings. A digest, if you'll forgive the expression.' Elliot looked at a young waspish woman whom he hadn't yet addressed personally and who remained, so far, the only person without a file. Elliot smiled at her as he slid it across. 'Michelle, it only seems fair...' His briefcase was now empty. His party piece was complete. He had nothing more to add.

Paddy was conscious that he hadn't said anything yet and instinctively he knew that his time had come. He stood up first, dragging others up with him and pointed at Elliot. 'He works for me by the way.'

Chapter 43

Elliot went straight from the meeting back to his hotel room to write a report for Tom. Paddy went to the Nelson because he needed a drink, but also because he had arranged to meet Tom. He was particularly excited at the prospect of telling him how well they had both performed. His enthusiasm was infectious as he slurped his pint of mild and Tom was pleased. Any smattering of good news was very welcome.

'I'm telling you, Tom, he was like a machine. Like a bloody ninja, he was. Of course, I was there supporting him all the way,' Paddy added.

'Of course.'

'But he's got these reports in his bag, which are like arrows. And he was firing them at these suits, one after another – bang, bang, bang! I'm telling you, it was a like a YouTube clip; it was actually quite beautiful.'

'Did he do the name thing?' Tom asked.

'The name thing? Yes. Fuck me. He did. Six people and he remembers all their names –'

Tom's phone pinged.

'That'll be Elliot's report coming in?' Tom half joked to which Paddy roared.

And entirely appropriately, it was indeed. Elliot's initial report, complete with his recommendations. Tom smiled and pointed Paddy's attention to Elliot's email sign-off.

"Paddy was awesome btw."

Paddy read it and beamed. 'I fucking love that kid.'

Tom chuckled. He needed to get going. He replied quickly that he was heading over to the Hyatt as soon as he could.

'OK, then, Paddy, well done again.'

'No bother.'

Tom got up to leave.

'And if Joe shows up, will you –'

Just then, Joe poked his head into the pub. Spotting Tom, he scowled, threw his right hand in the air and disappeared without saying a word.

Back at the hotel, Elliot was typically understated about the meeting and Tom didn't feel that he had much to celebrate. The Fruit Bowl was not a success and he was even more troubled about his growing feelings for Sarah, not to mention the further folly of buying any local land. He could probably explain The Fruit Bowl and its importance to the people closest to him, but he knew that none of them would understand and agree with his other plans and he felt increasingly isolated. He wanted to hear from Sarah but he daren't call her. As normal, his thoughts quickly reverted to his family again, forcing him to pause and consider just what he was trying to achieve and why. Yet, Joe's cruel accusations swirled around his conscience and he even wondered if there was an element of truth to it.

Sarah was also having a bad day. She slumped into her chair and thumped her desk in frustration. She bitterly regretted giving Nathaniel a detention now and it was no consolation that she had been right to do so. Nathaniel was the school's star football player and the detention would mean him missing the school match against arch rivals, Christopher Wren School. There were other sanctions available and ones that would have caused her far less stress, and so she was cross with herself for not taking them. And she couldn't rescind it either, not if she wanted to maintain any semblance of authority. Discipline and respect were the two absolutes of the Super Head and allowing such chinks wasn't an option. She looked at the clock, worked out the likely stage of the match and prayed that her school might somehow prevail, or at least not lose. Never in her life did she have so much invested in the outcome of a football match and she could only imagine the opprobrium heaped upon her if they didn't win. And of course, it would all be her fault because Nathaniel hadn't been available and with good reason. He had abused a girl because she objected to him fondling her breasts, so he could consider himself fortunate it was just a detention he faced and not the police. Not that the police would have been interested. Nathaniel would have denied it and the girl was most likely an ex-conquest of his anyway. Anne hadn't been much of a help either.

'There'll be other games,' Sarah had argued hopefully.

Anne had looked a little awkward.

'What?'

'It's a cup game – a knock out.'

Sarah groaned.

Paddy closed his stall early and reconvened his meeting in the Nelson with his usual set of friends as they speculated by how many goals St Edmund's would concede, especially without Nathaniel playing; word of which spread quickly. Tom wanted to support Sarah's stand, but he didn't, however. He said nothing and felt disloyal doing so. It seemed to him that they wanted Ed's to lose because blaming Sarah was more fun than a victory. It was bullying and Tom didn't enjoy the tone, so he made his excuses and left. He needed to call Nell and no doubt field yet more reasonable questions about his plans.

At just after 5.00 p.m., a disconsolate-looking Joe entered the pub. Evidently, they had lost. The question was, by how many? Benny reasoned that it was a two-goal margin, but Paddy knew better and was going higher, maybe even as many as four. Joe nodded in their direction as he waited for his pint he hadn't needed to order and then slowly trudged over to his mates.

'How many?' Paddy asked.

Joe sat down heavily. 'Five fucking nil.'

Paddy, George, Benny and Declan all roared with laughter. It was a good thing that Tom had left already because it was all her fault, that bitch from across the road.

Chapter 44

Tom was a bundle of nerves as he swung his car into the school staff car park. It was nearly 7.00 p.m. and he expected and half-hoped that Sarah would have left already. But there was only one car parked and it was her Audi. He took a deep breath, unclear what he was doing exactly. Was he there to discuss The Fruit Bowl and if so, why so late and without an appointment? Or was he there to offer her his support? Either way, it was all very awkward. Full of doubt, he walked slowly towards the reception building. The light in her office was on and he made a deal with himself, based on the assumption that the security measures in modern schools would save him. If the front door was locked and required him to ring through, then he wouldn't bother her, but if it was open, then this would be a sign for him to go on in to see her. Tom pushed gently on the door and much to his dismay, it was open.

Sarah couldn't really concentrate on a report after what had been a torrid day. It had started with a difficult staff meeting where low morale was the order of the day and this was followed by an inevitable showdown with a troublesome member of her teaching staff, Mrs Tranter, whose commitment was as poor as her attendance record. Mrs Tranter had taken almost two weeks' sick leave each term for the last eight years, the latest of which was to grieve for a deceased aunt. An aunt! Sarah had wanted to ask her how big her family was, because St Edmund's needed its staff at school, not at home. Mrs Tranter, however, was an experienced operator and enjoyed highlighting her prominent and long-standing union membership who would back her to the hilt. Sarah was becoming paranoid. She imagined the ensuing conversations between Mrs Tranter and her on-side colleagues, which increased her sense of isolation in the school. In desperation, Sarah had called her Head of Education at the local authority who offered her more precautions than support and it was with this sense of frustration that she had slapped the detention on Nathaniel. This had backfired badly. Joe had been in touch with the news of the defeat and had rather unkindly and sarcastically offered her his thanks.

She hoped for a better evening ahead but she wasn't allowing herself to get too excited. Her on/off boyfriend, Garth Montgomery, had arranged to take her to dinner after his nets session at Warwickshire County Cricket Club, but like his batting of late, he was hopelessly unreliable. It was an entirely unsatisfactory relationship that did nothing for her self-esteem and she was cross with herself for allowing it to limp on for so long. Her parents certainly didn't approve and for once she agreed with them. Garth was practically always away, playing in Australia or back home in South Africa during the winter, but Sarah was kidding herself if she thought the relationship would be any better if he had a more regular job. It was a relationship of physical convenience only which had a tawdry feel to it and she suspected that he had other 'Sarah's' in other towns across the cricketing world. He was already late and it wouldn't be the first time he'd fail to show up altogether. She had left the door open for him and had started to clock watch, so was relieved to finally hear a knock at her door.

Her face dropped when she saw Tom appear and he misinterpreted her shock.

'I'm sorry. Is it a bad time?'

'Er…' Sarah shook her head.

'No problem. It can wait until the morning, I'm sorry.'

'No… it's fine,' she said, trying to recover, her eye darting to the clock.

'Right.' Tom wasn't convinced. Had he made yet another mistake?

'No, it's fine. Er, what can I do for you?' she asked, too formally as she still struggled for some composure.

Tom shut the door. 'I heard about the match…'

Sarah sighed and shook her head.

'I was just passing and I saw that the light was on and well…'

Sarah smiled for the first time all day, her resolve weakened by exhaustion and a sudden burst of unexpected and profound joy. How kind of him to think of her like that? She looked at the clock again. It would suit her now if Garth didn't show up which of course meant that he would. It had been that kind of day.

'Well, Tom, thank you, that's very kind of you. But I'm expecting someone: my, er... boyfriend, actually.'

'Oh? Well, that's great. Look, I'm sorry.'

'No, don't be, please.'

Tom was acutely embarrassed which she sensed and was excited by. It was partly why she had used the word 'boyfriend' to gauge his possible interest. His reaction made her feel a little more confident, despite his now apparent diffidence and backing away. She had mentioned her boyfriend as a flag or a warning so now he knew where he stood which was a good thing, he reasoned. Now he would have less explaining to do to Beth who he spoke to every night, sometimes for hours with her photo in his hand.

'Look, I'm sorry. I'll get going, really.' Tom fumbled, desperate to get out of there.

'Well, actually, he's not really my boyfriend...' Sarah tailed off and a moment hung there between them. All his previous logic and rationale was now obsolete and the pathway ahead was suddenly complicated again. And he was pleased.

'Well, I just wanted to make sure you were OK, and you know, go through some stuff on The Fruit Bowl. But we can do it tomorrow or whenever...'

Sarah nodded.

'Thank you. I'm grateful that you stopped by. I really enjoyed our lunch the other day.'

'Yeah, it was great. We should, er...'

'Do it again?' Sarah nudged him.

'Yeah, sure.'

'Tom, I would love that.'

'Good, OK then.'

'Or even dinner?' Sarah suggested.

'Sure.' Tom had the door open now. 'So, I'll er... wait for you then...' Tom's eyes widened. 'By which I don't mean, you know...'

He stopped talking and she smiled demurely.

'Sarah, have a lovely evening. I've got to go. I'll see you in the morning.'

Sarah nodded and he left. Her spirits had soared. She slumped back in her chair and marvelled at how a terrible day can suddenly turn into something quite wonderful. Just then her mobile rang. It was Garth calling, which meant that he wasn't coming. Sarah would have been upset, but now she smiled and didn't bother to answer it. There was no need.

Chapter 45

The next morning, Tom was up even earlier, cross with himself for his impromptu visit to Sarah. He had lain in bed with Beth's memory all night and hadn't been able to sleep at all. It was still dark when he pulled on his running shoes and didn't bother to check the time as he hit the wet streets. Running was normally a release for him but this morning he was running like a love-struck teenager. Despite himself, he was also worried about The Fruit Bowl, now into its third lacklustre week. Sarah was a welcome distraction but one that came with huge anxieties and he ran on harder and harder until it was light.

His morning on the stall had not lifted his spirits much when he met with Elliot later and he didn't bother to ask how the morning had gone.

'I take it Michael is completely up to speed on everything?' Tom asked knowingly, without sounding angry and Elliot nodded.

'Conference call last night and a report.'

Tom shook his weary head. 'And does it conclude that I'm mad?'

Elliot almost smiled. 'Put it this way, he won't be signing off on any quantitative easing?' Elliot answered and Tom chuckled. It was a rare thing to hear a joke from Elliot. Tom rather enjoyed his straitened company. As well as being highly effective, Tom suspected that he quietly approved of what he was trying to do.

'And what is your take?' Tom asked.

Elliot took a moment. 'The Fruit Bowl? I rather like it. If we can create sufficient demand, I can see some obvious synergies and opportunities.'

'But?' Tom asked sensing that he had reservations.

'But I can't see any merit in purchasing land. Or not that piece of land anyway.'

Elliot qualified.

Tom nodded because he was right of course.

'The economics might be flawed, but the central tenets of the business are sound.'

Tom murmured. 'Flawed. How so?'

'Well… That one should remove personal sentiment from any business model.'

Tom scoffed. 'But isn't that a little naïve because most businesses begin as personal missions.'

'Yes, sure, but for them to thrive…'

'And what about charity?' Tom asked.

'Er…'

'Doesn't charity have a value and merit?'

Elliot didn't respond, out of his comfort zone now. Crunching numbers was his thing which provided him with exact and irrefutable answers. He also reminded himself of Tom's personal circumstances and these loosened his footing even more.

'OK then, why are you trying so hard to help me with all of this stuff? Tom asked. 'Particularly in getting this auction opened up for me?'

Elliot shook his head. He would not be answering this question, not until he had run it by Michael anyway. He considered the photocopy of a document on his desk which he had yet to share with Tom. On it, a section had been highlighted yellow:

…whereby the statutory powers and procedures of the council can be halted, queried and even reversed when it is judged by the electorate that their interests might be better served by other means. Furthermore, that due process and the express interest of the electorate can and should prevail if they can present a majority decision against the specific actions of the borough's privy council…

In plain speak then, a fully audited petition would most likely suffice but the truth was, Elliot reasoned there was insufficient time to collect sufficient signatures. And therefore, he could complete this task for Tom but in the safety that it couldn't ever be acted upon. It was obvious that Tom was being driven by his emotions, not logic and so he was making poor decisions and needed their protection as much as their support.

This was not the only thing that Elliot had failed to share with Tom. It seemed that his thorough submission to the council may have backfired because the council had responded very quickly with a letter of their own, couriered to Paddy's home. It thanked them for their full and comprehensive submissions and explained that the council would need time to assess so much information, and it suggested that The Fruit Bowl might cease operations until it had time to do so. It was a suggestion and not a command, but it was so worded as a warning and a veiled threat. Elliot read the letter coolly enough. It was a good move that he had not seen coming and he rebuked himself. And so, he did something for the very first time in his life – he took an executive decision - not to tell Tom or anyone else. He asked Paddy to do the same. He knew how Tom would respond and he reasoned that he had enough to contend with already. So, it was business as normal, which strictly speaking was not 'business' at all, but Elliot was happy to use the term anyway.

Later in the day, Tom called Elliot from the wholesalers and arranged to see him immediately. He sounded agitated and Elliot prepared himself as he waited in the business suite at the Hyatt. It was about the letter. It had to be. He should never have trusted Paddy to remain quiet.

'It seems that they want to stop it, The Fruit Bowl? Does that strike you as odd?' Tom asked.

Elliot mused. It was the question on his mind also.

'Why would they want to stop such a thing?' Tom repeated.

"Not their idea" syndrome?' Elliot offered.

Tom shook his head. 'But if it were to be rolled out across other boroughs and schools?'

Elliot didn't respond. He didn't like to remind Tom that this was highly unlikely.

'Anything else for me? You mentioned something about a petition? Tom asked.

Elliot explained the clause again and offered his opinion that there was insufficient time to garner such support. Tom tended to agree which was reassuring and something Michael would be happy to hear.

'How many signatures are needed?'

Elliot was alarmed.

'Twenty-two thousand I'm afraid. And in less than a week.'

Tom sighed heavily.

Chapter 46

It was just another routine exchange for the undertaker, but for Nell it had been an awful telephone call to take and it dredged up sad memories and some foreboding. Pilkington & Sons had handled the burial of Tom's family and with the laying of the headstone, they were signing off on their duties. Usually a headstone can be laid after a year, but in this instance, because the stone was so heavy, the land had to be allowed to settle for at least eighteen months. It wasn't an exact science but Pilkington's masons had visited the grave and taken some readings. They were satisfied that things could proceed and could do so with or without the family present. Nell didn't have an answer and promised to get back to them.

Joe was a little surprised and hurt that none of his mates sympathised very much with his injured nose.

'Come off it, Joe. You got what you deserved,' Paddy suggested. 'I heard you were being a right little twat.'

'Oh really, who from? Was it Lewis because…'

'Hey, calm down. I didn't need to hear it from anyone, OK?'

Joe looked a little hurt.

'You don't like him and you've been needling him ever since he arrived?'

'Yeah, well…'

'Well, what?' Paddy asked. 'You can't dislike someone just because he lives in London and has chosen to lose his accent.'

Joe felt a little undermined and embarrassed.

'I like him,' Benny offered rather unhelpfully and Declan agreed.

'Actually, there is something that annoys me about him,' Declan added, and Joe was suddenly hopeful.

'Yeah, my Missus thinks he's bloody lush.'

Everyone roared their approval.

'She's even added him to her special list – men she can go with without any consequences. He's right up there with Clooney and Nick Knowles.'

'Fock me, Nick Knowles?' Paddy feigned horror.

'I know, embarrassing.'

'My Mary has only one list and with only one name on it!'

'Yeah, well, you should buy her a telly then.'

More raucous cheering and hilarity, which Joe didn't feel a part of.

'Maybe that's it, Joe?'

'What?' Joe skulked.

'I think you're jealous of him?' Paddy reasoned.

'What, because he's successful?' Benny asked.

'Yeah, that as well.'

Both remarks were direct hits and hurt Joe more than Tom's fist had done. His own failings had nothing to do with Tom but he was indeed jealous of him – a feeling that he wasn't enjoying at all. He resented the way he had just arrived out of nowhere and the way that people had responded to him – Paddy to begin with and now even more so, Lewis. When Lewis had been at Aston Villa, he had been assigned a nutritionist and he even suggested to Joe that The Fruit Bowl was a good idea. The truth was that Joe had isolated himself and his pride was the obstacle blocking his way back in to the fold.

'And he's helping me out no-end with my accounts?'

'I've heard that Elliot lad is a wizard.'

'Harry Potter he is, I'm telling ya.' Paddy quipped. 'So, if you could cut him some slack, Joe, that would be great?'

Joe tutted and looked to the ceiling.

'And if you can't do it for yourself, then do it for me, eh?' Paddy suggested. Joe felt suitably admonished. He forced a smile and gave a tiny nod. His nose wasn't broken after all and his ego would heal as well. Suddenly, the cloud lifted a little.

It had been a busy morning at the centre for Joe. What had started as a normal coaching session had descended into mayhem when one child insulted the mother of another and a huge fight ensued and quickly spread. Fortunately, Lewis was on hand to break things up but not before metering out a punishment of his own to the boy with the loose mouth, as sensitive as he was to mother insults. Joe was supposed to log the incident but decided that a stern word would suffice and busily got on with tidying up after the kids had left for the day. As he pushed some tennis rackets back into a cupboard, he saw Tom's Fiat pull into the car park. He'd had a day to dwell on his mate's advice and he even wondered if he needed to apologise to Tom, which would be new territory for him. Pulling at his nose gingerly as a reminder, he looked over to Lewis and assured him that everything was going to be fine.

Tom was rather desperate now concerning his faltering trial. If Paddy was right and The Fruit Bowl needed some cool staff then he had done precious little about it. Tom, therefore, needed to act on the matter himself. He didn't know what to expect but he wasn't really in the mood for any more of Joe's hostility. He had already apologised and didn't see that there was much else he could do. He locked his car remotely and walked quickly along the kiddies play area towards the Centre. Lewis had appeared from the building and he acknowledged Tom with a little nod as they passed each other, which pleased him and emboldened him to his task. He entered the Centre and immediately held his arms out in a gesture of hope and goodwill.

'Joe, please, I haven't come here for round two.'

Joe smiled, for the first time since Tom had first recognised him as the football prodigy.

'No, sure, I'm not much of a fighter myself.'

Tom was relieved at his conciliatory tone.

'I haven't been very welcoming, have I?'

Tom didn't know how to respond.

'And I'm sorry for that.' Joe added.

Tom smiled and gestured that it was in the past.

'No problem. And since we're on apologies, sorry again, for

the nose.'

Joe nodded. 'Yeah, I didn't see that coming.'

'It was my first punch as it happens.'

'Well, not bad, then.'

They both chuckled.

'Joe, I need to ask you a favour.'

'Steady on,' Joe joked. Paddy had again mentioned that his help was needed on the stall. The reasoning was flattering for him to hear, especially since he didn't feel particularly cool anymore.

'With your permission, I'd like to take Lewis out for the day.'

Joe's face fell. He hadn't seen this coming; being passed over for Lewis. The request wrong-footed him and instantly rekindled his resentment. Tom had checked with Social Services and established that his community sentence could be signed off by any responsible party, but only with the express permission of his supervisor.

'Just for a couple of hours. I'd like to take him to the wholesalers.' Tom carried on explaining himself but Joe had stopped listening. It made good sense of course. Lewis's cache and cool was certainly more current and there was little doubt that Lewis had responded to Tom. He hadn't said as much, but it was there and it heightened Joe's sense of failure again.

'Yeah, fine, do what you want,' Joe scowled, unable to conceal his disappointment.

'Really?'

'Yeah, why not?' Joe spat.

'Thanks Joe, I'm really grateful.'

'Yeah, whatever.'

Tom went outside, a little confused by Joe's inconsistency and nervously approached Lewis who had seen but not heard the exchange.

'Hey, Lewis. How are you doing?'

'Yeah, man, superb.'

Tom registered his point, which he was hoping to address.

'I was just chatting with Joe and I wondered whether you might like to come to the wholesalers?'

Lewis looked over towards the building, perhaps for Joe's

approval, only he wasn't there. Secretly, he was pleased but he was mindful not to show it. After all, it wasn't Alton Towers he was being taken to, but he was pleased nonetheless.

In the car on the way to the market, neither man said very much at first as an awkwardness hung between them. Lewis studied Tom, trying to figure him out. He had an air about him that Lewis admired. He wore nice clothes, had an expensive-looking watch and sunglasses, and immaculate nails. Even his haircut looked expensive. He was a lot like the professional players he had known at Villa. He had their confidence and sheen, which he found attractive. Plus, he was nothing like the other men more closely associated to him – his half-brothers or the crew on his estate – and that appealed to him equally. However, his similarity with millionaire football players ended with his choice of car. No self-respecting pro would drive a Fiat and this intrigued Lewis even more about him.

'So, how's things, Lewis?' Tom asked, breaking the silence.

Lewis laughed to himself as he considered his life and how things had turned out. 'Yeah, man, things are superb.' It was a repeat of a line he had used earlier. Tom picked up the heavy irony and peered at him via his screen mirror, and they both laughed a little.

'Are you going to try and change me?' Lewis asked.

Tom knew what he meant and considered how he should respond.

'Is that what people try and do?'

'Yep, that's it. They try to change me.'

'Into what?'

'Exactly. Miss Frost, Joe, teachers, coaches.' Lewis turned to look at Tom. 'And now maybe you?'

Tom considered the various scenarios and how each might play. 'Yeah, maybe, maybe not.'

'Yeah, right,' Lewis drawled suspiciously.

'Because I don't see how I can help you, not really.'

Lewis looked at him curiously.

'How do you mean?' Lewis asked.

'Like to play football for England. Only you can do that. No one can play for you, right?'

True enough and Lewis tutted as a Porsche from the opposite direction blasted by.

'But I'd like to see it happen though.'

'Yeah, so would I.' Lewis said, brooding on his ambitions. Tom didn't add anything. What he was suggesting was implicit. He was mindful of Paddy's warning about his incendiary temper and issue with authority; he didn't want to provoke him. Lewis finally turned to face him.

'Why are you doing this, man?' He asked.

'What, talking to you?'

'No, man, this juice thing?'

Tom sighed and didn't answer. The same old question, over and over.

'That's what people want to know.'

'Really? Is, that right?'

'Yeah, man.'

'Like who?'

Lewis tutted. 'Everyone. No one gets it, especially when the word is you're rich.'

Tom nodded a thank you to his newest best friend, Paddy bloody Porter.

'So, come on then, why?'

Tom thought of the real reasons. He saw the jug of orange juice on his counter at home and his wife smiling as she poured it for their boys and the arguments and laughs it always inspired.

'It's complicated.'

Lewis huffed, let it drop. 'And what is it with you and Joe?'

'That's complicated as well. Maybe you should ask him. I'm disappointed I hit him. I was wrong and I shouldn't have done it.'

'Why? He was cussing you, right?'

Tom shook his head and didn't bother to answer.

'Cos fighting is wrong, right?' Lewis asked.

'No, not always.' Tom answered, taking the young man by surprise.

'No, sometimes fighting is good. Sometimes fighting is absolutely the right thing to do,' Tom answered, wrong-footing him again.

'Yeah, like when? When is fighting good?'

Tom took a moment. He hadn't expected such a deep conversation but he sensed an engagement with the kid and he was happier for it. 'Like when you're fighting for something you believe in, or for something you want. That's what life is, right? It's just one big, long fight.'

Lewis stared at him, his eyes narrowing with interest.

'You fight to get a job and then you fight to keep it. Or you fight to get promotion. You fight to get in the team. Fight to keep your place. Fight for the team to win promotion. You fight for a girl. Fight for what's right. And for every fight, there must be a winner.'

'And a loser?' Lewis finished for him.

'Exactly. One guy gets the girl; one guy doesn't. That's it. Welcome to the world. Just one long fight. Winners and losers. That's it.'

Lewis listened, pondering his own life and its constant and ongoing fights. He reflected on how so often he had thought he had won but in fact the opposite was true. He had been told about the incident between Paddy and Tom in the playground at his old school and asked for Tom's version of events, which was much safer ground for Tom and he was happy to oblige.

'The boy was called Connor. He was a tough kid. Probably a bit like you.'

Lewis smiled knowingly. 'Oh yeah, here we go.'

'What?'

'How many times have I heard this speech man?' Lewis spat.

'What speech?'

Lewis tutted. 'How I'm gonna end up just like him if I don't get my shit together?'

'No, that's not it.'

'Has Joe put you up to this?'

'No, course he hasn't. You brought it up, remember? Not me.' Tom shouted.

Lewis shook his head, doubtful again of Tom. 'So, what then?'

'What do you mean?' Tom asked.

'This Connor kid? What is he now? Cos he's either a crack-head or he's in jail. I know it, man. I've heard this so many times. So, come on, which one?'

Tom shook his head. 'Actually, neither – he's dead.'

The words shocked Lewis and his mouth fell agape. They drove on for the rest of the journey without saying a word, both lost in their separate and troubled worlds.

As Tom parked up, he mooted the idea of Lewis helping on the stall and he seemed to consider it momentarily before dismissing it out of hand.

'There's no way she'd let me anyway.'

Tom assumed that he meant Sarah and he was encouraged that he had at least considered it. And he was pleased that Sarah might hold the key.

In the enormous warehouse, Lewis was struck by the sheer amount of stock, just like Tom had been on his first visit. He also became intrigued and even enchanted by the array of fruits on offer and what could go into The Fruit Bowls. Tom had quickly rejected Lewis's suggestion of melons and kiwi fruits but undeterred, Lewis grabbed a box of mangoes. They didn't look particularly ripe and wouldn't juice very well, so were not suitable. Tom shook his head again and suddenly Lewis became angry. Aggression was the boy's default.

'Fuck sake! Are you going to say no to everything I want?' Lewis shouted.

'Hey… calm down. To start with, they need to be peeled which is difficult: tight skins. They have a large stone that can't go through the machines. Plus, these aren't even ripe. But other than that, they're perfect.'

Lewis didn't enjoy Tom's superior tone or logic and dropped the heavy box to his feet, making a loud noise and commotion that drew people's attention. 'Fine. Fuck the mangoes.'

This put them in a stand-off that Paddy had warned was inevitable. Tom stared at the young man, almost as tall as him, but with some obvious growing yet to do. Lewis's jaw bulged and Tom could sense that his fists were clenched. But he had no intentions of backing down.

'You want mangoes, do you?'

'Yeah, I do. I want mangoes?' Lewis felt somewhat foolish for saying so.

'Fine, well pick them up and I'll buy them. But on Monday morning, you're on the stall peeling them.'

Lewis's eyes narrowed, realising the corner he had painted himself into.

'Don't worry, I'll square it with *her*, but you have to turn up,' Tom added.

Lewis nodded a little. 'Right then, fine.'

Tom smiled. Progress at last. Lewis bent down to pick up the box and Tom helped him.

Chapter 47

Tremendously buoyed after his visit to the market with Lewis, Tom hoped that matters might be changing in his favour and in a moment of exhilaration, he made the decision to adopt Elliot's unlikely plan to force the auction open. It would give Paddy the pivotal role he had been craving all along. And it was something for which Paddy was ideally suited and might even be able to pull off.

'So, the question is, Paddy, can you get enough people to sign?' Tom asked and Paddy laughed dismissively.

'What sort of stupid question is that? Of course, I can.'

'Really? You're sure?'

'Course I am. But why though? A petition for what?' Paddy asked, although he didn't much care – he was just delighted to be given a role. He enjoyed the feeling of being needed and from the look of him of late, Tom could certainly use a tonic.

'What's it for, though? The petition?' Paddy asked again. 'I'll need to know if I'm to persuade anyone.'

'It's silly really. There's an auction at the council – selling off all sorts of stuff – but some of the lots are closed bids only and I would like to see them open, that's all.'

Paddy scratched his head full of wild hair.

'So, it's going to upset the council then?'

'I guess.' Tom answered sheepishly.

'Right, then, I'm in. No problem.'

'But, Paddy, I'm going to need it by next week, even by Wednesday.' Tom sounded a little needy now, which Paddy loved.

'So?'

'Next Wednesday Paddy? You really think you can do it?' Tom asked.

Paddy smiled broadly and soaked up his moment. Tom was doubtful but he was grateful to hear Paddy's confidence and see his swagger. And who knows? Tom wondered to himself.

Sarah did not have much time. She was rushing off to a two-day conference in Telford but was pleased that Tom had asked to see her and furthermore she didn't care how it might look to any prying eyes.

'I can see that you're busy,' Tom said, as she crammed her laptop into a bag.

'I am, can it wait until I'm back?' She asked. Looking at him, she could see that it was important. Flustered, she sat down and appealed to him, sensing his feeling of awkwardness.

'I was wondering whether Lewis could help out on the stall?'

This was not what she was expecting and she could not hide her surprise.

'Has he agreed to?' she asked, more than a little shocked. That feeling again of being undermined and put out.

'I think so.' Tom answered tentatively.

'Well, that is a surprise, well done you. May I ask, how?' she asked.

'I took him to the wholesalers and we talked it through. Actually, I did most of the talking and in the end, it was the mangoes what did it.'

Sarah didn't laugh and she didn't have time for an explanation, but she could see how important it was for him. And who knows? Maybe it would help Lewis as well.

'Supervised at all times, obviously?' Sarah said a little curtly, at least to register her true feelings.

'Absolutely, of course.'

'Fine, I'll email Anne.'

'Thank you, Sarah.'

The stall limped along for the following two mornings and was still nowhere close to being a success. Certainly, a lot was resting on Lewis's young shoulders and his debut on Monday but by now, Paddy thought that the task was even beyond the football hero.

'But it was your idea,' Tom protested.

'Yeah, but that was at the beginning when I thought we stood a chance. And you should have told Joe because he isn't going to be happy.'

'Do you know what? I don't care what Joe thinks.'

'Oh, really?'

'Yeah, really. You worry about getting the signatures and I'll get on with the stall.'

Paddy looked to the skies. 'I'm telling you it won't work. Unless Lewis is wearing a pair of football boots, he's bloody hopeless.'

'Fine, then, get him to wear his boots.'

Paddy scowled.

Chapter 48

Lesley was irked when he heard rumours that some kind of petition was planned. He hated nothing more than initiatives by his electorate. They could vote every four years and, in the meantime, they should shut up. But he wasn't unduly concerned. Petitions were a toothless weapon and he would use their pile of paper as a foot rest. He was concerned, however, about this irksome man, Tom Harper. The question remained, just what was he up to? One thing he was certain of, though; it wasn't about providing a bunch of fat kids with a dose of vitamins each morning. His investigations had established his glittering city background and a man of his means didn't squeeze fruit unless there was a reason. But what was it? The petition didn't worry him but Tom Harper did because he could sense something was afoot. He just needed to establish what he wanted and then they could strike a deal. Isn't this how things are done? He sat alone in his office, pondering his options. His strategy of squeezing Tom into revealing his hand had failed and so it was time to force things into the open. He called Mark Hooper, and instructed him to set up a meeting between him and Harper. It was time for a frank exchange of wants and needs.

This was a strange request, Tom thought, re-reading the email on his phone. He didn't know what Councillor Irwin wanted to see him for and the urgency intrigued him. He called his assistant and they agreed to a time of 2.00 p.m. that very afternoon. Elliot offered to accompany him but he refused. Until Lewis started work on the stall, he had little to do and the prospect of meeting the head of the council rather appealed to him.

Lesley took his lunch at his desk. He perused his papers one more time with one eye on the clock that was edging towards 2.20 p.m., a suitable time to keep anyone waiting. It was just shy of being rude but it was long enough to demonstrate his status. He brushed his desk of any errant crumbs and jumped out of his chair to welcome Tom warmly.

'Mr Harper, how kind of you to come. Do come in,' Lesley began without an apology for his poor time-keeping.

Tom shook his hand firmly and sat down in his comfortable chair facing Lesley's large and impressive desk. It was a modern office in an old building with no expense spared on the fittings and furniture. A thick rug lay on the highly-polished floor and a rather beautiful-looking coffee machine sat in a wall recess to the right of the grand bay window, with its view to the town square.

'Coffee? Tea?' Lesley asked, but Tom shook his head. 'Fruit juice?' he added in a jocular fashion but making a point also. There followed some further banal pleasantries to which Tom barely responded. He wasn't really interested in the hopeful signs of spring and when the summer would arrive. Perhaps wrongly, Tom took an almost instant dislike to the man sitting opposite. The Councillor had an air about him and it occurred to Tom that he hadn't been summoned because he wanted to help him.

'And what is it that you wanted to see me about?' Tom asked directly, momentarily wrong-footing Lesley, but he quickly regained his composure.

'Well, I thought that we should meet - given all these initiatives of yours?'

Tom noted the use of the plural but didn't respond.

'We could start, though, with this fruit juice venture.'

Tom shrugged. It was more a statement than a question so he didn't feel much need to answer.

'Because it's rather taken everyone here at the council by surprise,' Lesley stuttered.

'Oh, really? Why's that?' Tom asked.

'Well, your motives, to be honest, because it seems to be a little 'small beer' for a man such as yourself?'

Tom's eyes narrowed, wondering what this man knew of him.

'Make no mistake, a firm like Tel-com's investment in Bromsworth would be most welcome.' Lesley laid upon him that he had done his research.

But, Tom was not overly concerned. He was being naïve if he thought no one would do any digging into his affairs. His business history was easy to establish and he was fortunate that it hadn't come to light already. But he couldn't be sure what else Lesley knew about his life and resented him for looking.

'You see, it's important that the council understand all of the issues. And when an illustrious individual such as yourself simply arrives on the scene, I need to see that the interests of my constituents are being served and if so, then I need to ensure that you're given all the help you need.'

It was a broad and bland statement and one laced with inference, which Tom was perfectly aware of and his mood hardened a little more. He fixated on what else the councillor might have learnt.

'Anything else you know about me?' he asked. He was short and unfriendly now.

'No. Should there be?' Lesley replied, interested that he had obviously struck a nerve.

'For your information, I am no longer running that company in London.'

'Oh?'

'And what else did you find out? Anything?'

Lesley shook his head but he knew now to dig a little further. Clearly, the man had something to hide, which might be of use and of some value when the dancing stopped and they inevitably cut their deal.

'You seem upset?' Lesley put to him frankly. 'You can hardly blame me for establishing a little bit of background.'

It was a reasonable point and Tom was cross with himself for being so direct and apparent.

'And you would like to understand my motives for establishing this fruit business?' Tom asked.

'Absolutely, I'd like to understand everything. I'm particularly interested in your speculative searches with the borough. Any connections there?'

Tom was seeing a clearer picture now.

'I assume that you're looking to develop in the area?'

Tom didn't respond. 'Something non-residential perhaps? A storage facility, that kind of thing? The sort of thing that I might be able to help you with?'

Again, it was a clever use of language. Nothing to suggest impropriety but crystal clear nonetheless that the councillor would like to be included in his plans. But Tom had no intention of sharing his ambitions with him. 'Nothing really very specific. Just lots of options really.' Tom answered deliberately vague.

'Really? And may I enquire about their nature?' Lesley finally asked and in doing so, showing more of his hand than he wanted to.

'No, not really. Would you be this interested if I was buying a house in the area?'

Lesley's thin lips broke into a smile. 'Well, I would be surprised if there was a house in Bromsworth that would suit a man of your considerable means.'

Tom bridled. 'Oh, I don't know – if yours were to come up for sale...'

The antipathy between the two men now clearly established. Battle lines drawn but Lesley was a wily operator and he raised his hands in submission. Whilst he enjoyed their point-scoring off each other, it wasn't getting them very far and he needed to establish the common ground between them. There is always common ground. Every man has his price.

'OK, look...' Lesley began in a more conciliatory tone. 'We seem to be getting off on the wrong tack. I'm really just trying to establish what your intentions are here in Bromsworth, and to see whether I might be able to help.'

'Well, there is considerable waste in the fruit industry and what with the diet of children –'

'Right, yes. I get all of that. I've had the reports, but what about the land speculation? That's what interests me – or the council I mean,' Lesley snapped, cross with himself for his momentary lack of control. He fidgeted under his desk as he waited for Tom to enlighten him, but he wasn't very obliging. Lesley's heightened reaction certainly firmed up Tom's suspicions about why the site was being sold by sealed bids. And then it occurred to him that

Councillor Irwin himself might have some skin in this game. It would explain his hostility and if he was right, then the petition must have been a worrying curve ball for him. But whatever his plans, he needn't worry too much. It was unlikely that Tom would be in any position to buy the plot, not least because of Michael's fierce opposition, but no matter, he enjoyed the effect his interest was having on the councillor and it pricked his curiosity. He hadn't even explained his lofty intentions to Paddy or to Sarah, and so he had no intentions of explaining them to Councillor Lesley Irwin.

'I'm sorry, but I thought we were here to discuss The Fruit Bowl.'

'Yes, yes, we are.' Lesley almost shouted now. 'Isn't that what we are discussing, the Fruit Bowl? Isn't that all part of your strategy?'

Tom was now genuinely perplexed. 'Yes, it is. My hope is to provide kids with fruit juice.'

'And that's it, is it? This whole thing is just altruism? Out of the goodness of your heart.' Lesley barked.

He had lost control now, sick of his lack of progress and frankly the man's bloody impertinence.

'And I understand that you're personally funding everything, until you get funding from my local authority?'

This sounded like a threat, but Tom did not feel particularly worried by.

'Was there anything else?' Tom asked.

Lesley managed a faux smile. 'I just don't want to see anyone waste their money, that's all.'

'Well, thank you. That's very kind of you. Then I assume you'll be supporting our grant applications?'

Tom got up to leave and Lesley didn't bother to see him out. The meeting was over and it hadn't gone the way that Lesley had hoped. He picked up the phone and called Danny.

Chapter 49

We, the undersigned, as individual members of the Bromsworth electorate, would like to see the sale of the land, known as THE QUADRANT, Barrow Road, BROMSWORTH, scheduled for sale by sealed bids auction on 25th April, be conducted as a lot in an open auction. As stated in the constitution of the BROMSWORTH COUNCIL, section 8, clause 6.2, we understand that this wish shall be granted if the undersigned represent a majority of the Bromsworth's electorate. We understand this to be the case and state for the record that this is our intention – and that this intention is registered with our lawyers, Stafford & Hay, Lombard Street, London, EC1 2NN.

Paddy read the petition a couple of times and finally gave up. He would just pretend that he understood it. He studied the laminated map of Bromsworth that Elliot had provided, with the boundary clearly marked in thick red pen. Elliot had been very insistent that the petition needed to 'be rigorous and bear up to scrutiny'. Paddy stared at him blankly.

'It needs to be genuine, Paddy – only people from the borough and strictly by postcode. Only genuine people signing and signing only once. No repetition. And no Spider-Men or Wayne Rooney's.'

'Yes, sir,' Paddy shouted and gave an ironic salute as he stamped down his heavy right boot. He was excited at the prospect of galvanising his town even though he didn't know what for. He understood that the truly successful leader was one who could delegate effectively and so he decided to appoint Mary his second in command, with specific responsibility for the women's vote. Mary didn't understand the motives of the petition either and nor did she care. She was just delighted to see the effect it was having on her husband. He was determined and fixed on success – qualities she had long yearned for in her man – and she suddenly found him overwhelmingly attractive: another first in quite a long time.

'Right then, Paddy Porter,' Mary pleaded, 'you've got to be organised.'

'Yes, I know that.'

'You can't just go charging off willy nilly. You'll need a system.'

'Yes, I know that. And I have a system.'

'Right, then show me.'

Paddy didn't respond. The last thing he needed was an argument so soon into the venture with his number two.

'You heard what he said – "no repetition."'

'Yes, Mary, I've got that. And no Donald Ducks. I got it.'

'OK, fine. And we'll need to identify key people as well,' Mary went on, 'like Robbie at the Post Office. And George at Preston's. That's gotta be a thousand people right there alone.'

Paddy thought for a second. Key people? This was indeed a good idea. His decision to bring Mary in was a good one. She was bright and capable. Paddy congratulated himself for bagging such a formidable woman. The house was quiet and he smiled at her fondly.

'Are the kids out?'

'Yeah, why?'

He flicked his eyes suggestively upstairs, but she scotched his chances immediately.

'What?'

'Oh, go on,' he pleaded.

'For God's sake! Get off! We've got work to do.'

'Oh, come on, Mary; it wouldn't take long.'

'Yeah, I know.'

Petitions are essentially a waste of trees. They serve to make a point, provide a photo opportunity but little else. But this petition had teeth and Lesley could see how it could possibly affect his plans. Understandably, he was seething when he had established what its intention was. When his elderly mum rang to say that she had signed the blasted thing, Lesley almost broke his toe kicking the bin across his office.

'What fucking clauses?' Lesley cursed. It was a rhetorical

question since Lesley had presided over the council's constitutional changes himself. It was just lip service. A sop to the clamour for more open and transparent local government, which he had glibly agreed to, never imagining that it would ever be enacted by his apathetic electorate, more than half of whom didn't even bother to vote. It was the speed at which Tom Harper and his people reacted that he found so unnerving. But they didn't have time to complete this petition, he assured himself. The last petition dumped on his desk had contained six thousand signatures and had taken over a month to collect, so this was a complete impossibility.

With Mary's guidance, Paddy had formally organised his assault on the unsuspecting Bromsworth public. They appointed a team of eight to take care of the residential districts and another team of eight to account for the businesses. Elliot continued to feel torn – loyal to Tom of course, but also aware of Michael's influence, his clarity and legitimate concerns over Tom's intentions. Elliot enjoyed seeing Paddy so energised by the petition and yet he hoped that he would fall some way short and assured Michael that this would be the case. But that said, Paddy's verve and apparent order and method were somewhat worrying and Elliot felt the first pang of alarm.

In the Nelson on Friday night, Paddy was full of enthusiasm as he updated Tom on the progress that he and his team had made.

'Hey, look; even Joe's signed it,' he enthused.

'Oh, great.'

'Yeah, and he's getting his staff signing up as well.'

Tom was relieved. He would need Joe's support over the stall if Lewis was to become properly involved and he was determined to make this happen. Perhaps, Joe might join them after all, as Paddy had originally suggested. Paddy, however, remained doubtful about young Lewis.

'Lewis, saying that he'll turn up and actually turning up - are two very different things.' Paddy reasoned. It seemed that Lewis had dampened almost everyone's expectations of him over the years. He had promised so much and delivered so little was most people's view and now Tom was pinning the legacy of his wife and boys on such a character. Lewis was playing in a local football match this coming

Sunday, his first fixture since his conviction, and Tom had said that he would go along to watch. The football pitch was where Lewis felt most happy and Tom's mind turned again to the plot of land and he wondered.

The petition would fall short but it still galled Lesley how everyone seemed to universally approve of the bloody Fruit Bowl, even his myopic staff. And he felt further undermined since everyone seemed to consider Tom Harper favourably as well. Outside Tesco's on Sunday morning, Lesley glared at the people with their clipboards and enthusiasm. Danny, his business partner had become very anxious about the whole thing and suggested that he send Tom a message of his own, one less subtle than talk about a Health & Safety audit. A breezy young woman came up to Lesley and stuffed a piece of paper in his face and asked whether he lived in Bromsworth. Cheeky little bitch! I am fucking Bromsworth! Lesley wanted to shout in her face.

'What's the petition for?' Lesley asked, half-seriously.

'It's about the fat cats at the council.'

Lesley didn't wait to hear anymore and turned on his heel, grabbing for his mobile phone. Perhaps Danny was right. It was gloves off, now.

Tom allowed himself a lie in and got out of bed at just before 7.00 a.m. He felt stiff and rubbed at his aching neck in the shower. His body felt tired, as if he had spent hours in the gym the previous day. Only, he hadn't. He hadn't done anything other than his normal run, so put it down to stress. He wondered if Sarah was back from her conference and whether he could call her? He didn't really know. Another reason for his anxiety was fielding regular calls from Michael who had now broken cover and was bypassing Elliot altogether.

Aside from Lewis's match that afternoon, he had nothing planned and couldn't decide whether this was a good thing or not. Before the accident, he longed for a Sunday morning with just a pot of coffee and the newspapers, but his children would never allow more than just a cursory glance at the headlines. Now a whole day with nothing to do was the thing he needed least. It heightened his loneliness and sense of loss.

He shaved quickly and considered his face, wondering if any of the lines around his eyes were new - to go with the grey wisps creeping over his ears. His eye brows were certainly fuller now and trimming them would be his only concession to male grooming, and he pulled out a rather prominent grey hair as well. His confidence in The Fruit Bowl had been pummelled over the weeks. Michael sent him a timely mail: a spreadsheet of The Fruit Bowl's costs to date, which all appeared to be wasted and hardly the legacy he imagined. But he remained resolute. Lewis was starting on Monday and this could just be the spark. Plus, he would see Sarah again tomorrow and there was no use pretending that this was not something to look forward to. He pulled on his running shoes and headed for the lift, walking quietly past the dirty trays of last night's room service hardening in the hot hotel corridor.

It was a bright and warm morning and Tom ran hard along the tow path of the canal connecting the Midlands with the Black Country further north. Birmingham is a city with more canals than Venice: a fact often quoted to shock and amuse rather than to inform. Tom stopped running, sat down heavily on a bench and immediately attracted a swarm of flies, buzzing around him like a pack of photographers on a red carpet. He brushed them away but it made little difference and he contemplated the still water in the canal – perfectly calm except for the gentle wake created by a mother duck and her recently hatched family. Tom laughed at the utter perfection and beauty of the familial scene before him. The mother looked so proud with her chest puffed out and her beak aloft, but also defensive, her eyes alert to any possibility of danger posed to her young. In the distance, he could hear the tolling of a church bell. He looked at his watch and a thought occurred to him; he pulled out his phone.

The mass was already into the first or second reading as Tom sloped into a pew to the left of the altar. Irritatingly, but as if the norm, the back pews of the church were fuller, forcing Tom towards the front where he couldn't sit down without disturbing anyone. He had run back to his hotel for a quick shower and then hurried to the church and as such, he was hot and bothered and hardly inconspicuous. A lady was reading from the pulpit. Tom rubbed at his face and tried to recall the last time he had attended mass in the church.

Father Franey was sitting on the altar and seemed to acknowledge him: another of his lambs returning to the flock? Tom looked about the congregation within his eye-line and spotted Paddy immediately, a good head taller than anyone else in the church and smartly dressed in a dark jacket and clean shirt. He spent most of the service looking at his boys sternly and occasionally pointing at them threateningly. He hadn't noticed Sarah, who was sitting slightly behind and to his left in the main body of the church. She had watched him arrive with great interest and was delighted that he had sat in a position that allowed her to study him at her leisure. She too was looking forward to Monday and seeing him again. His hair was still wet from his shower and he had nicked his lower jaw shaving. She found him as confusing as she did attractive. For all his obvious abilities, he looked troubled and this morning in mass, she thought that he looked lonely. There was a sadness to him and a vulnerability that she hadn't seen before and it made her warm to him even more.

The service continued and Tom found himself lulled into something akin to peace as the kindly priest's words about kinship washed over him. Even the cadence of the sentences felt comforting; he understood why the needy seek solace in church. The service ended in what seemed like a surprisingly short time with a lacklustre and ill-chosen hymn that no one could really get the handle of and people began filing out before it was over. Tom waited until the final note before joining the queue of people who had done their bit of spirituality for another week. Outside, Sarah made sure that she positioned herself so that they would meet and Tom was delighted to see her.

'Hello.'

'Sarah, hi. How was the conference?'

'Oh, you know, thrilling. I didn't have you down as a church type,' Sarah smiled warmly and they shook hands.

'No, well, it's been a while actually. And you?' Tom asked.

'Lapsed as well, but it rather comes with the job now.'

'Yes, of course.' Tom looked over to Father Franey shaking people's hands. Spotting Tom, he waved and smiled at him and gestured whether he was OK. Tom assured him as best he could and the old man smiled in return.

'Father Franey used to teach me you know.'

Sarah nodded wilfully. 'Well, he's a wise old man. He could teach us all a thing or two.'

Tom agreed and wasn't sure what else to say. He would like to suggest lunch but she probably had plans, but perhaps a walk, since it was such a nice day. Just as he was about to suggest it, Paddy bounded over and completely spoilt the moment.

'Jesus! Doesn't he go on!' Paddy gasped, referring to the unnecessary length of the service. 'Anything over an hour is just wrong. There's no need for it.' He nodded at Sarah. 'Have you signed the petition, headmistress?'

'Not politically expedient I'm afraid. I was going to ask you about that.'

Paddy pointed at himself. 'Ah, well don't ask me; he's the man for explanations. I'm more the Operations Director, if you know what I mean.'

Tom shrugged. He would rather not and Sarah didn't press him.

'Tom, are you OK for Sunday lunch?' Paddy asked.

'Yes, fine, thanks, Paddy. My sister's coming up to visit,' Tom lied.

'Oh, that's nice, or is it?' Paddy shot back at him.

'What about you, Sarah? Another cricket match?' Tom asked, catching her a little off balance.

'Er, no. No more matches for a while actually.'

Tom wanted to ask why but thought better of it.

'I have work to do, actually. Big job and all that,' Sarah added hurriedly, trying to sound upbeat. But then a lady made a move to speak with her, no doubt a parent at the school with something on her mind.

None of the Sunday papers held his attention for long and an hour later, on a walk on his own, he found himself sitting on the same bench he had sat on earlier in the day, when his phone rang. Probably Michael, he scowled as he fished in his pocket and was delighted to see Sarah's name. He answered it immediately and was unable to mask his excitement, but he could instantly hear in her voice her disquiet and that she was not phoning with good news.

'Sarah, what is it?' he asked.

His face fell as she explained.

'Stay where you are. I'll be as quick as I can.' He ended the call and broke into a hard run, away from the canal and towards the school.

Chapter 50

By the time Tom arrived at the school, the shed and his stall had been almost completely razed to the ground and the fire crew was gathering in their spent equipment. Sarah was standing huddled outside the cordon established by the fire crew. She looked ashen, but managed a smile when she saw him arrive. Tom hadn't quite believed her on the phone, but there was no mistaking it now. Everything was destroyed, but it wasn't the cost that concerned him: it was what it represented. The fire crew was satisfied that everything was now safe and was gathering to leave. Sarah gestured a thank you in their direction as she approached Tom. Neither of them knew what to say to each other and just stared at the remains. Tom noted immediately that no other damage had been caused to the school itself or to the nearby kitchens: no windows smashed or doors forced, nor the graffiti that is usually associated with vandalism. It didn't take Colombo to establish that his stall had been the sole target.

'Shall I ring the police?' Sarah asked but Tom shook his head. 'But you'll need a crime number for the insurance claim. You are insured?'

Tom shook his head in a general sense of despondency and anger; he wasn't interested in making any insurance claims. He just fixated on getting his stall open again and could think of absolutely nothing else. The stall represented his family and someone had decried this memory. He felt a wave of revulsion and was determined to see it open again.

'Do you have any bags? Heavy duty bags?'

Sarah's eyes widened. 'You're going to do this now?'

'I have to. Lewis is coming tomorrow. I need it open.'

Sarah looked doubtful on both counts.

'I'll just need a trestle table and I can pick up some new machines in town today. The shops will still be open, right?'

'Tom, you can't possibly think of having this open for the morning?'

Tom shook his head. 'I have to. I can have this cleared up in no time. Paddy will help me.'

Sarah shook her head in bewilderment. 'Fine. Then we'll do it together.'

'No…'

'Yes. Leave Paddy to have his family lunch.'

Tom could see that she was determined. And anyway, he wanted her company and not Paddy's; this was not the time for chivalry. 'Thank you, but haven't you got work to do?' he asked.

'Yes, I have – this!' And she turned and marched off towards the school with Tom in tow. They retrieved shovels, a wheelbarrow and a roll of heavy-duty rubble sacks, and proceeded to clear the site. Tom insisted on doing the heavy side of things, shovelling the weighty rubbish sodden from the fire hoses into bags that she held open for him, and then he dragged them over into a pile by the school gates to be collected by Paddy in his van. Sarah returned from her office with a coffee for them both and a packet of biscuits. Her face was dirty with a black mark running across her forehead. She seemed energised now and her eyes flickered with excitement.

'I've had an idea,' she began urgently.

'Right?'

'What if we make rebuilding the stall a year 12 project, for DT? Chris Bales is the teacher, and he's always looking for things for his pupils to work on. This is perfect.'

Tom smiled. His heart leapt for her.

'It's perfect,' Sarah continued. 'It would harness their energies and encourage them to use the stall and with twenty kids on it, they'd have it up in no time, plus it could come out of the school's budget. You can look on it as your first grant. What do you think?'

Tom was delighted and smiled broadly. He was so happy, he didn't know what to say.

'Well, say something.'

'Yes, Sarah, I think it's a brilliant idea.' He was tired and emotional. His throat swelled at her kindness and at the thought of getting the stall back up and running again. She considered him again; suddenly his vulnerability had returned and, in that instant, she realised that there was something else at work, something that he hadn't told her and now she needed to know.

'Tom. What is it?' she asked gently. 'What is it about this stall?'

He shook his head, wondering what to do and why he felt so incapable of sharing the truth. It was nothing to be ashamed of, certainly not, and yet it still seemed too personal and hurtful. Of course, he would have to tell her at some point and now seemed like a perfect time, but she looked a little fretful now, scared even. He stepped closer to her, took her hands in his, considered her beautiful face and appealed to her for more time. She seemed to understand and didn't push him. He pulled her towards him and hugged her gently and he wondered if she could feel him almost cry a little as he whispered, 'Thank you.' Then he released her and stood back quickly. She could see that he was tearful and typically now, he looked embarrassed. His eyes quickly refocused as he looked about the stall and the great progress they had made together, but there was still more to be done and it was back to business.

Chapter 51

On Monday morning, Tom paid for the produce at the market as Paddy loaded the van.

He remarked, in passing, that mangoes were a big mistake, which Tom ignored. He was tired and not really in the mood to explain. Naturally, Paddy was seething about the attack on his stall and indignant that Tom hadn't called the police, and assured him that he would ask around. He was confident that he could establish exactly who was responsible, but Tom wasn't particularly interested. He just wanted the stall open and with Lewis helping, he could gauge whether it had a future. He fervently hoped that it would. The trestle table made a sorry sight against what had gone before and Tom had also bought a cheap gazebo in case the heavens opened. With his recent run of fortune, he fully expected that they would. Benny came along to show his support in the hope that he might be needed, but by 8.30 a.m., Lewis was a no-show and Tom was bitterly disappointed. The remnants of the fire naturally pricked the kids' curiosity and drew a few more over than usual, but it still couldn't be described as a success and even Tom struggled to remain optimistic. He kept looking towards the car park in the hope that Lewis might emerge. Arriving late would be better than not showing up at all. The only good thing to happen was that Sarah hadn't turned up either to see his failure. Paddy fussed about, uncomfortable with the awkwardness of it all. He wanted to tell Tom how well the petition was going but he sensed that the timing wasn't right and left him to wallow in his gloom. Tom was unusually quiet. He didn't enjoy being wrong and was imagining what Michael would say. His nightmare would be that Michael followed through with his threat to visit Bromsworth to see for himself what was keeping Tom so busy. And he was hopping furious with Lewis when he considered how hard he and Sarah had worked to ensure that they opened. He picked up a mango and kicked it hard towards the car park, watching it run along the asphalt and reduce in size as it bumped along. So much for not wasting fruit, and the gesture embarrassed him and he hoped that no one had seen him do it. Paddy couldn't stand it any longer and felt that he had to say something.

'Hey, Tom, come on, man. Early days, eh?'

But such an assurance felt hollow because of course, it wasn't true and they both knew it.

'And the petition is coming along fantastic.'

Tom groaned. Michael and everyone else would have a field day if he ever got into the position to buy the land. His eyes were dull and his shoulders slumped. Realistically, he should cancel the petition before it put him on a collision course with every person he knew and trusted.

'Paddy, I'm really sorry, but never mind the petition.'

Paddy's eyes widened. 'What?'

'I'm sorry...'

'But I've been busting my balls.'

Tom sighed. 'Yeah, well, you and me both.'

'But, why?'

'Just, because, Paddy!' Tom shouted. 'Because of everything. Look around you! And believe me, I'm sorry. I'm sorry about everything.' He turned on his heel and walked off towards his car. He needed to go and find Lewis for himself.

When he arrived at the youth centre, Joe was immediately more agreeable. He had heard about the fire and was pleased that he felt no glee about it being torched. Tom welcomed his concern, tired of arguing and clashing with him. He looked around the yard. 'I was hoping to see Lewis.'

'No, he's not here.'

Tom nodded. 'No, he was supposed to help out on the stall this morning.'

Joe was immediately guarded again: keen to defend his young charge.

'Well, can I call him, or arrange to meet with him?' Tom asked hopefully, but Joe didn't seem very willing.

'Joe, please. It's important.'

'What about?'

Tom shrugged. Wasn't it obvious? 'Joe, please, can I have his address?'

'No! No way.'

'I just want to talk to him.'

'Yeah, fine, but you're not going to his house. No way. Plus, I'm not allowed to give you his address.'

'But why? Data protection bull-shit. Is that it?'

'Look, I can't go into it.'

Tom shrugged. 'Because?'

'Just because, that's why.' Joe stated.

Tom almost laughed at the use of the phrase he had only just used himself with Paddy and now he realised how irritating it was.

'Look,' Joe reasoned. 'I can call him for you and ask him to come here, but that's as much as I can do.'

'Right, fine.' Tom could imagine the red tape and protocol that came with a boy like Lewis and he didn't want to compromise Joe, not after what had happened between them already.

'But I can't promise anything. He was a no-show and he doesn't take to being told off.'

Tom sighed.

Anne wasn't very comfortable either when Tom arrived at the school, looking urgent and politely asked for Lewis's address. At first, she declined but he was insistent. Ideally, she would have waited for Sarah's approval but she was in a board meeting and couldn't be disturbed. She certainly trusted Tom and wanted to help, especially since what had happened over the weekend and she also knew that Sarah would want her to assist him. Tom could see that she was softening and thanked her even before she had agreed. She gave a furtive glance across the empty reception area and quickly tapped at her screen and grabbed a pink Post-It pad on her desk. Tom thanked her and was quickly on his way.

He plugged the postcode into his sat-nav and waited for a moment for the machine to get its bearings and plan the route. It was a four-mile journey or twelve minutes according to the machine.

He was unsure what lay in store for him and with the traffic being quiet, he reached his destination within the twelve minutes allocated.

Facing him was a sprawling mass of high- and low-rise, very neglected-looking properties. A central tower block dominated the skyline with a series of lower buildings surrounding it on all four sides. It was a mass of concrete: grey, cold and desolate. An old worn out sign announced that it was the Burton Estate and was next to the mean-spirited sign, 'No ball games'. When Tom grew up, the estate hadn't existed and he wondered what it had replaced. A mangy looking cat without a collar strolled past and eyed him briefly. Poverty hung in the air like a fog.

An aggressive-looking man with an over muscled and equally ugly dog watched his car pass and Tom was grateful that he was in his rental. The car park at the first of the satellite blocks was absolutely choked with drivers resorting to improvised parking spaces on the lawn flanking the building. It was a brave traffic warden affixing anything to a windscreen in this estate and probably pointless because no fines would be paid anyway. Tom drove around to the other car parks in the vain hope of finding a legitimate space. All the visitor's sections were full and in the last car park, the handicapped bay was occupied by a bright turquoise car that had been modified beyond all recognition of what make and model it had once been: a Vauxhall Nova, Tom guessed, but he couldn't be sure. Its owner was almost certainly deranged but probably not handicapped or infirm.

Eventually, Tom found a spot that looked like it would cause the least amount of aggravation. Technically, he wasn't blocking any other vehicle in, but this provided him with little confidence as he pulled on his hand brake and locked his car.

Looking up at the flats, the satellite dishes blurred and lines of laundry fluttered in the brisk air. He checked the address again and quickly made for the building ahead of him. He pulled a heavy metal door open with its reinforced wired central glass panel and a pungent smell encased him. A lift door faced him with a stairwell off to his right. He pushed the button and waited, staring at the red light. A smell of urine greeted him as the doors opened and two spent condoms lay discarded, but he expected that the stairwell had horrors of its own, so he entered the lift and pushed the button for the tenth floor. All the flats were identical and equally rundown. Number 1068 was where Lewis Adele lived. It had a blue front door that must have been kicked in at some point and been badly repaired. The windows of the property were filthy and almost obscured the wire mesh running through them. It was hardly residential. Tom rang the bell and waited, nervous now and wondering if he was making a mistake. Joe had been adamant. But he hadn't said that he shouldn't visit Lewis's home; he had said that he couldn't, like it was against the law or something. Suddenly, Tom hoped that nobody would be in and he could be on his way. Joe could set up a meeting for him elsewhere, through the formal channels which was a much more sensible idea. But suddenly, he could hear movement from within the flat. Then he heard a woman's voice screeching from within.

'Lewis! For fuck's sake, get the door!'

Now he was in two minds whether to run off or not. But intrigue got the better of his instinct to leave and he waited. After all, he now knew that Lewis was in and he just needed a chat with him.

'Lewis!' The woman screamed again at the very top of her voice and then Tom could hear angry and exasperated footsteps from within. He braced himself. A door chain slid into place and then the door opened ajar. A woman in her early thirties stared at him angrily through the gap. She was wearing a dressing gown and Tom could sense little else underneath.

'Who the fuck are you?' she snarled, baring her yellow teeth.

'Er…' Tom began, startled.

'Has Ringo sent you?'

He didn't respond - trying to compute what exactly was playing out before him.

'Cos, if he has, you can tell him that I've only got one cunt.'

Tom's mouth fell open and still he said nothing.

'Well, speak then, 'cos I'm fucking working here,' the woman snapped. She was an attractive woman – or had been at least but now she was an incredibly ugly proposition.

'I'm sorry. I'm a friend of Lewis's.'

Immediately, her face dropped with exasperation and anger

and the door slammed shut. She continued to shout out for Lewis as the chain disengaged and the front door finally flung open. He saw the woman walking away from him down a dirty and narrow corridor, but his attention was quickly diverted, because Lewis had appeared from an end room, pulling off his headphones.

A look of sheer terror gripped his face when he saw Tom in the doorway and he athletically bounded toward him, smashing the front door shut with his foot. It barely remained in its straining frame and an enormous row ensued from within with both Lewis and the woman hurling abuse at each other. He couldn't catch every word or what was said but he didn't need to.

He turned and was about to leave, when suddenly the ailing door was wrenched open again and Lewis burst out of the flat and nearly flattened Tom. He rushed past him and flew down the stairs, and the women stood in the hallway and stared harshly at Tom.

'Why did you come here, you cunt?'

Tom apologised faintly and hurried away. He wanted to chase after Lewis but given his youth, he knew it would be hopeless. He heard the front door slam shut again as he went for the stairs. When he emerged from the building, he expected to see no trace of Lewis and was wondering how he would ever be able to explain himself to Joe. Anne would most likely be in trouble as well and he hoped that he might be able to protect her by at least taking full responsibility for his actions. But Lewis hadn't vanished. He was sitting on the bonnet of a car with his knees under his chin and his fists pressed against his temples as tears streamed down his face. He looked at Tom with total contempt. Tom approached with arms splayed and an expression of remorse, which had little effect. As Tom crossed the road and mounted the pavement, Lewis leapt from the car and launched himself at him, his two extended arms pushing hard into his chest, sending Tom sprawling backwards and into the road. Tom fell heavily and hit his head and scraped his shoulder, but he sat up quickly and immediately apologised to the young man bearing down at him with his fists clenched and his right foot poised.

'What the fuck are you doing here, man?' Lewis spat venomously.

Tom got up with as little fuss as possible. He grabbed at the back of his head briefly, looking at his fingers for any signs of blood, and pulled his jacket down. 'Lewis, I'm sorry.'

'Fuck, sorry! Who told you where I live?'

'I don't know,' Tom started feebly.

'You fucking do-gooders, you make me sick, I swear.'

Tom couldn't think of how to respond.

'And now you've seen my life. Still think you save me, you fucking prick.'

Tom shook his head and just repeated his apologies again, over and over. Lewis began pacing back and forth, like he was trying to expend his excess energy. Inevitably, a small crowd of onlookers had gathered but at a safe enough distance, aware as they were of Lewis and what he was capable of. Lewis snarled over at them and collectively, they all backed off a little. He then turned to look at Tom again.

'Lewis, I'm sorry,' Tom repeated.

'What the fuck are you doing here, at my house? Huh?' He kicked the air in frustration.

'I wanted to talk to you.'

'Yeah, about what? What do you want to talk to me about?'

'About the stall.'

Lewis's reddened eyes rolled back in his head. 'Oh, what? And why wasn't I there this morning? Is that it?'

Tom's face gave himself away and Lewis seized upon it.

'Yeah, well, yesterday, where the fuck were you?'

Tom was momentarily confused.

'I had a game, remember? You was going to watch?'

Tom's face fell. With the events of yesterday, the fire and the clear up, the match had completely slipped his mind. The fire had caused much more damage than he had first imagined. The stall could be rebuilt easily enough, but Tom worried that his relationship with Lewis fared less chance and without it, he reasoned that the stall was finished as well.

Lewis threw his hands in the air as he turned and skulked off. A thought flashed into Tom's mind and he quickly chased after him. He caught him by his arm and pulled him round. Lewis stiffened, with his free hand cocked, but Tom tightened his grip and his authority appealed to be listened to.

'Lewis, please! Listen to me!'

'Why? Why should I listen to you?'

Lewis tried to wrestle free but Tom's grip held firm, his confidence restoring.

'Because I have something to tell you and it's important.'

Lewis shrugged himself free and glared at Tom. The crowd had grown a little bigger now, hoping for a fight or anything to break up the monotony.

'But not here,' Tom said, gesturing to his car before moving off with a reluctant Lewis in tow. His car had been scratched: the work of a key or possibly a knife and it went across three panels, but it wasn't his car and not his problem, and he barely registered it.

Lewis got in and sat low in his seat. He didn't bother with the belt and Tom didn't insist as they drove off in silence.

'Where are we going?' Lewis wanted to know, but in truth Tom didn't know: just somewhere quiet and private. He recognised a landmark and he figured that they weren't too far from The Quadrant, which seemed as good a place as any. It would certainly be quiet. He fumbled with his sat-nav and hit recent destinations. Lewis applied his seatbelt now to stop the blasted safety ringing and finally, silence prevailed once again. Tom followed the directions for the short journey of just over a mile. When they arrived, Lewis got out of the car quickly, still seething and he ran his finger along the newly scratched paintwork of Tom's car with some satisfaction.

'Well, go on then. What?' Lewis snarled.

Tom nodded and took his time as he walked about the car, gathering his thoughts, planning how exactly he should begin.

'Right then, to start with… Lewis, back there, at your home; I can't believe what you're dealing with.'

Lewis tutted aggressively. 'Don't talk to me about my home. You don't know nothing about me.'

Agreed, but Tom knew enough. 'Sure, that's right, but you don't know anything about me either.'

Lewis shook his head angrily. This was a tactic used on him so many times and he had long grown tired of it. 'Fuckin, please, don't tell me that you're feeling my pain, man. Cos believe me, you ain't. You don't feel pain like mine – not ever. Do you get me, bro?'

'Is, that right?' Tom asked, his own voice rising now.

'Yeah, that's right,' Lewis shouted back.

Tom took a moment. 'Don't assume you know about me and my pain,' Tom shouted angrily, which took Lewis by surprise. 'Are you going to listen to what I have to say?' Tom appealed, quieter now, more measured, and Lewis nodded.

'OK, first up, we can't change our pasts, right? What's happened has happened. And it will always be. That's it. Nothing we can do about it. And God knows, I would literally give anything to change mine. But equally, we can't allow our past to blight what's to come – our futures. Because the future is something that we can affect.'

Lewis was quiet now and almost pensive, thinking of Tom's words, but also waiting for his explanation.

'And I think that we can help each other deal with our pasts.'

Lewis finally snapped. 'Oh, yeah, is that right?'

'Yeah, I figure it is.' Tom said defiantly.

'Right, fine. So, come on then. What's your past? Cos right now –'

Tom nodded and raised his hand. His throat was now tight and dry. 'Do you remember asking me why was I doing the stall?'

Lewis's eyes flickered as he recalled the conversation.

'This fuckin' stall man, seriously?'

'And I said that it was complicated and that I didn't really know?'

'Yeah.'

'Well, that was a lie. I know exactly why I'm doing it and I'm going to tell you why... And then hopefully you'll get it.'

'Go on then.'

'Sixteen months ago, I was married to a beautiful woman called Beth. We had three gorgeous boys and you were right; I had it all. Back then, I was the man. I knew it and I was unbelievably happy. My life was fucking perfect.'

'What? And you've split up? Fuckin so what man?'

'Lewis,' Tom said sharply. 'They died. Seventh of February. 8.26 a.m. They all died in a car crash on their way to school.'

Lewis's mouth hung open. 'Oh...'

'Yeah. They all died.'

It was Lewis now almost lost for words and he stared hard at Tom. 'What were their names?'

'Beth, my wife, and then Daniel, Luke and Jack. Luke and Jack were twins.'

Lewis pulled at his face and didn't know what to say and Tom understood. He was just a kid after all.

'I haven't told anyone. Not Paddy, Joe, Ms Frost.'

Lewis nodded again. 'I won't tell no one, man.'

'Thank you.'

'And I'm sorry,' Lewis offered.

'Yeah, thanks.'

'I mean, what I said about pain.' Lewis added.

Tom bowed his head a little. He felt a good degree of relief at finally being able to share his tragedy and it seemed that the level of trust he was investing wasn't lost on Lewis. Being flattered was the wrong word, but Lewis understood the gravity of his sharing such information and for him to be the first to hear it.

'My wife used to make a juice drink for my boys each morning –'

Lewis stopped him. He got it now and didn't need Tom to elaborate. 'Fine, man. Listen, and I will help. If you think I can.'

Tom was pleased and grateful. 'Thank you. I'd really like to give it another go.'

Lewis took a moment and seemed to be struggling. 'About my mum,' he began.

Tom shook his head but Lewis was insistent.

'No, no, I need to explain. She's an addict. Has been all my life...'

Tom listened intently. Drugs had never really touched his life. He'd smoked the odd spliff at university but nothing since. Rumours of cocaine being rife in the city might be true but Tom had never experienced it himself. So, it was the odd documentary and newspaper article that kept him abreast of this misery. As Lewis explained his wretched home life, it occurred to Tom why Lewis felt the need to explain himself. It was because he loved his mum and he didn't want Tom to feel ill-will towards her. Lewis explained that he had twice been taken into care and twice his mum had got herself clean and rescued him as he called it. But each time she had re-lapsed and selling herself was the only way to feed her habit.

'They'll do anything to get their junk – and I mean, anything.'

Tom nodded even though he didn't understand, not really.

'So, it ain't her; it's the junk what you saw. She's doing her best and she does love me, just like you loved your kids.'

'I know she does.'

A moment of need hung in the air between them. They had both exposed something incredibly personal to each other. Material that made them vulnerable but also stronger for having shared and explained.

Tom clapped his hand on Lewis's shoulder and shook him to and fro. Lewis recognised the importance of their exchange. He was happy to help Tom but most pleased that he had defended his mum. Tom raised his other arm and the two embraced like a father would his son.

After dropping Lewis back at home, Tom sat alone in his car for a moment and stared at the estate. He recounted the whole morning and the experience he had just shared with such a young man who he barely knew. Back at his hotel, there was a raft of messages from Paddy and Elliot, but he ignored them all and turned off his phone. He needed to be alone. He hung the 'Do not disturb' sign on his door and informed switchboard that no calls were to be placed to his room. He closed his curtains, got undressed, slipped into bed and fell asleep. It was 11.00 a.m.

Shortly before 6.00 p.m., Tom turned off his shower after another punishing run by the canal. He felt better for the sleep and the run, but realised that his feeling of wellbeing was mostly because of his exchange with Lewis and his feelings for Sarah. He trusted Lewis that he wouldn't tell anyone but he reasoned now that he would need to tell people anyway before too long: chiefly, Paddy and Sarah. He had almost told Sarah after the fire, but had backed off and now, as he drove to school, he was pondering his options. He wanted the stall to be a success before he would tell anyone. It had to be. He needed it to be a success on its own merits and not because people felt sorry for him. To be a worthy memorial to Beth and his boys, it had to be a success. He pulled his slightly battered hire car in to the school car park and looked over at the temporary stall. Then he turned his attention to Sarah's office. Noticing that her light was on. This time, he hoped that the front door would be open and it was.

Tom knocked on her office door and waited for her to call him in. It was obvious that she was delighted to see him.

'I thought you were going to be the cleaner.'

'I could always pretend,' he laughed. 'How are you?'

'Yeah, I'm OK,' Sarah lied.

'Busy as always, I can see.'

Sarah agreed but she ceremonially shut her laptop to signify that her work for the day was over and rather hoping that he might have plans.

'Because I wondered whether I could take you to dinner?'

Sarah smiled broadly. 'Absolutely, yes, you can. I'd love that.'

'Er, great.' Tom wasn't sure if they were heading off now or later. Sarah picked up on this and looked doubtful.

'Are you meaning now? Because you look ready, but I'm certainly not. Could I go home first and freshen up?'

'Of course, I'll pick you up if you like?'

Sarah began scribbling something on a pad and quickly ripped the sheet out and handed it to him.

'I could be ready for, say...' she did a quick calculation, 'eight.'

At just after 8.00 p.m., under instruction of his sat-nav again, Tom made the final left turn and parked his car, a little down from her house. He glanced at himself briefly in his mirror and thought that he looked a little anxious, which was understandable given that this was his first date in more than twenty years. The street was a mixture of semi and detached Victorian houses with a short row of modern-looking flats in the middle, most likely filling in the Luftwaffe's handiwork. It was a street much like the one he had grown up in, only it was in a nicer neighbourhood and the houses were much better kept and cared for. A grass verge bordering the kerb added to the sense of civility. Boxes of recycling were stacked outside most houses and a fox was out on duty patrolling his patch. It eyed Tom with a nonchalant air before disappearing into a front garden. Quickly, he came upon her house. It was a neat brick house with a well-kept front garden but no recycling box, he noted. He rang the bell and waited. She answered quickly, her hair recently dried, she looked lovely and was ready to go. She had her coat and bag already with her and there was no need to invite him in.

'Shall we go?'

'Er, no. We can't, not just yet,' he answered.

'Oh?' She looked confused.

'Not unless you want a nightmare tomorrow morning, or a week of pain.'

'What are you talking about?'

He smiled.

'One word – recycling.'

Her mouth opened as she remembered and quickly disappeared back into the house, calling out that she wouldn't be a minute. She reappeared through her side gate, pushing and kicking an array of green boxes ahead of her and carrying a brown caddie bin, carefully and at arm's length. Tom helped her position them before she pulled her front door shut and locked it on the dead lock.

'Thank you for that. Do you like French?'

Tom feigned disappointment. 'Sure, but I was hoping for an Indian, because Paddy and the boys said they might join us.'

Sarah laughed, bashed him on the chest and pushed past him.

Chapter 52

Rather unnecessarily, the maître d' scooted around to ease Tom into his seat, having first made sure that Sarah was sitting comfortably. It was an attractive restaurant to the west of the city centre called The French Table. At the higher end of the Birmingham restaurant league, Sarah usually reserved it for special occasions, which this most certainly was. A waitress arrived with a basket of bread accompanied by a little saucer of oil, pepper and salt and then handed Tom the wine list. Tom caught Sarah's eye and gave the list to her.

'Any preference?' she asked and Tom shook his head.

'I'm going to have fish, if that helps.'

'Good, me too.'

Sarah ordered a white burgundy along with a bottle of still water and didn't really listen to the waitress as she announced what the specials were. The restaurant was quiet, which suited them both. Sarah scanned the menu as the wine arrived and she waited to taste it and predictably, indicated her approval.

'Are you ready to order?'

They nodded even though they hadn't really decided, so they ordered somewhat on the hoof. It didn't matter as neither of them really cared too much about what they ate.

The starters arrived quickly and like the opening gambits of their evening together, they were perfectly enjoyable but not enough on their own. By the time their sea bass arrived, Sarah was becoming a little impatient.

'Do you know what?' she asked.

'What?'

'This is all starting to feel a little bit unbalanced.'

'What is?' Tom asked.

'You and me. Our friendship.'

'How do you mean?'

'Well, you see, you already know quite a lot about me. You know what I do, where I work, where I live now and where I'm from.'

Tom rolled his eyes a little, knowing where she was heading.

'Where I went to university, what I studied, what my dad did for a living…'

'Yeah, OK, I get it.'

'And I know next to nothing about you,' she stated expectantly.

'Yeah, well, I don't like to bore people.'

'Oh, I'm sorry but have I been boring you?' she asked.

'No, that's not what I meant.'

'Well?'

Tom breathed out heavily. Where to start?

Sarah tutted. 'You're the talk of the staffroom. Mary and her girls – they don't think you're real.'

'Er…'

'The rumour is, you're from another planet and have been sent here to show up their men.'

Tom chuckled at this flattering joke. 'Are you telling me that I've got the pick of any of the dinner ladies at my old school?'

'Yes. Apart from Mary, obviously.'

'Obviously.' Tom laughed and finished his second small glass of wine.

'Well then?' Sarah asked. 'Are you?'

Tom sighed. 'Am I from another planet? Can I trust you?'

'Absolutely not. So, go on.'

'Actually, they're right. I come from a place far away…'

Sarah chuckled. 'Good, and are there others like you? Can we put in orders? I'd like one like you, only a little taller.'

Tom laughed, which delighted her. 'This fish is excellent, by the way.'

'Yeah, don't change the subject. We're currently on you and exactly who you are.'

Tom gave her a pained expression. 'OK… how about I've just been released from prison. Or no, I know… I'm a spy.'

But Sarah didn't laugh anymore and waited for a proper

explanation, which she deserved.

'OK, fine. I'm from London, well, Buckinghamshire actually: a place called Gerrard's Cross.'

Sarah looked to the skies. 'Married? Single?' she surprised herself by being so direct, but she was pleased as well. Tom was pleased also and flattered, but he pondered a moment on how to respond.

'Er, married? No,' he began, which was technically true and Sarah gestured because he hadn't answered her other question yet. 'Single, actually.' The words felt strange to him and made him feel uncomfortable for the first time in the evening. Immediately, he thought of Beth. Sarah sensed some awkwardness and assumed that he was probably divorced.

'Kids?'

'Er... no. No kids.' Again, his answer wasn't fluent and a little awkward.

'You don't seem sure?'

'No, I am - categorical. No kids.' And he left it at that, not feeling that he could elaborate, or explain that this reality made him weep every day and made him feel empty and almost dead inside.

Sarah was relieved if a little surprised, but something troubled her; his being so unencumbered seemed frankly implausible.

'What then, gay?' she joked. Tom smiled, happy for the levity.

'Er, no, but actually I've never tried it, so who knows?'

Sarah giggled quietly, still trying to understand the conundrum sitting opposite her. He wasn't married. He was single and without kids. But there was no mistaking either that he was very guarded, but now she didn't wish to probe, scared of what she might discover. His guard remained as he quickly deviated to information about his career and she decided to let things go. He was too good to be true and for now, this was how he could remain.

'I work in London, in the city actually.'

Sarah winced and held her hands up theatrically in faux horror. 'You're not a banker, are you?'

'No.'

'Oh, thank God. That would have ruined absolutely everything!'

Tom laughed. 'No, I used to run –'

'Actually, don't tell me. I don't want to know. Not when you're so far ahead. Just leave it at a professional, working in the city.'

'Fine.'

A thought occurred to Sarah. 'I mean, you are a professional? You're not a security guard, are you?'

Tom smiled. 'I'm currently in the middle of a career break.'

'Ah, the sabbatical?'

'I guess.' Tom squirmed a little.

'Or the late gap year. That's what they call them now.'

'Yes well, it sounds a lot nicer than mid-life crisis.' He chuckled.

'And how far into it are you - your crisis?'

Tom laughed again. He liked her confidence and turn of phrase. 'Am I being charged for this session, doctor?'

'Well, that depends on whether I can help you or not and that depends on how acute your crisis is.'

'Oh, it's definitely acute. Maybe even, grave.'

'So, let me ask a series of questions so that I can make my assessment.'

'Very good. Fire away.'

'OK, do you own any of the following: a very large motorbike?'

Tom laughed. 'No.'

'OK, good. A power boat?'

'No.'

'OK, any of the following: a juke box, pinball machine, Jacuzzi or a spiral staircase?'

Tom shook his head proudly and Sarah looked encouraged.

'So far, so good. OK. I can't make any promises, but it seems to me that your situation could be retrievable.'

'Thank God.'

'One last question: do you already own, or are you considering buying, a sports car?'

Tom dithered, recalling Daniel's horror when he discovered the brochures in his study and Beth too had been equally unenthusiastic, so he shelved the idea.

'A while ago, I did test drive one.'

'What, Porsche? Ferrari?'

'Maserati, actually.'

'But you didn't buy it?'

'No.'

'Good.'

'So, have I passed?' he asked.

'Well, materially yes, but circumstantially, no.'

Tom murmured his confusion.

'Well, when successful city types –'

'I never said I was successful,' Tom interrupted.

'Maserati?'

'OK, fair enough.'

'When successful city types take their "gap year"' – she spoke the words slowly and used her hands to make the speech marks – 'it's normally to build a well in Africa or a school in India, and rarely, I believe to squeeze fruit in Birmingham.'

Tom laughed hard. It was an excellent point and well made.

'You see, it's almost the classic rich man's crisis but –'

Tom stopped her quickly. 'Er, excuse me, but I conceded successful, not rich.'

Sarah shook her head at him. 'Really, you should never trust Paddy with anything.'

Tom tutted ruefully.

'And anyway, you have an air about you.'

'Oh, do I?'

'Yes, you do. Plus, you seem to be paying for everything. You're staying at the Hyatt, in a suite.'

Tom looked at her a little surprised.

'I'm friendly with Douglas, the GM there. Plus, Bromsworth is tiny. It has no secrets.

And for what it's worth, I think that The Fruit Bowl is a wonderful idea.'

'Thank you. So, do I.'

'I glanced through one of the reports that Elliot sent to the council – oh, my God, the waste!'

'I know. It's appalling.'

'And I'm sure that your dad would approve.'

Tom dithered a moment but quickly recalled the explanation he had given for its origins. 'Yes, of course.'

'And I'm sorry that Lewis didn't show up this morning. That must have been a blow.'

Tom nodded. 'It was, but he had his reasons and we've worked them out.'

'Oh?'

'I went to his house.'

Sarah's eyes widened and Tom was quick to allay her concerns. 'It was fine, really.'

'Well, then, you were very lucky,' she said. 'How did you get his address?'

Tom shook his head. 'Actually, I'd rather not. But it ended very well.'

'Did you meet his mum?'

'Yes, I'm afraid I did.'

Sarah sighed. 'Poor kid.'

'Poor mum as well,' Tom added.

'Yes, absolutely. Can you imagine?'

'No, not really,' Tom answered. 'Can I ask you something? About Lewis?'

Sarah shrugged and looked a little awkward.

'The teacher that he assaulted?'

Sarah looked away.

'That was you, wasn't it?'

She just sighed. 'Lewis struggles very badly with rejection…'

'Oh dear.'

'You have to admire his confidence I suppose – trying to chalk off the head.'

Tom couldn't imagine anything worse or more compromising for her.

'But it wasn't my decision to press charges or to exclude him,' she protested. 'But try explaining that to Joe, so I got the brunt of it all. I'm a little easier to shout at than the local authority.'

'Bloody hell, Sarah! That must have been awful.'

'It was. It was a complete bloody disaster. But Lewis paid the highest price of all with Villa letting him go. He was the big solution, you see. Lewis turns pro, gets his mum off the streets and clean, and away from the estate.'

Tom considered all the ramifications and his mind quickly wondered to the land and his plans.

The waitress delivered their desserts and coffee at the same time, as requested. Their wine was finished; Tom was driving and Sarah didn't want another glass on her own. The restaurant had gradually filled up as they'd been eating and now an elegant lady approached their table.

'Hello, Sarah,' she said and although she was greeting Sarah, her eyes practically never left Tom.

'Hello, Muriel.'

'You must be Tom?'

Sarah rolled her eyes. 'Tom, this is Muriel.'

'Hello, Muriel.'

'Muriel is chair of education at the West Midlands Forum.'

Tom shook Muriel's hand and hoped that she would leave.

'Sarah's told me all about your venture. Very commendable. How's it going?'

'Er, well, I think,' Tom answered as briefly as possible, without appearing to be rude.

'Well, it's very nice to meet you.' Her approving eyes still fixed on him.

Once she left, Sarah looked to the skies. Tom smiled and lifted the flap of the leather folder to look at the bill.

'We're not going to argue about this, are we?' Tom asked. 'I mean, we've already established that I'm rich and that I'm mid-crisis, so to help with my self-esteem, I should be allowed to get the bill. You never know, it might help.'

Sarah smiled and made no protest at all. She looked beautiful when she smiled. She leant forward and put her hand gently on his to thank him and instantly, a surge of excitement coursed through him.

'Thank you,' she added before excusing herself and heading

to the bathroom. He felt flustered and scared about what might lie ahead for the rest of the evening. Perhaps she was just a tactile person and was being friendly and grateful for dinner. But second guessing her emotions were a waste of time and so he decided to concentrate on his own, and whether or not he was falling in love. If he was then it was supposed to represent progress, but this wasn't how it felt. He kept imagining his family. He imagined Beth and wanted to see her. He wanted Sarah to be Beth and for them to leave together and go home to their boys.

Tom sat in his car on the garage forecourt while Sarah was in the shop. He was over-interpreting everything, looking for signs and meanings, including this stop at the garage because she needed some milk. Did she need milk for an innocent coffee, or was it for their cornflakes in the morning? He felt like a nervous teenager. He didn't know what he wanted or what he should do. He thought of Beth again and the words of advice and wisdom from practically everyone on the subject and he reasoned it to himself. His family and Beth would want him to be happy; they wouldn't want him to be lonely and on his own. They would want to see him complete again or at least as complete as he could be in their absence. But such sentiment was easier in words than practice and he worried again if he was ready. Suddenly, he wanted to speak with someone, with Nell, and he wondered if he had time to place a call. His phone had been off all day and quickly he pushed the power button. He could see Sarah in the queue and for once, he felt lucky for living on such a congested little island. The phone came to life and as soon as it armed itself with a signal, it sprang to life with a series of message alerts, texts and missed calls. Tom was going to ignore them all to place a call instead, but then by chance his phone rang. It was Nell. Sarah was nearly at the front of the queue now. Perhaps this was all fate.

'Nell, hi.'

'Jesus, Tom!' Nell screeched, her voice full of frustration. 'I've been trying you all day.'

Tom too was urgent now as he saw Sarah being served and he didn't have time to apologise or to explain his radio silence.

'Did you get my messages?' Nell blurted.

'No, I've been busy. I've –'

'About the headstone?'

Tom panicked now, as his mind raced.

'The undertakers have called.'

Tom's face fell. It had been on his agenda of late as he knew the time was approaching but with the stall and other matters, it had slipped his mind. And now a crushing sense of guilt fell upon him as he imagined his family's bare and freezing grave.

'Tom, are you still there?'

Staring blankly, for the first time, he felt he had failed them. People had told him that he would move on and that his memories would fade.

'Tom!' Nell called again.

'Yes.'

'Do you want to be there when they place the stone?'

Sarah was on her way back to the car now. She was beaming at him and looked so happy. She was holding aloft a plastic bottle of milk and a small jar of Nescafe, like they were in a scene from some cheesy advert. Tom did his best to look happy but the moment was gone.

'Tom?' Nell continued.

'Yes, I want to be there. Tell them I'll call. I'll call them tomorrow. I have to go now.'

Sarah could sense that something was awry even before she got into the car and naturally asked him who he had been on the phone to.

'My sister, Nell,' Tom answered coldly.

'Oh! Is everything alright?' she asked, more out of politeness than interest, and he gave a cursory nod and started the car. His frivolity had gone, replaced by a more formal tone and she suddenly felt embarrassed for her little scene with the coffee.

'And you're sure everything's OK?' she asked as he filtered back into the traffic in light drizzle now. He nodded but he wasn't convincing. They rode along for the next mile in an uncomfortable silence with just small talk about the weather, which made Sarah angry. Something had happened, no doubt about that, and because of it, their evening was over. Just ahead of reaching home, to save her own dignity, Sarah brought the evening to a close herself.

'Tom, thanks for a lovely evening, but I have a very early start in the morning.'

He didn't argue and Sarah just wanted to get out of his car. He could sense how upset she was but his mind was a whirl and he needed to be alone. He was overwhelmed by Nell's news and he needed to go back home to sit with his family again. Sarah was clearly confused and upset and quickly unbuckled her seatbelt. The solution would be to tell her the truth, but the moment past and she got out of the car. There was no kiss or even a hand shake. She turned to look through the window as he lowered it. He tried to smile, to thank her and to apologise. She smiled back that she understood — only, she didn't. She didn't understand at all.

'I'll call you,' he called after her, but she didn't turn around or acknowledge him. In her haste to leave the car, she had left her jar of coffee.

Chapter 53

The police car pulled up behind Tom's Fiat on the M40 heading for London. It was a marginal speeding offence and on a busier night, they probably wouldn't have pulled him over. The officer ambled up to the car and was alarmed when he saw that the driver's window hadn't yet been lowered and that the passenger had his head in his hands. He signalled a warning to his colleague still in their car and tapped gently on the window with his torch.

Tom lowered the window.

'Is everything all right, sir?' the officer asked.

Tom rubbed his reddened eyes and breathed out heavily. No, not really, but there isn't much you can do about it.

'Was I speeding?'

'Yes, sir, you were doing eighty-five miles an hour.'

Tom sighed. Fair enough. Fair cop, as it were. He seemed hardly bothered.

'Have you been drinking, sir?'

'Yes,' Tom answered quickly, without thinking of the consequences, and the officer straightened a little and explained the procedure. Still, Tom seemed completely disinterested. The test was negative but Tom didn't look relieved in the usual way that motorists did and the officer was intrigued.

'May I ask why you were speeding, sir?'

Tom looked at the young man. He had already noted that he was wearing a wedding band and he hoped that he had children at home. 'I'm going back to London to see my family.'

'Right, and why the rush?'

Tom almost laughed at the question, because there certainly wasn't any rush.

'Not going, anywhere are they?' the officer asked.

'No, actually, they're not. My wife and children… I had three boys. They died… in a car crash actually.'

The officer's face softened immediately.

'Nearly two years ago now and I'm going home to have their headstone placed.' It felt helpful to him to share the truth again, even if it might be a little unfair on the policeman.

The officer had heard some extraordinary excuses in his career from motorists seeking to avoid a fine and he had learnt to spot those telling the truth and those who were lying. And on this occasion, not a part of him disbelieved Tom.

'Well, I'm very sorry to hear that, sir.'

Tom nodded.

'And are you going to be OK, driving back tonight?'

Tom managed a small nod. 'Yes, I'll be fine, thank you.'

The officer thought for a moment. 'And you'll keep an eye on your speed?'

Tom agreed and the officer gestured that he was free to go. He thanked the officer, got back in his car and pulled on his belt.

'We're going to follow you for a few miles or so, just until we're happy that everything is OK.'

'Yes, of course.'

'And once again, I'm very sorry about your loss.'

'Yes, thank you.'

Sarah felt completely bewildered by the events of the evening, her mind a mixture of hurt and confusion. She had so many questions and none of which she could answer, making her frustration complete. Her tea went cold as she sat in her lounge trying to make some sense of her evening with Tom. And the more she thought about it, the more hurt and humiliated she felt. Humiliated because she had made her feelings for him abundantly clear in the restaurant, by touching his hand and stopping to get a jar of coffee. She thumped the arm of her chair as she recalled her smiling and holding the jar aloft. She shouted angrily at herself and worried about what he might think of her now, which itself made her cross. She hadn't done anything wrong and why should she worry about his feelings anyway? But she did. She worried that she might look desperate to him or even worse, easy, and the whole evening, which had been so wonderful, now made her want to cry.

The more she ran through the evening, the more vulnerable and upset she felt. He had seemed distracted at times but he did tend to whimsy. They had enjoyed their meal. Their conversation flowed easily. He enjoyed her ribbing him about his crisis or he seemed to at least. He laughed and found it funny. And they discussed serious subjects as well; it wasn't all frivolous. He couldn't have misinterpreted her feelings for him and she was confident that her feelings were reciprocated. So, what happened then? She no longer believed that it had been his sister on the phone and her imagination charged off in all manner of destructive directions. He hadn't been comfortable discussing his personal status and now Sarah felt she knew why. She played with her phone, desperate to call him, but managed not to. That would only fluff his ego further but it increased her sense of hurt. Of course, she hoped that he might call, but he didn't and by 2.00 a.m., she turned her phone off, sick of its silence and the rejection it reminded her of.

The following morning, Paddy arrived at the stall at just after 7.00 a.m. The project to rebuild it had begun in earnest and good progress had already been made by Mr Bales and his students. It was going to be bigger than before and the framework was almost complete. It was a surprise that Tom wasn't present yet, but he was astounded to see that Joe and Lewis were.

'Morning lads,' he called out and they nodded in his direction. Tom would be thrilled to see them and Paddy hoped that they might just make the difference. After all, it was his idea. It was very odd that Tom hadn't arrived already and Paddy placed a call to his mobile but got his answer phone. Lewis unpacked the mangoes and seemed keen to start preparing them.

'Hey, Joe, shall I peel these?' he asked but Paddy answered for him, keen to establish his number one status on site. Paddy provided him with a clean bucket and a sharp blade and managed to avoid cracking any insensitive jokes about the dangers of letting him loose with a knife. Lewis looked at him ruefully before he got on with his task, which wasn't easy and he recalled now how Tom had warned him about tight skins.

By 8.30 a.m., it was clear to everyone that The Fruit Bowl was set to have its most successful morning to date. Joe and Lewis were indeed the draw that was needed. They provided the magic and that nebulous ingredient of cool. Nathaniel and his crew were quickly drawn over and seemed happy to take up the free drinks on offer and with such boys came a posse of girls, attracted more by pheromones than the vitamins on offer. But there was still no Tom to enjoy it all, which was a terrible shame and took the gloss off the morning. Paddy worked hard, shoving carrots into the machine to try and keep up with demand and Lewis likewise, surprised everyone by his dogged commitment to the cause. Joe was particularly impressed by the change in his attitude and he wondered just what could have happened to have caused it.

An attractive girl who had never been to the stall before reached the head of the queue and smiled demurely in Lewis's direction, but he was too busy to really notice. Paddy decanted another full jug into the serving hopper, busied himself with another batch and muttered to himself about Tom being missing.

Sarah looked over from the car park. Her first and obvious assessment was just how busy the stall looked, which was a good thing. She could also see that Lewis was indeed present and seemed to be hard at it, but she also noted Tom's absence.

Paddy smiled in her direction and gave her the thumbs up. She did her best to look pleased but even at a distance he could sense that something was awry and that she wasn't very happy. His sensors were not so blunt that he couldn't connect Tom's unusual absence and Sarah's demeanour. Something must have occurred, but he was reduced to guessing and he hoped that Mary might have a better idea.

At just after nine, they served their last customer on what had been, far and away their busiest morning ever and for the first time, they had nearly ran out of stock. Lewis and Joe enjoyed the impact that they had and were happy to take all the credit for themselves. Paddy slapped Joe hard on the back and shook Lewis firmly by the hand, genuinely thanking him.

'So, where was he then?' Joe asked and Paddy just shrugged.

'I don't know. He never said anything about not coming.'

'Have you called him?' Joe asked.

'Yeah, twice.'

'Well, maybe he's got something on,' Lewis interjected, which drew both Paddy and Joe's attention. It seemed odd for Lewis to have an opinion and there was a sense of knowing about him also.

'Why? Did he say something to you?' Joe asked, but Lewis shook his head immediately and a bit too vigorously, which pricked Paddy's intrigue again.

'What exactly did he say to you, son?' Paddy asked.

'No, man, nothing; just how much this means to him and how much he wants to see it work.' Lewis looked directly at Paddy now. 'For you, man, as much as for him.'

Paddy looked a little embarrassed and was delighted by the distraction of his mobile ringing. He fought with his jeans pocket to release it without losing the call, but it wasn't Tom. It was Elliot and he couldn't explain Tom's absence either and now the confusion really thickened. If Elliot didn't know, then no one did. Elliot too, sounded alarmed. He needed to speak with Michael, especially when Paddy announced that the petition was well on course. Elliot grabbed at the remains of his hair.

'But, Paddy, Tom called the petition off?' Elliot insisted.

'Yeah, but he didn't mean it, did he?' Paddy answered. 'I figured that was just talk because he was upset about something.'

Elliot needed to get off the phone.

'But, Paddy, you said you were going to be short, that you wouldn't be able to get enough signatures.'

'Yeah, I know, but I've had an idea.'

Tom sat in his empty house. The undertakers would set the stone first thing the next morning and so he had little to do for the day but wait. He called Sarah but got her answerphone again and didn't leave a message – too much information to impart. He had already left a message of apology but he had much to explain besides. He resolved to do so as soon as he got back. The timing felt right but for now he wanted to enjoy some closure with the people who should still be with him in his fine house. He had ignored calls from Paddy and Elliot and felt guilty for doing so, but it was probably to say that Lewis hadn't shown up and he didn't want to hear bad news. But then Paddy sent him a picture of the queue snaking out from the stall, with Lewis doling out drinks. It was a happy picture and made him feel proud. Elliot then called again and Tom took his call. Elliot was as efficient as ever and didn't ask Tom to account for his absence or where he was. He did, however, mention with some alarm that Paddy was continuing with his quest for signatures and he sought some assurances about Tom's plans for the land. Tom smiled at the thought of Paddy pushing ahead despite his say so and if anything, it strengthened his resolve.

'Tell Paddy to carry on,' was all he said and ended the call.

Paddy had his brainwave in the Nelson, where most of his other flashes of inspiration had occurred to him throughout his life. Everyone had agreed at the time that it was a brilliant idea, but now that he was standing outside Villa Park on a match night, the whole idea seemed much less attractive. It certainly seemed apocryphal that Birmingham should be playing Villa on this night, with a stadium packed with Brummies', many of whom would live in Bromsworth. On paper, it was perfect and seemed as if the stars had aligned for them. But it is one thing talking about addressing forty-two thousand, seven hundred and eighty-eight people – the exact capacity of the ground – and quite another thing doing it. Joe had refused point blank to replace him, which Paddy derided him for, given that he once aspired to play on the very pitch that Paddy was now expected to make his announcement from. Similarly, Elliot was determined that Paddy was the only man for the job; local popularity and his sheer size being two critical factors. A few strings had to be pulled at the club, which had a 'no appeals' policy in general as they already supported various charities in an official capacity, but an exception was made in this instance. Paddy had some influence with people that he knew, but it was Lewis's involvement that had really made the difference. The youth team coach rated young Lewis very highly and if his involvement with Paddy's new business helped to straighten his head out, then Paddy Porter was a useful man and should be helped by the club.

Sarah had sat through a staff meeting and was uncommunicative and distracted. Anne put a few calls through to her office, none of which lasted very long. She was pleased that she had a missed call from him, but she noted that he hadn't left a message and she was cross with herself for allowing him to have such an adverse effect on her. It didn't seem fair and she finally justified to herself that she had every right to find out the truth. She placed a call to her friend, Douglas and arranged to meet him.

Douglas Monroe was the general manager of the Hyatt and he knew that something was wrong the moment Sarah had called. She had never arranged to meet him at work before and certainly never during school hours. His ego momentarily allowed him to believe that she might finally be interested in him, but reality quickly prevailed when he saw her and greeted her warmly.

'Something tells me that this isn't just a social call,' Sarah seemed nervous and anxious to get to the privacy of his office, as if she was keen to avoid being seen.

'Is everything alright?' he asked as they sat down. Sarah apologised in advance because what she would be asking would flout every aspect of hotel protocol. But Douglas demurred once she had finished and fired up his laptop. Quickly, he confirmed that Mr Tom Harper had returned to the hotel last night but left again shortly afterwards and hadn't returned since. And he hadn't checked out. Douglas hit another key on his machine. 'His room has been made up already today and we haven't been told when to expect him next.'

Sarah nodded and girded herself for her next question.

'Can I see his room, please?'

Douglas blanched a little. He could sense that she had good reason and was kind enough not to ask why.

'I apologise Douglas. I know it's an awful position to put you in…'

'I'll need to accompany you.'

'Of course. Thank you.'

'Do I need to search you?' he asked, to which Sarah looked confused. 'I can't have you cutting up his suits.'

They walked quickly and silently through the hotel. Douglas

rather enjoyed the subterfuge and theatrically warned his concierge to keep a look out for Mr Harper without explaining why. He knocked politely on the door, called out his name and waited, just in case, before he slid his master card into the slot, waited for the green light to appear and then gently nudged the door open. They both entered the room. All appeared normal. His small travel case was open in the lounge area and was the only indication that the room was even occupied. The bathroom was busier though with an array of belongings neatly gathered to one side.

Sarah knew exactly what she was looking for and made straight for the bedroom, whereupon it was the first thing that she saw. A photograph of him and his family in a silver frame. She had been right all along and it explained everything. She held the photo and sat down heavily on his bed. She shivered and suddenly felt cold in contrast to the warmth and happiness captured in the photograph. Douglas appeared in the doorway but didn't ask any questions and gave her the moment she needed. She looked at the photo again and studied it. His wife was beautiful and so were his boys, which came as no surprise at all. As unsurprising as it was that they existed, she felt cross with herself for being so naïve. She shook her head briefly and wondered what sort of man Tom could be to leave his family for pastures new. She shook her head and asked herself how she could have been so stupid. Wasn't it her intelligence that was supposed to mark her out? So how then had her antennae failed so miserably when it came to her emotions and avoiding situations just like this one?

'Sarah, I'm sorry, but we really need to get going.'

Standing in the tunnel, waiting for the half-time break, Paddy's sense of terror increased when he considered what he was wearing. He slapped his head and admonished himself for being so bloody stupid. He was wearing black jeans and a black sweat top – what the hell was he thinking? How would he cope if the entire crowd broke into a rendition of the football classic 'who's the wanker in the black'? He looked at Elliot with a pleading eye but Elliot shook his head firmly.

Paddy was introduced to the crowd at Villa Park by the announcer, but no one could hear very well and those that could, weren't interested as he plodded out to the centre circle to general indifference. Even his giant frame didn't make much of an impact in such a big space. He waited for his moment of quiet but it wasn't forthcoming, so he began anyway.

'Hello, everybody, my name is Paddy Porter and I'm from Bromsworth.'

A predictable clatter of boos rang out from the people around the stadium who hailed from elsewhere in the city.

'Yeah, thank you; it's a shithole, I know, which is why I'm here making a tit of meself, 'cos I need your help. We've got a petition together to try and buy some land to build a kids' hospice, so if you're from Brom, we'd love your support by signing it after the game. Thank you.'

A small ripple of applause started to gather at the mention of the children's hospice and Elliot's eyes almost popped out of his head. Immediately, he sought assurances from Joe that he must have heard him wrong. Paddy had indeed mentioned the idea of a hospice when he had approached Aston Villa; but he never intended to include it in his on-pitch appeal though, but his nerves overcame him and it just came out. Now, as he walked off the pitch to generous applause, he was less worried about the consequences and more trying to savour the moment. He felt like a star striker coming off to be rested after bagging his hat-trick. He looked around and almost bowed. He waved briefly and clapped the crowd back. Elliot was already on the phone, and Michael would now have to wrestle with the legal ramifications that come with the walking liability that was Paddy Porter.

Chapter 54

It had been raining most of the night and the ground at the cemetery was soft and yielding. Tom held Nell's hand as the stone was lifted by crane from the flat-bed truck and gently worked into place on to its concrete footings. The blossom on the trees was in full bloom and a non-fruit cherry tree, with its vibrant pink nearby, was doing its best to mark the occasion. A worker quickly grouted the join to the foundation slab with some ready mixed render as another brushed and cleared behind him. They worked quietly and efficiently and then respectfully, they departed. Tom squeezed his sister's hand as he stared at the large piece of granite with his family's names and appropriate dates beautifully inscribed, and the newly cut flowers arranged in front of their communal grave. It still felt odd, almost surreal, reading their names and knowing that they were all so close to him and yet so far. Fervently, he wanted to believe that there was a heaven and that they were all together and happy. The stone was already wet from the water that was hanging in the air and it made it glisten in the light. It was the final piece in a process that would last for the rest of his life and he wondered what lay ahead. He was somewhat assured that he desperately wanted to see Sarah again and more importantly, to explain himself to her. Something he should have done already. But as everyone had explained, he would know when the time was right. Tom had tried calling again last night and again this morning, but still hadn't managed to speak to her. He would have liked to leave immediately for Bromsworth, but had promised to meet with Michael and Jeremy, and in the evening, he was having dinner with Nell.

Mary and Joe had verified the numbers. The names were in and the almost impossible total had been achieved. Paddy fired off a quick text to Tom:

Fruit Bowl now a raging success and the petition is complete. Wherever you are – STAY AWAY!

Most people had said that it couldn't be done but none of them had reckoned on the formidable Patrick Porter. Lorraine placed the bottle of champagne on their table in the Nelson and his friends cheered loudly as the cork popped. Just to be on the safe side, Elliot had done an audit of his own and agreed that everything was in order. No mention had been made by anyone about Paddy's unfortunate announcement at Villa Park and Elliot decided not to mention it to Tom in any of his communications.

Sarah listened to his message over and over and became angrier each time.

Hi Sarah, it's Tom again. Trying to get a hold of you because I need to explain. I can explain everything. And will do when I see you tomorrow. I'll be back tomorrow.

Just who the hell does he think he is? His choice of words, 'need to get hold of you,' was unfortunate, but the fact that he thought he could explain himself was what really rankled her most. Her mum had called and immediately suspected that something was wrong – a mother's intuition? But Sarah was reluctant to share her problem, as embarrassed as she was. Her parents were aghast at her inability to form a decent union and her liaison with Garth, the itinerant cricketer, had been a new low for them – until a married father of three that is. She brought a mountain of paperwork home with her, which served as a useful distraction at first, but quickly her attention reverted to Tom and the photograph. She berated herself again for being so naïve and loathed his sense of confidence. 'I can explain everything.' No, you bloody well can't, she hissed.

She refilled her glass and played with her phone. She had half a mind to call him and tell him that she already knew and that it changed everything. But she didn't call. She didn't want to speak to him and wished she had never allowed him to set up his wretched stall.

Chapter 55

Mark Hooper knew exactly what he was signing for as the van courier unloaded the heavy boxes and a legal letter accompanying them from a firm in London. A council porter humped the boxes onto a push trolley and followed Hooper back into the bowels of the council building to deliver the bomb to his boss. Lesley waited until his door was shut before he opened the letter. He knew what it was and tried to remain calm, but he could feel his anger welling deep from within. Mark Hooper knew what to expect and didn't hang around. Lesley read the letter in silence and then calmly put it back in the envelope. He placed it on his desk and then leapt to his feet and began assaulting the offending boxes with his feet and fists.

As expected, his legal department at the council were hopeless. Lower second-degree law graduates from various Universities of Tokenism, the lot of them, and none of whom could provide him with an opinion or a suggestion that he found remotely helpful. It seemed that the auction would have to be conducted in an open and more traditional manner. And, so what? seemed be to the consensus view of his staff.

'Are you, all right?' one of his legal advisers asked.

'Yes, I'm fine,' Lesley twitched. 'Why wouldn't I be fine?'

'Well… You just seem upset, that's all.'

'Well, actually I am upset. You see, I've dedicated my entire working life to public service and now it seems that the electorate are fucking well telling me how to do my fucking job. So, if you must know, then no - I am not all-fucking-right.'

The lawyers quickly took their leave, leaving Lesley alone with his fears.

'I mean, what can he possibly want with this land?' Lesley asked, a question that continued to torment him. 'A garden of remembrance? Fine, then just ask and cut me in.'

Lesley had made a considerable effort to find out all he could about Tom. It wasn't great when the news of Tom's family and his loss came to his attention. It was desperately sad of course and even Lesley was moved, although not to a point where it altered his position. If anything, Tom Harper's loss made him even more heroic and Lesley was mindful to keep it to himself. Everyone being so mawkish these days – the legacy of Princess Diana's death and compounded by the bloody internet, Lesley reasoned – and matters were always heightened when kids were involved.

Tom tried Sarah again but her phone was now off completely and he hoped that she was OK. She hadn't returned any of his calls, which surprised him a little and made him a little anxious. He was on his way to see Michael and he wasn't much looking forward to it, especially now with Paddy's great breakthrough. It made things more acute and sharply focussed. It was a financial folly of course, but he didn't care and a further dollop of adrenalin dripped in to his system. But Tom needed to see Michael; he needed his assurances. They had agreed to meet at a venue, away from Michael's office, and the RAC club on Pall Mall was as good as any. Michael was already there when he arrived and welcomed him warmly.

'How was it, this morning?' Michael asked kindly.

Tom shrugged, not really knowing how to respond. The stone was beautiful but no replacement for his family.

He sat down and Michael ordered a pot of coffee for them both and a selection of sandwiches.

'So, you're looking well,' Michael said as cheerily as he could. The truth was that Tom was looking rather tired and drawn.

'Yeah, I'm fine, thanks. There's been an awful lot going on.'

'Yes, so Elliot tells me. The stall is finally a success I hear?'

'Yes, in my absence it seems,' Tom joked.

'Something about a young football maestro?'

Tom nodded and smiled at the idea of Lewis being factored into the thinking of Michael Millhouse, one of the most successful lawyers in the city of London.

'That's right: Lewis Adele. I've never seen him play but I'm told he's brilliant – a future premier league player.'

But Michael quickly glazed over, unable to maintain much interest. 'Good,' he said by way of conclusion, keen to move on to more pressing matters.

But Tom had other ideas. 'His mum's a prostitute and a drug addict.'

'I see.' Michael managed.

'No dad.' Tom continued. 'He was at my old school but was excluded for assault, for which he was convicted and Aston Villa released him.'

Michael did his utmost to look concerned but it was his client, who needed his skills and his compassion and not some kid he had never met.

Michael's plan was broadly to support Tom with his plans for the stall. It was clearly more than just a distraction for him and something that Tom was determined to see through. It was broadly affordable, especially if some local funding could be found and was infinitely preferable to his client diving down the financial black hole of land speculation.

'And what about this auction then, Tom? If you could please enlighten me about that? And your intentions for any land you might acquire?'

Tom tutted a little but said nothing. The prospect of buying the land was only a possibility because of the efforts of Paddy, but Tom was still unclear about his intentions. Michael opened a document: no doubt the sale of lots including the site called The Quadrant.

'Well,' Tom began, 'I have this rather romantic notion of

buying a plot of land and turning it into a sports facility for my old school. Their playing fields were sold off…' Tom tailed off as he saw the gloom envelope Michael's face.

'I was rather hoping that you might talk me into it?' Tom concluded and at which Michael guffawed.

'Well, Tom, I will not be doing that, I'm afraid.'

'No.'

'No. I'm afraid I err firmly on the side of reason and logic. And not emotion.'

Tom was disappointed but not surprised. 'Difficult though. To put a value on something like this?'

'No, not really. It's perfectly simple because there isn't any value in it.'

'Apart from altruism, you mean. Or don't lawyers get this?'

'Oh please, leave off with this hardened heart stuff,' Michael returned. Tom rubbed his face and didn't respond. He looked like he didn't care how much it might cost.

'Tom, we don't know what lies ahead. You're a very wealthy man but I've seen larger fortunes than yours squandered.'

'That's a bit dramatic, isn't it? I'm not buying a football club.'

'No, but it is a vanity project though?'

Tom shook at the accusation. Michael wasn't going to be persuaded, which troubled Tom because he was seldom wrong on anything. But Michael wasn't finished yet either. He needed Tom's assurances that he wasn't going to proceed and so he took a more conciliatory tone.

'Look, Tom, it's laudable what you're hoping to do, but I'm sure there are other more affordable ways that you can help your old school.'

Tom didn't care to be patronised and stopped him. 'Yeah, well, you needn't worry too much, Michael.'

'And why is that?'

'Because I can't buy anything without your approval, can I?'

Tom said accusingly and stood up for good measure.

'Actually, you can,' Michael snapped back. 'If you bothered to read your mails…' Michael added angrily.

Tom waited for him to finish.

'…then you'd see that you have full access to all your funds and accounts. Which is a worry, because you can do whatever you bloody well want. It's your money.'

Tom felt contrite as Michael waved a dismissive hand at him. Tom was still unclear what he might do and if anything, having access to his money made him feel anxious.

Chapter 56

Lesley put aside the fact that he had been completely out-manoeuvred at every stage and now Danny was threatening to pull out of the deal altogether. Lesley had to convince him to hold firm. As yet, nothing had changed, aside from the format of the sale; they should proceed as normal and hope that their budget of £1.8 million would be sufficient. Lesley assured him that it would be. A businessman would have to be out of his mind to pay more for a plot of land that he couldn't develop.

Sarah was driving herself demented and needed to confide in Anne about the photograph. Anne was immediately sympathetic.

'Oh dear, Sarah. I'm sorry. But we did wonder, didn't we?'

Sarah agreed and sighed heavily. She didn't wish to see him again, which of course was impossible now, given that his stall was suddenly a success, which she now resented on several levels. She looked out from her office window at Paddy and Joe arriving with a new load of carrots and apples ready for the next morning. The new stall was really taking shape. The roof was on and the trimming was being applied. To everyone concerned, it seemed that the stall was a force for good and yet it made her feel so hurt and angry.

Back in his lounge, mid-morning, Paddy sipped his mug of tea as Mary busied herself with tidying on her morning off. They had gone to bed discussing Tom and he was still their subject of speculation now.

'Maybe he's married after all; you've said yourself, men like him…'

Mary supposed, but she was tired of their guessing game. 'Paddy, all we really know is that we don't know anything about him.'

Paddy agreed. She was right enough.

'Maybe he knocked her about?' Paddy suggested.

'No, I don't think so. And if he did, she'd have given him back as good as she got.'

'Yeah, I guess. Actually, I can see her giving him a good kicking.'

Mary threw his under-pants at him, catching him full in the face. It was time Paddy got back to his own stall. Sean would want relieving and she had stuff to be getting on with.

Tom couldn't concentrate on anything other than Sarah and he wasn't much company for Nell over their early evening dinner. She wanted to help her brother, but didn't feel able to support his plans for the field. Like Michael, she suggested there had to be other more affordable ways to help their old school. The land was hardly mentioned and Nell suspected that it was something else that was absorbing Tom's attention anyway. She had a hunch what it might be. A women's intuition and gave him plenty of scope and opportunity to bring it up. Finally, she gave up waiting and decided to force the issue.

'Tom, are you going to tell me?'

'Tell you what?'

Nell clutched at his hand. 'That you've met someone?'

Tom looked shocked at first but then quickly relieved.

'What's her name?' she asked, absolutely convinced now.

'Wow, and I always thought Michael was intuitive.'

Nell was dismissive. 'Michael's a man.' She smiled and looked delighted for him. She reached forward her other hand and held him affectionately.

'Sarah,' Tom said, smiling a little painfully.

Nell said nothing and just waited.

'You're not going to believe this, but she's the Head at St Ed's.'

Nell chuckled a little. 'Well, you always were the teacher's pet.'

Tom laughed and squeezed his sister's hands as he quickly became tearful. He blew out hard and explained how they met and how his feelings had grown despite his efforts to fight them. Nell smiled. She'd forgotten all about the land, which didn't seem important anymore as Tom recounted his last evening with Sarah and how he had run away from her. But Nell understood.

'But you do have to tell her, Tom, about the accident.'

'I know. I will. As soon as I get back tomorrow, I will.'

'It will probably come as a great relief, to you both.'

Tom nodded. 'Certainly, explain some of my recent behaviour anyway.'

He paid the bill and kissed Nell good night. Sharing his news with his sister created a huge sense of relief. And that Nell was so approving was a fillip also. He was pleased to be heading to his empty house again where he could sit quietly and try to make sense of it all.

Chapter 57

Normally, he would just let the house phone ring because if it was important, whoever it was would call his mobile, but something forced him to catch the call and he wrestled to get his front door open. He lunged across his hall just in time. It was Theresa, Beth's mum and he was pleased now that he had hurried. She was unlikely to have called his mobile and he wanted to speak with her to see how they were. They talked at length about his exploits in Birmingham and what he had been up to and she was pleased to hear that he had been busy. She sounded older, her voice wavering slightly; he could still hear the pain in her voice which would never go away. Tom sensed that she had called for a specific reason and it was most likely about the laying of the stone, which she would want to visit. Not that she needed an invitation to her daughter's grave, but knowing how proper she was, Tom extended a formal invitation to them both to visit tomorrow if it suited them. The relief in her voice was palpable and Tom felt guilty now for not staying in closer contact since the accident.

'If we came at, say, ten, dear?'

It wasn't ideal because he wanted to get back to see Sarah as early as possible. He hadn't of course mentioned her to Beth's mum. Tom assured her that it was fine. They could all have lunch somewhere and then he could get back on his way to Bromsworth. The auction was the day after and he had a lot to plan for besides.

He checked his mobile phone for messages and considered ringing Sarah again but decided not to. It was now too late and he settled in the snug with the remote control and a bottle of beer he didn't really want. He flicked through the channels trying to find something of interest and predictably ended up looking at what sport was on offer. It was mainly football, which felt appropriate in the circumstances and he started watching a match between two teams he didn't recognise. His attention wandered to Lewis and his ambitions as he watched the young men who had made it in the professional ranks. A player went down injured, after an innocuous challenge and yet he writhed on the ground in agony. The commentator was unimpressed and joked about Oscars and insurance pay-outs. Tom sat transfixed, staring at the screen as the player suddenly sprang back to life and was miraculously OK again. Tom's eyes narrowed and his mind continued to race. It was beautiful and perfectly apt, and so extraordinary that he had missed it until now.

He tore upstairs to his office, leaping two steps at a time. His mind frantic, he recalled the first piece of mail he had received from the Life company and the rage it had caused, not to mention the cost as he proceeded to trash his kitchen.

Naisi had tidied his office and had left it immaculate, as ever. He quickly located a pile of mail that she had gathered to forward onto Michael's office: some private post, bank statements mainly and other circulars. Knowing exactly what he was looking for, he rifled through the pile of unopened envelopes until he found it. It occurred to him how inappropriate the company's name was, emblazoned across the envelope – because nothing about Beth's life could ever be described as 'Standard'. He was so excited he could hardly breathe as he ripped open the envelope and read the letter quickly. It was fate, he decided. He loved his wife so much and for the first time since the accident, he felt happy when he imagined her. He wished he could tell her this and hoped that she knew.

He looked at his watch. It was too late to call anyone and he couldn't leave now for Bromsworth either because it would upset Beth's parents. He read the letter again and quietly wept. Tears of hurt and loss but also, immense pride and love. There seemed little point of going to bed now because he knew that he wouldn't sleep. Against Nell's advice, he placed a call to Sarah's mobile but got her answer service. Once again, he didn't leave a message. He would see her tomorrow and explain everything. And finally, he had complete clarity. He knew exactly what he was going to do and that everything was going to be all right.

Chapter 58

The girl working in the call centre at Standard Life took her caller through security. The man gave hazy responses and got a couple of questions wrong, but eventually got his passwords and memorable dates in order and his account details appeared on her screen, along with a red flashing 'alert' and her dull day brightened just a little. Quickly, she assimilated the salient information and given the circumstances and the amount of money involved, this call was set to become a career highlight for her.

'Mr Harper, I just need to ask you a few questions.'

'Yes, fine,' Tom answered quickly because it was already a little after nine and Beth's parents were capable of arriving much earlier than they had agreed.

'I can see from my screen that we've sent you eight letters since February last year without hearing back from you.'

Eight letters. Tom rebuked himself.

'Yes, I've been busy,' Tom answered blandly to the employee's surprise. She pushed a key on her console to alert her supervisor.

Theresa laid a beautiful wreath at the foot of the gravestone to accompany the flowers that Tom and Nell had left the day before. It was a bright morning with the sun warming them all as best it could. Ted was as upright as ever, his reserve unswerving, but inside Tom could feel that he was hollow. Theresa demonstrated their emotions for them both and she cried softly into her hanky before her daughter and three grandchildren. Finally, she stood back and grabbed for her husband's hand. Tom wrapped his arm around her, tenderly.

In an award-winning pub, with a Michelin-starred restaurant on the river along from the cemetery, Tom ordered lunch and they sat drinking their sparkling waters. Tom was desperate to head up the motorway as soon as possible, but he was also keen to share his plans with them. Naturally, they were pleased for him because he seemed so energised and they liked the idea of The Fruit Bowl of course. Their grandsons had long regaled them about the funny drinks that their mummy made for them. Ted and Theresa smiled and enjoyed the idea that Beth's Fruit Bowls might live on.

'And, Tom, what about you?' Theresa asked gently, much to her husband's dismay, but Tom gestured that it was fine. They had a right to know and he felt sure that they would be pleased for him.

'Actually, there is someone, I think.'

Theresa's face softened and instinctively she reached out for his hand. A tear appeared instantly and filled her right eye. 'You think?'

'Actually, I know.'

The old lady smiled and seemed very at peace with his news.

'But nothing has happened. We've just had dinner...'

Theresa stopped him. She didn't wish to pry and didn't want to make him feel uncomfortable. Tom was grateful. He looked at her as the next words gathered and stuck in his throat. 'But I do like her.'

'Good, Tom. That's good. You deserve to be happy again and she's a very lucky lady, whoever she is.'

Ted cracked a little as well now, his lip quivering as he leant over to clutch at Tom's shoulder and to assure him also. Tom was grateful to them both for everything they had done for him.

After an eventful morning at school, Sarah was rushing to a meeting at the local authority when she was caught by Mr Bales, the DT teacher. He was delighted by the shape of the newly constructed stall and was seeking out her approval. Sarah did her best to share his excitement.

'Chris, it looks great. You and the boys have done a terrific job. Thank you.'

Paddy waved over at her enthusiastically and she returned the gesture but without the same enthusiasm. She had already noted that Tom was still absent, which was a good thing as far as she was concerned. Maybe he had left for good?

Chapter 59

Tom charged up the M40 quickly, taking his chances with the ugly cameras that lined the road, his mind racing even faster. He got Paddy on the phone, who almost exploded with excitement at how things had improved in his absence, but he was delighted that he was on his way back nonetheless. Naturally, he had lots of questions and Tom had the answers, but all in good time and not as he raced along in the outside lane.

The stall did indeed look very impressive and Tom admired it inside and out with Paddy hopping about like a kid at a theme park. Tom's eye wandered to the car park and then to the school. Sarah's car parking space was empty and Paddy anticipated his next question.

'She went out this morning somewhere.'

Tom nodded. 'How does she seem?'

'Er... I've seen her happier,' Paddy answered. 'Is there anything I can do to help, you know, between you two?'

Tom laughed at such a ridiculous notion. 'Er, no thanks, Paddy.'

'No, OK, I get that. So, where have you been then?' Paddy asked expectantly.

Tom sighed a little.

'I had to head home to London to get some stuff sorted out. Chiefly, my head.'

'And did you?'

Tom nodded. 'Actually, yes.'

Sarah's car pulled into the car park. Tom knew by Paddy's eyeline. He turned around briefly. Paddy winked at him.

'Whatever it is, Tom, be honest.'

Tom smiled back at his friend who couldn't have known how powerful his words had just been.

Having seen Tom arrive at the school, Anne had immediately

called Sarah to warn her. Just like Paddy had been, she too, was full of questions, but Anne couldn't enlighten her of course.

Sarah tried to calm herself as she approached the school but without much success. She was furious that she should be made to feel nervous on her way back to work, and how he thought he could just show up again as if nothing had happened. She spotted him instantly but avoided his gaze. She had stopped her car briefly after taking Anne's call to gather her belongings so that she could be out of her car immediately and into her office without being interrupted. But Tom had other ideas and was upon her as she locked her car remotely. She could feel his presence as she hurried towards the school and she wondered who might be observing and how it would look. It was all very public and hardly the place.

'Sarah, please, can I have a word?' he called after her.

She stopped still and took a moment before turning around, her face hurt but defiant. She took a few steps forward. 'This is hardly the place.'

'Well, I tried calling you.'

'Yes, which I ignored, which should be clear enough for you to understand.'

Tom was a little confused. 'Right, but I can explain…'

Sarah stepped in closer now so that she could speak much quieter and know that she couldn't possibly be overheard. 'No, Tom. No, you can't explain. Now just leave me alone.' She turned quickly and made on her way. Tom thought to chase after her but he too was conscious of his surroundings and decided against. Paddy was a long way off, but he could read easily enough that it hadn't been a happy exchange. Paddy shook his head. Tom was an enigma all right. For a man with so much ability, he did manage to frequently get things very wrong. Tom gathered himself and began walking towards the stall.

Chapter 60

Paddy started his van with a disconsolate Tom slumped in the seat next to him. Paddy didn't say anything and waited for him to explain.

'Paddy, there's something I need to tell you.'

'Jesus, do not tell me you're the fockin tax man.'

Tom didn't laugh at his joke and Paddy half-apologised as he got the van in gear and they headed off. 'Has something happened?' Paddy asked.

'Yeah, you could say that. Where are we off to now?'

'Wholesalers. Why?'

'Let's go back to your house. It's a long story and I need to start at the beginning.'

Paddy and Mary sat still on the sofa in their lounge as Tom continued with his story. Tears streamed down Mary's face but she didn't make a sound and Paddy was silent as well. No jokes now from the big man. It ended with the laying of the stone and had taken barely fifteen minutes. Then, he looked up at them both and just shrugged.

'I probably should have told you right at the very beginning, but I didn't –'

'No, no…' Paddy shook his head quickly. He understood Tom's reasons exactly. It was why he was back in Bromsworth – precisely *because* no one knew. Paddy got this immediately but he could not begin to imagine the hurt of what Tom was dealing with. Neither he nor Mary knew what to say.

'Tom, you poor devil.' Paddy reached forward and grabbed his friend into his massive arms and hugged him hard. When he released him, Tom's face was wet with tears.

'How did you cope?' Mary asked, and Tom thought for a moment and half-chuckled.

'I didn't.' He shook his head as he recalled. 'At first, I just went sort of numb, you know, disbelieving. Then I kept thinking that it wasn't real and that it hadn't happened and that everything was going to be all right. But of course, it was real. It had happened. They were dead, so then I became angry, really angry.' Tom paused as he recounted those days. 'I couldn't sleep. Literally, I'd go for days and weeks without sleeping, which meant no real respite. I couldn't ever escape from it. And I became so exhausted and so angry, I ended up in hospital with a full-blown mental collapse.'

Mary returned with a steaming pot and three mugs on a tray: the universal medicine. Paddy was at a loss for anything to add but fortunately, he didn't need to because Tom kept unloading and filling the impossible void.

'And that's why all of this has been so important to me,' he said, looking directly at Paddy and hoping that he would understand. Paddy nodded immediately.

'You see Paddy - it was in hospital that I recalled our incident together – you, me and Connor.'

Paddy's eyes narrowed.

'So, without the accident, that memory would have probably remained buried and I would never have come back here. Why would I? But the accident did happen and because of it, I remembered you. And so, it felt like I remembered you for a reason. And I needed to do something about it but I didn't know what.

Paddy was now totally choked. A heavy tear rolled his cheek, impeded by his bristles. 'Yeah, well, Tom, I wish you weren't here now.'

'No.'

'I wish you'd never remembered me or come back to Brom. Because that'd mean it hadn't happened and you'd be at home now with your family.'

Tom nodded his head gently. Paddy recalled the story Tom had told him about how The Fruit Bowl had originated and things finally clicked into place for him. 'It wasn't your dad, was it?' he stated. 'What squeezed the fruit? It was you. You did it for your boys?'

Tom closed his eyes and tears streamed down his face as he recalled their family routine. 'No, it was Beth. It was her thing…'

Paddy smiled and leant forward again to grab his friend and he squeezed him tightly.

Chapter 61

Paddy drove Tom to Sarah's house and he didn't argue. They had been for a walk and had talked at length about the same things over and over, even sharing a laugh about the recent success of the stall. Tom thanked Paddy for the petition and made his way along Sarah's street to her house and waved as Paddy's car drove past him. There wasn't much consideration for logistics because it could have been that Sarah wasn't in and Tom would have been stranded, but it was after 7.00 p.m., and her hall light was on, and other lights upstairs also. He rang the bell and waited nervously. He prayed that she wouldn't have company. He heard a noise before he saw movement through the obscured stained glass, her slim figure approaching and finally the door opened. They stood staring at each other. She didn't look altogether surprised to see him but she looked no less pleased than she had done earlier in the day.

'Hello, Sarah.'

Sarah looked over his shoulder, the way she would if she was expecting someone else.

'Can I come in, please? I have something that I need to tell you.'

Sarah sneered as she considered her options. Slamming the door shut was tempting but instead, she turned and walked into the house, leaving him to follow her. She still hadn't said anything.

Sarah was sitting in the chair in the bay window with her arms crossed. Tom sat opposite, wondering where to begin. Her eyes darted quickly to and fro, like she was busy and had things to do. She looked at his hand and scoffed derisively.

'My God, you're wearing your wedding ring now. Remembered, have you?' Sarah's vigilance surprised him as he thumbed his wedding band. He had taken it off when he first travelled to Bromsworth, but he wanted to wear it now – since he was allowing his past to accompany him again. Now he wanted everyone to know about Beth and his boys.

'Yes, which is what I need to explain –' he began confidently until she stopped him.

'How dare you?' she hissed. Was he so arrogant that he thought he could just explain this away? 'No, you can't, because I knew you were married all along.'

Tom's face fell.

'Oh, don't flatter yourself, you horrible bloody man.'

'What are you talking about?'

'I knew deep down that there was something not right. That there had to be a wife or someone, and kids as well because you were just too good to be true.'

Tom tried to interrupt, but she was in full swing now and wouldn't be deterred.

'So, after you just took off, I went to your hotel suite and I saw your family photograph.'

Tom's eyes widened.

'And don't you dare judge me.' Her voice was rising now as she stood up to show him out. 'And somehow you think you can explain yourself?'

'Sarah!' Tom shouted. 'Sarah, please listen to me.'

Suddenly, he looked awful, his face buckled with hurt. 'Yes, I am married. I have a wife and three boys.'

'Get out.' Sarah screamed.

'But, Sarah, they died. They all died.'

His words hung in the air and it took a moment for Sarah to register them. She felt winded and shook her head trying to compute the information and then she suddenly went limp. Her knees buckled. She fell forward and he caught her.

'What? What did you say?' she murmured.

'My wife and boys; they were all in a car accident.'

Sarah started crying now as he hugged her, her tiny frame heaving gulps of air and sobbing uncontrollably.

Tom eased her across the floor and lowered her carefully into a chair. She looked up at him as he pulled a photograph from his jacket pocket.

'This is my wife, Beth, and my boys.'

'Oh, my God,' Sarah shivered.

'I should have told you earlier. I wanted to and I even tried once, but –'

'Oh, my God, Tom. I'm so sorry.' Her head was a cauldron of emotions: of relief, guilt and above all else, love. She had gone from loving this man to absolutely despising him and now the one scenario she hadn't considered allowed her to love him again and she was completely overcome. He knelt in front of her and looked at her affectionately. She pulled his head onto her lap and wrapped her arms around him with her head resting on his. He kept talking about why he left her as he did, but she wasn't really listening and she kept apologising over and over.

Finally, after some time, Sarah broke from their embrace and held his heavy head up so that she could see him properly. He looked exhausted, his face lined with tears, and hurt etched all over. Her mind still flitted with conflictions and associated guilt. His news was devastating and yet it was also wonderful news: an equation for her to dwell on later and alone. But one thing was certain now and she had no compunction in telling him.

'Tom, I probably shouldn't say this now but I think I love you.'

Tom squeezed his stinging eyes shut again as he clutched her hands.

'I do, I really do, I love you. And I know that sounds crazy when we've only really just met and we haven't even kissed...'

At this, Tom leant forward and he kissed her gently. For a moment, everything was calm and made sense. Their tears spilling down their faces adding to their moment. They broke off to stare at each other. He wiped her wet eyes and smiled and then they embraced again.

Chapter 62

On the morning of the auction, Lesley sat nervously with Danny, his somewhat reluctant partner. Both men were anxious and fidgety.

'Maybe he knows about the recycling plans,' Danny suggested again and Lesley had to restrain himself.

'Jesus Christ! We've been through this already?' he snapped.

'Yeah, well. Something's not right.'

'Yes, I know that.' Lesley slammed his fists on the table. 'But he doesn't know what we're up to. No one does; not even my bloody wife.'

Danny sneered and Lesley tried to calm himself and his partner down.

'Everything was fine until this bastard rode into town on his big white fucking horse.' Lesley moaned.

'Yeah, and I'm wondering whether you didn't invite him.' Danny asked.

'Right. And why would I do that, you moron?'

'So, you can turn me over.'

'Don't be ridiculous. I'm a public officer. You have stuff on me, remember?' Lesley didn't like conceding such a thing but it was true and it seemed to work. And so, they were back to square one; the unknown.

'And anyway, according to my assistant, he's taken off somewhere anyway.'

Danny looked hopeful. 'Good. Hopefully he's finally got bored of the place.'

Lesley murmured his agreement although he didn't believe it, not for a second.

Tom sat at Sarah's kitchen table and watched her busy herself with breakfast. To be fair, she had been caught unawares and was struggling to put together a spread to be proud of. The cereal selection was meagre, her supply of milk was a concern and she wasn't too confident about the eat-by date on her bread either. But Tom didn't care. It would take much more than a green spot on his toast to dent his mood and his sense of relief. It was the most alive that he had felt since that fateful morning. The preceding night had been a watershed, but he still felt torn. They had hardly slept as they sat chatting and crying before eventually falling to sleep briefly just as it started to get light. And then an hour later, they both woke at the same time, as if an alarm had sounded and finally they made love and then predictably, his tears flowed again. Sarah held him as tightly as she could because she understood completely.

'Are you sure I shouldn't run and get a new loaf?' she asked, dusting off a misshapen slice of brown bread and she inspected closely also for green spots.

He shook his head and she smiled.

'God, I'm so embarrassed.'

It was just after 8.00 a.m. Sarah would usually be at her desk already and Tom would be squeezing fruit, so they were obviously a bad influence on each other and their relationship was doomed! Tom's phone pinged a reminder of the auction. He placed a call and Paddy answered immediately.

'Oh, good of you to call.' Paddy began mischievously. 'We're all here working, by the way.'

Tom chuckled. 'That's good to hear.'

'Yes, and where are you, might I ask?'

'No, you might not. I'll be there in an hour.'

'Fine.' Paddy sounded delighted.

'Oh, and Paddy?'

'What?'

'Not a bloody word.'

'No, of course.'

'And Paddy?'

'What, now?'

'I bloody well mean it.'

They showered quickly. So that Sarah wouldn't be any later for

work, she left Tom to get a taxi back to his hotel and drove herself to school. On arrival, she did well to avoid the beaming gaze of Paddy Porter. His demeanour said it all and she counted herself lucky that he didn't have a banner up for their newly loved-up headmistress. Anne watched her also. Immediately, she sensed that something was afoot and deliberately got into Sarah's eye-line with her quizzical look. For all Sarah's professionalism, she couldn't help smiling. Anne grabbed at Sarah's shoulders knowingly and they giggled like teenagers ahead of their first school disco.

Tom arrived at the school a creditable forty-five minutes later, smartly dressed in a black tailored suit and a brand-new white shirt that he had brought with him from home. He looked like a different man and Paddy beamed as he approached. He walked over to join him, leaving Joe, Lewis and Benny to look on. The two men shook hands warmly and then briefly hugged.

'Don't ask,' Tom said.

'No, I won't. It's wrong to pry. And I don't need to anyway because I already know.'

'Oh?'

'Yeah, I saw Ms Frost arrive a little earlier and the look on her face - safe to say, you were freaking awesome.'

Tom shook his head at his incorrigible friend. Paddy continued to beam. Since Tom's revelation, Paddy had thought of little else and now he felt very protective of him – as he must have done thirty years ago in their school playground. An incident now that he wished he could recall.

'You haven't told anyone?' Tom asked.

'No, of course not. And, how are you?' Paddy asked in a rare moment of seriousness.

'Yeah, I'm good. I'm really good. But there's something else I need to talk to you about.'

'Jesus! What now?' Paddy joked, reverting quickly to his old self.

'I'll tell you in a moment. Let me say hello to the lads, first.'

Tom was warmly welcomed with back slaps all round. The morning stall had been another success and spirits were high.

'You'll need to stay away, Tom,' Paddy quipped and the others cheered. Lewis was quiet but no less excited about the success and he shared a brief moment with Tom. Just a look of sincere thanks between them. Tom felt that he owed him a more fulsome thank you but it could wait for an appropriate time. Paddy had mentioned something also about a half-time announcement at the Birmingham derby, which Tom couldn't really take in.

'Paddy, are we going to Smithwick's now?' Tom asked, although it was more of an order than a question.

Paddy quickly gathered his belongings and they got on their way.

On their way to the wholesalers, Tom had to calm Paddy down.
'So, you stayed over?'
Tom dithered a moment. 'I thought you didn't pry?'
'You did. I know it.'
Tom conceded a small smile.
'You stayed at hers?'
'Yes, but in her shed. I slept in a wheel barrow.'
Paddy beamed at his friend.
'Well, that is fucking fantastic.'
Tom smiled and shook his head.
'And, if I might say so, you are punching…'
'Paddy, please!'
'OK, sorry. I'm sorry.' He sat, fidgeting like a child. Tom looked at him via his mirror.
'No one, Paddy. Not even Mary…'
Paddy frowned at the mention of his wife and quickly, Tom relented.
'Fine, but only Mary.'
'Absolutely.'
'It's Sarah's business and no one else's.'
'Absolutely. Quite right.' Paddy remarked.
'But if you wouldn't mind…'
'Yeah, anything.'
'If you could tell Joe for me. About my family and what happened.'

'Really?' Paddy seemed surprised.

'Yeah, it's easier than me telling everyone.'

'Yeah. I get that.' Paddy agreed.

'People should know now.'

'Yeah, sure. If that's what you want.'

'It is. Because this is a new Tom Harper – the one who can finally face his past.'

Paddy slapped him affectionately across his chest.

'Good on ya, Tom. You're a bigger man than me.'

Tom smiled. 'Thanks Paddy. And, when you tell people...'

'Yeah, what?'

'Please explain, that they don't have to try and console me.'

'Oh.'

'I know that they'll want to. But I don't want people's sympathy. Does that make sense?'

Paddy nodded. 'Yeah, I get that. I get that completely.'

'Thanks, Paddy. You're a good friend – a bloody good friend.'

'I am indeed. If I say it myself, I'm a blinking marvel.' Paddy joked and they both roared with laughter.

As they arrived at Smithwick's, Tom took on a more serious and business-like tone. 'Now, I need to talk to you about this afternoon.'

'Why? What's happening this afternoon?' Paddy asked.

Tom was cheered by his not knowing. It was highly apposite because had it not been for Paddy Porter, then there wouldn't be anything of note happening this afternoon.

'Er, a certain Council auction?'

'Oh, my God! Of course, my petition!'

'Yeah. We're going to buy some land.'

Chapter 63

Auction day at the town hall was always a busy occasion and especially so that afternoon, with the wide variety of lots available, from old computers that the council no longer needed, through to a series of repossessed council properties and finally the late addition and star lot – a piece of derelict land.

Elliot arrived early and took up his seat. He looked anxious, switched his phone to silent and checked for any emails from Michael. There were none. Michael was reasonably confident that he and Nell had managed to get through to Tom, but Elliot was less sure and had his number on speed dial just in case. Unlike Michael, he knew the full story and worse, he hadn't shared all the information with him. Withholding information from Michael Millhouse was always a poor career decision but, in this case, he had little choice and at least he was siding with Tom Harper. But still he fretted. He touched the breast pocket of his jacket again and felt the heavy envelope within, a reminder of his position and a constant source of worry for him.

The council auction room was half-empty when proceedings began and gradually started to fill up as lots came and went. Danny Green was present from the beginning and sat patiently as the gavel came down on a load of old tat. The auctioneer looked bored and relieved to be moving onto a couple of derelict properties. Lesley pushed his way quietly into the room, nodded at various colleagues and studiously avoided any eye contact with his business partner. Scanning the room, he noted Elliot's presence but was relieved to see that he was alone. Lot 65, two derelict maisonettes, was sold to an uncontested Asian buyer and Lot 79 moved a little closer.

Tom and Paddy arrived in good time as a series of retail units and associated residences were offered and returned unsold, the all-conquering on-line sales putting a dampener on retail speculators. They found two seats at the back of the room near to Elliot and with a good view of the now-almost-full room. Lesley Irwin stared coldly in his direction but Tom ignored him and studied the sale sheet. Elliot nodded a greeting to the two men, before firing off a text, as promised, to Michael.

Tom is here.

No doubt, this would prompt a phone call. Elliot watched carefully and sure enough, a moment later, Tom reached into his pocket and retrieved his device. He looked in the window, pushed a button and put it away again. Elliot gulped and tried not to think about Michael bouncing around his office in London.

And there it was – Lot 79 – the star attraction - six acres of land known as The Quadrant. A wave of excitement caught hold of the room as a photograph of the site appeared on the screen behind the auctioneer.

'Six acres in all, with full municipal planning.'

Lesley glared at the auctioneer. Just get on with the fucking bidding, why don't you?

'This lot has a reserve price of eight hundred thousand, which is where I'm going to start the bidding...'

Danny raised his card without looking at the auctioneer.

'Thank you, sir. I have eight hundred thousand pounds.'

Danny waited as the auctioneer's attention was diverted to his left and slightly ahead of him. A balding man in his fifties.

'Thank you; I have eight hundred and fifty thousand.'

Lesley considered the new bidder and appealed to Mark Hooper for his take, just away to his left, but he shrugged. He wasn't local or known to either of them. Lesley wondered if he might be bidding on behalf of Tom.

Danny bid again.

'Thank you. Back with you at nine hundred thousand.'

The fat man motioned to the auctioneer again.

'Thank you; nine fifty. Nine fifty.'

Danny raised again.

'One million. One million pounds. One million and fifty.'

It was against Lesley and still way below their budget, but the unknown bidder was unnerving him and intriguing Tom, also.

Danny committed another fifty grand to the cause with a tiny eye movement and so it went on.

'One point one, thank you, sir…'

When £1.2 million was reached, the auctioneer suggested that it might be better to proceed in increments of one hundred thousand and both men agreed, keen to appear more confident than the other.

'Do I have one point three?'

Within moments, Danny was agreeing to £1.5 million and now, for the first time, the counter bidder was reticent. Lesley felt a surge of adrenalin shoot through him. He had been panicking unduly because £1.5 million would be a wonderful result.

'Against you, sir, at one point five.'

The bidder played with his tongue and glanced over at Danny.

'One point six?' The auctioneer nudged.

The man didn't move.

'One point five five?'

Danny could barely contain himself, but then the man nodded.

'Thank you. Back with you, sir. I'm looking for one point six?'

Danny motioned immediately. Yep, £1.6 million, not a problem, and there's plenty more where that came from.

The auctioneer, expressionless, now turned his attention back to his opponent.

'It's against you sir, at £1.6 million. One point six five?'

The man stared ahead, completely motionless.

'One point six five is what I'm looking for.'

The man took a further moment but still made no gesture. Lesley grimaced and wrestled with his instincts to leap to his feet and punch the air.

'OK, then, are we all done?' The auctioneer appealed. 'Going once at one-point-six…'

The fat man barely flicked his head. Back in the game.

'Thank you, sir. One point six five.'

Lesley seethed and Danny immediately countered.

'Thank you. One point seven.' The auctioneer stated, his attention back at the fat man. The bidder nodded again.

'I have one point-seven-five. Do I have one-point-eight?'

The room was silent now. Completely breathless and still. £1.8 million was a pivotal figure. Calling in all his investors, this was Lesley's ceiling and the strain on his face was plain to see, as Danny raised his finger and his last throw.

'Thank you, sir. I have one point eight million pounds.'

Mark Hooper didn't dare look at anyone and kept his eyes fixed at the floor. His hands clammy and his throat dry because Hooper had provided Tom with this invaluable information and for which he would be relieving Elliot of the brown envelope in his breast pocket. If matters proceeded in Tom's favour.

'Are we all done at £1.8 million?'

Tom savoured the moment a little longer.

'Going once at £1.8...'

Lesley gripped at his sleeves. A bead of sweat running down his brow.

'Going twice...'

Tom pointed to the ceiling and the auctioneer's keen hawk-eye locked on immediately.

'One-point-eight-five...'

The fat bidder was out. Tom was in and Lesley audibly winced.

'Thank you. I have a new bidder. Back of the room at £1.85 million. Against you at the front, sir.'

Danny almost crunched his teeth to dust. Looking around now, he stared directly at Tom. Just what the hell could he want with this land? Municipal planning you dumb-fuck not residential. Danny and Lesley had discussed just this scenario and they agreed that if they were going to lose out, then they should punish the victor. Danny gestured again, his hand quivering now.

'Thank you. One-point-nine?'

Tom's eyes narrowed. He enjoyed the ball hanging heavy in his opponents court; more landmine than tennis ball.

Tom raised two fingers in the air, appropriate in the circumstances. Let's get this done, shall we?

'Two million pounds.'

A flurry of excitement spread through the room as the milestone was reached. More than twice the reserve.

'Ladies and gentlemen, are we all done?'

Danny closed his eyes heavily.

'Selling then at two million pounds...'

Lesley shuddered. Two years of planning up in smoke.

'Sold.'

Tom smiled. He was up and out of his seat as the gavel came down and then immediately out of the room. Lesley almost collapsed.

Paddy was dancing on the spot with the drama of the whole thing, even without knowing Tom's intentions for the land – the numbers involved, the way Tom had been so calm. The whole thing had been impossibly exciting and he could barely contain himself. Understandably, Elliot was less excited. He hastily met with Mr Hooper and gave him his ill-gotten dues and then corralled Tom to one side for a quick exchange.

'Tom, I imagine that Michael is on the M40 as we speak and is –'

'Elliot, don't worry, everything is fine. Really. I can explain it all.'

'But Michael gave me...'

'Even to Michael.'

Elliot stood down although he didn't look at all convinced.

'Elliot, seriously, don't worry. You've been magnificent up here and Michael will be very grateful when he realises.'

'Thank you.'

'No, thank you. As soon as he arrives, we'll all sit down.'

'Or stand? Because we might need a ring.'

Tom smiled. Elliot was doing jokes now. Bromsworth had been good for him also.

Tom wanted to go now to see Sarah but before he did, he needed a quick word with Paddy who still looked fit to burst.

'Paddy, not a word to anyone, remember?'

'Got it.'

'About the land as well?' Tom added.

'Really? Oh, come on! It's out there already.'

Tom smiled. 'Okay, but keep it from Joe, just until tomorrow.

We'll all go there together after The Fruit Bowl.'

Paddy smiled broadly. He held up his huge hand for Tom to slap and then they hugged again.

Sarah kissed Tom as he closed her office door behind him. To all appearances, it looked like just another of her long succession of daily meetings, but it felt completely different and clandestine. They hugged briefly as though they could be seen and quickly broke off to consider each other.

'How's your day been?' He asked.

'Better now. Yours?'

'Yep, good. I've just bought a hunk of land for too much money but I don't care because I have a crazy plan for it.'

'Oh?' Sarah enquired.

'What this school really needs is its playing fields back. Right?'

Sarah stared at him, aghast.

'Have you gone mad?'

Tom chuckled. Maybe? He enjoyed seeing the excitement on her face. Her desk phone rang, which meant Anne could no longer postpone the realities of her job. Tom kissed her goodbye and quickly invited her to dinner at the Hyatt that evening. Nell had called and was on her way up with Michael and it seemed a great time for the two women in his life to meet.

Michael and Nell had already arrived when Tom got back to the hotel and in contrast to his earlier meeting with his lawyer, this was a meeting he was looking forward to. Despite his lack of sleep, Tom looked vibrant and full of life. Gone was the anxiety that fixed his stare and he even seemed taller and less slumped than before. Nell looked beautiful and was delighted to see her little brother, hugged him warmly. Michael too was pleased to see him looking so well, but he was barely able to mask his fury at his recent acquisition. They shook hands formally but Tom smiled broadly and held eye contact.

'You look well, Tom.'

'Yeah, thank you. Actually, I feel great.'

Michael didn't answer.

'Michael, please, sit down. You're angry I know. But I can explain everything.'

'Oh, I doubt that, Tom. Elliot's filled me in. You've bought some land with municipal planning.'

Tom beamed his confirmation.

'Two million pounds?' Michael winced.

'Well, yes and no,' Tom began, which no one understood.

'Meaning what exactly?' Michael asked, rapidly losing his patience.

'I didn't buy it.'

Michael was about to protest.

'It was bought for me.'

This stopped Michael completely and he appealed for an explanation.

'Beth bought it.'

Instantly, the room fell silent at the mention of his beloved late wife and his confusing answer hung heavily in the air.

'Michael, you were right about the land. You all were. Yes, I wanted to buy it and it felt right to do so, but I couldn't justify it, not with the investment it needs. And yet it still nagged at me. And it felt as though things were beyond my control. I explained it to you, Nell, do you remember?'

'Er…'

'I explained that I felt compelled to come back here to Bromsworth. To find Paddy, because it felt right but I didn't know why.'

Nell nodded.

'But now I do.'

Nell smiled now.

'I've met people here, people who have helped me without even realising it. And being here – where we grew up, it made me want to do something for the place.'

Michael enjoyed the sentiment too but was much more interested in the economics of the transaction and hopefully something to allay his worries.

'Yes, Tom, this is all very well but if we can please get to the part about –'

'I'm getting there.' Tom answered. Michael sighed and sat back in his chair. 'I met a kid called Lewis: a brilliant football player but with all sorts of problems. And Elliot found a loop in the council's constitution.'

Michael glared at Elliot.

'I met Sarah, the headmistress of the school. The petition was a success – all incremental things that led me to the same conclusion, that it was the right thing to do even though economically, it is madness.'

'Quite,' Michael added. 'And Beth is involved, how?' Michael now demanded.

'Which is why it's all so perfect, because, in the end, it was Beth who bought the land, not me…'

Michael scowled at this because Beth had no such resources or not that he knew about anyway.

'…whether I had been in denial, I don't know?' Tom continued. 'But the perfect solution had been right there in front of me the whole time, only I couldn't see it.'

'Jesus, Tom! Which is?'

'Beth had an insurance policy on her life.'

The room fell quiet again: so, quiet it was almost possible to hear people's individual minds clicking into place.

'We argued about it at the time. It was after the twins were born and she became quite depressed. The doctors said it was normal. Post-natal stuff, you know, but it went on for some time: six months maybe.'

Michael and Nell both looked stunned.

'I know, you'd never have known, right? And I wasn't going to tell anyone. Beth was determined to keep it quiet because I think she was ashamed - you know, to have so much and all that. But it got worse before it started to improve and she became quite fatalistic.' The words choked Tom a little as he recalled her trauma and no doubt, her ultimate fate too. 'She started to worry about the boys and how I would cope if something ever happened to her. I tried to tell her that it was nonsense but she wouldn't listen. Plus, we already had plenty of life cover but she was insistent. She got online and started to download life insurance policies. She wanted a specific and individual policy on her life, in her name only and with a debit from her personal account so that she could see it each month. It was mawkish and I hated the idea but she was adamant. And so that was it.' He looked at Michael and Nell directly.

He let the information percolate and settle before continuing.

'And do you know, the strangest thing, is that it was this very insurance policy that sent me over the edge and ultimately back to Bromsworth.'

'How do you mean?' Nell asked.

'It was when I opened the letter from the insurance company about the pay-out; that letter was the thing that finally pushed me off the cliff - when I smashed up the kitchen and ended up in hospital. That was the day. So, you see, the whole thing somehow feels connected. Maybe even that Beth has been steering me the whole time since the accident. That she knew that this is where I could heal. I couldn't have known this and it's difficult to rationalise even now. But here we all are. This is what has happened and this is the only way I can explain it.'

Michael was incredibly touched and almost as relieved. He was also a little troubled because he was supposed to be receiving all of Tom's mail and so what else might he have missed? Unlikely, his office could not have missed all such correspondence? He didn't, however, receive private mail and perhaps this explained it. It didn't matter now of course but being a pedant, it troubled him. But the result was the same and bloody marvellous it was too.

'I was so furious. I didn't want an insurance pay out. I wanted Beth. And so, I think my mind just blotted it out completely. It's my only explanation,' Tom continued. 'And then,' Tom snapped his thumb. 'Just like that, it popped back in to my mind again. I was watching football at home. I don't even know who was playing. It was something the commentator said and then, all-of-a-sudden, there it was – like finding a key to a padlock and the perfect solution. That I could only justify buying this land by doing it with Beth.

Which is perfect, right?'

Nell was bleary eyed. 'Tom, that is so beautiful,'

Tom laughed. 'Yeah, it is. It's beautiful. Just like Beth. And the beautiful game, right? And my boys loved their football. So, what better way to survive them than a football pitch for their dad's old school as a gift from their mum?'

Chapter 64

Lesley twitched a little as Tom explained his intentions for the land. The Council Head had invited Tom to a meeting and he was happy to attend. After all, for the development to move ahead, he would be working closely with the council.

'Two million quid for a blasted football pitch?' Lesley raged. 'Are you out of your mind?'

'I assumed you'd be thrilled.'

Lesley didn't respond. Didn't need to. His face said it all.

'The council got a great price and will get a wonderful facility to boot. A win win, surely.'

Lesley bit hard. 'How philanthropic of you?'

'Thank you. It's very gratifying. I can highly recommend it,' Tom answered.

Lesley sneered. 'Well, we don't all have such means, do we?'

'No, but isn't everything, relative?' Tom was enjoying their exchange and his upper hand. 'Am I missing something? Council Head celebrates new facility. But you seem almost aggrieved?' Tom prodded.

'Me? No, I'm not upset.' Lesley answered too quickly. 'If it's good for the people of Bromsworth then it's good for me.'

Tom eyed him carefully. He wouldn't reveal that he had been betrayed by his assistant. Tom knew he was working with Danny Green but he didn't know what intentions they had for the land. Plans that he had now scuppered.

'I will need the council's support of course?' Tom probed.

Lesley looked away, barely able to look him in the eye.

'And with The Fruit Bowl as well…'

Lesley tutted.

'…once you've approved the reports that is?'

And with this, Lesley finally snapped. 'You don't get to

patronise me. I don't answer to you or anybody else in Bromsworth.'

Tom smiled confidently.

'I read about your family and your loss.' Lesley offered, regaining some of his composure. He hoped it might spark some information from the man, to at least help him understand but Tom remained unforthcoming.

'Did you?' Tom got up to demonstrate that their meeting was over. He had made his point and Lesley knew exactly where he stood.

'A car accident?' Lesley added, clutching now.

'Yes. That's right.'

'I was sorry to see that.'

Tom looked at him. 'Thank you, Councillor. It was the accident that brought me back here.'

As planned, later that evening, Tom and Sarah sat down for dinner with Nell and Michael at his hotel. Sarah was understandably a little nervous meeting them both, but they welcomed her warmly and quickly she relaxed. Nell responded to her immediately and couldn't conceal her delight for them both. When Sarah excused herself to go to the bathroom, Michael and Nell both assaulted Tom with their comments of approval.

'Bloody hell, Tom! You are so predictable,' Nell began. 'She's almost as beautiful as she is clever.'

Michael agreed and Tom chuckled proudly.

Dinner over, they all retired to the lounge bar for a glass of port. Tom was suddenly tired again and made mention of the early start he had on his stall. For so long, it had all seemed so completely incongruous to Michael, and yet now it made good sense. Nell was aware that there might be other reasons that Tom wanted to retire early and she was keen to avoid any awkwardness about where Sarah might spend the night. Finishing her drink, she made her excuses, kissed Tom and hugged him and then did the same to Sarah. Michael took the hint and polished off his drink also, leaving Tom and Sarah alone.

'Tom, I would love to stay, but knowing Douglas as I do...'

'I understand.' He leant forward and kissed her briefly. 'I'm completely exhausted and I'll be at the school in the morning for six.'

Sarah couldn't recall ever feeling so happy. 'So, I'll see you then.' They kissed again before she got up to leave.

The next morning, out of his suit and back into his jeans, Tom was impressed that Paddy had been true to his word and hadn't mentioned anything to Joe or Lewis. They all worked hard and it was fitting that that morning should be the most successful yet in the fledgling life of The Fruit Bowl. A long and steady queue snaked throughout the morning. Teaching staff queued also and Sarah chatted freely with her colleagues. At just before 9.00 a.m., Michael and Nell arrived. Tom was delighted to see them both and quickly served them a drink, introducing them to Paddy and his team. For a moment, Joe reverted to form and eyed Michael with suspicion having seen his enormous black BMW. In contrast, Paddy was demur to Michael for no good reason other than that he had silver hair, looked wealthy and was a friend of Tom's. He was very taken by Nell and almost picked her up off her feet when he realised she was Tom's sister. After such a busy morning, there was much clearing up to do, but it could wait until later because Tom wanted to take a ride out to The Quadrant and bring his new friends with him.

Between Michael's car, Paddy's van and Tom's Fiat, they all drove the short distance to The Quadrant. On arrival, Tom walked arm-in-arm with Nell, while Michael did his best to conceal his alarm at how bleak the place looked. The existing building would have to come down and the ground would need excavating, but so what? It was a happy day and Michael could share Tom's vision now and more importantly, offer his full endorsement.

'Well done, Tom. This place is going to be wonderful and you can rest assured that I will be eking out as much public funding as is humanly possible.'

Tom smiled. 'Thank you, Michael. I wouldn't want to do it without you.'

'Really?' Michael joked and they both laughed.

'The Fruit Bowl as well?' Tom asked.

'Absolutely. Natural synergies as well as vitamins.'

If Lesley Irwin harboured any ambitions to wrong-foot Tom

and obstruct either of his projects, then Michael would flatten him and Tom would enjoy watching.

'So, what's going on then? Why are we here?' Joe asked as he wandered over with Lewis.

'Well, this land was bought yesterday by a private consortium.' Tom looked about the place. 'Of which I am a part and the question is, what to do with it?'

'Right?' Joe looked bemused, his eyes darting from one person to the next, looking for clues.

'Joe, we're going to turn this land into a new sports facility for St. Ed's and we're going to need someone to manage the place.'

Joe could scarcely take in what he was hearing. He spun around in a full circle to take the place in and was probably already counting out pitches.

'Are you serious?' Joe asked, almost overwhelmed.

'We expect to be league champions, Joe?' Tom smiled.

Lewis too was looking on disbelievingly. Joe rubbed at his watering eyes. It was incredible news. Luckily, though, Paddy was on hand to settle things for them both.

'Obviously, I'll be Head of Sports. But Joe, you can be my number two.'

Joe screamed with joy and jumped into Lewis's arms. It really should have been the other way around but this seemed right enough for now and especially so when Paddy bent down and practically picked them both up off their feet. Michael stood back and savoured the beautiful scene before him, wondering how he had ever questioned the judgement of his favourite client.

Epilogue

Lesley Irwin did indeed attempt to obstruct Tom, but quickly realised that he had little leeway in which to operate. Opposing such laudable initiatives was difficult anyway, but there are ways and means. Armed with red tape and procedure, Lesley calculated that he could grind any progress to a halt and by doing so, cut himself in, but such an avenue was quickly slammed shut in his face. Michael turned out to be particularly aggressive adversary and no less efficient. He even visited Lesley with a threat of his own about a forensic audit of all council proceedings and transactions, and his mention of including Danny Green's business matters finally shut Lesley up for good.

The grant for the works at The Quadrant came through just four months after the auction and not a moment too soon because work had already begun in earnest, and all on Tom's slate. The building was razed and the ground work was done quickly. The concrete slabs were broken up and then three meters of earth was excavated and replaced. A local firm of architects drew up plans for the pavilion; planners considered proposals and utilities discussed the supply of water and power. Perceived wisdom, according to the construction firm appointed, was to build the pavilion first before any thought was given to the actual pitches, but this would delay things by up to eight months and possibly even a year which wouldn't do at all. So, it was agreed that one pitch on the far side of the plot should be completed immediately and a series of Portakabins were brought in as temporary facilities. Work began on the pavilion and a shiny sign erected, complete with drawings of what could be expected. Naturally, Sarah was in full support and was the new darling of her local authority. The first fixture was agreed and approved for May 6th.

The Fruit Bowl continued to strengthen with Paddy now running it on an official basis and as such he became St. Edmund's newest member of staff, giving up his ailing stall altogether. Tom supplemented his school salary income without his knowledge and didn't much care if the grants were not forthcoming. Publicity for the stall became national and Paddy and Mary enjoyed their trip to the BBC in London for *The One Show* and Bromsworth Council were quick to revel in the glory as grant applications were quickly prepared.

Naturally, *The Bromsworth Echo* covered both stories extensively. Lesley Irwin talked passionately of his pride in both initiatives and how the people of Bromsworth under his stewardship had set an example to councils up and down the land, demonstrating the successful provision of services, and most importantly, within budget. The light that Lesley could bask in was certainly warm and agreeable. There was even talk of further honours but it was of little consolation to him. He was terrified of his impending retirement without the golden egg he was expecting to gorge upon. His wife suggested that they might like to buy a static home on the coast somewhere – Wales, perhaps? – and Lesley shuddered at the thought. He hadn't imagined a caravan featuring in his twilight years and nor, for that matter, his wife either.

'Well done, Lesley,' colleagues would say to him on both ventures and he would thank them through gritted teeth.

There was excitement when it was announced that Lewis Adele was being readmitted to the St. Edmunds to re-sit a year, with a view to completing his GCSEs. Naturally, he was the first name on the sheet of St Edmund's 1st XI for their first home tie in over two years, and practically the whole school turned out to watch.

Tom and Sarah firmly established themselves as a couple, but still protocol prevented them from any public displays of affection. Sarah twirled the ring on her finger that Tom had bought for her. They hadn't set a date, but Tom had no doubt who would be his best man as he looked over to the other side of the pitch at the gentle giant, a head taller than anyone else, bellowing encouragement to Joe's team.

Tom had stood proudly as he watched both teams run out onto the pitch. Naisi had flown back from Brazil after her wedding. Her news about being pregnant made Tom weep and he demanded to be the Godfather.

Lewis looked like a man amongst boys as he sprinted about the pitch, neither his team mates nor opponents able to touch him. There were rumours that scouts were present, including people from Aston Villa. But none of them were as important to him as the presence of his mum. She had gone into rehab for the very last time, determined to finally emerge healthy again and with her supervisor alongside her, she lined the pitch with the hundreds of other people.

It was certainly a day and a scene to behold. Half-time and a 3-0 lead, thanks largely to Lewis. The home team laughed and enjoyed their fruit bowls, which Paddy had made especially.

Tom had done his share of crying over the last few years, mostly on his own and at night when he felt most lonely. But that day, the single tear that fell down his face was welcome. It represented his salvation. His boys and his wife would be proud of him and pleased for him. It was just as people had explained and promised. Tom had died with his family on that fateful morning. But now, he felt alive again.

OTHER BOOKS BY

DOMINIC HOLLAND

Only in America

The story of *Only in America* was inspired from my experiences with my first screenplay, *The Faldovian Club*. I sold the screenplay and found myself involved in some very exciting meetings – until the project finally died and without being made.

The publication of the novel, *Only in America* and subsequent sale of its film rights involved me in further film adventures with even more exciting meetings – until it suffered the same fate as The Faldovian Club. A bitter disappointment until I realized that my ill-fated forays in film were a great contrast to other members of my family and their attempts to crack Hollywood – and that such a tale might make a funny story which I wrote and called *Eclipsed*.

"This book is so charming and funny. A genuine page turner, I read it on holiday and missed big chunks of Venice"

Sandi Toksvig

"A fine stand-up comic has turned in to a first class, laugh out loud novelist. Read and enjoy"

Barry Cryer

"The only book I have ever read in one sitting. Of all the books by comedians turning their hands to novel writing - this is the funniest, most enjoyable and satisfying"

Nottingham Post

"As soon as you pick it up, you forget about everything that you have you to do, and you read it from cover to cover and you laugh out loud and love it."

Jenny Hanley

"Witty and charming. Astonishingly good. Quite irritating in fact."

Angus Deayton

Open Links

This book was written for the Anthony Nolan Trust - the largest bone barrow register in the world. Anthony Nolan saves many hundreds of lives each year. All monies from this book go to Anthony Nolan to help grow their register in the hope that somewhere, sometime, someone with blood cancer will be tissue matched and be given a chance of life. By buying *Open Links*, you will be contributing to Antony Nolan's noble work. Thank you.

Open Links is available as a paperback and available at **www. thebrotherstrust.org**

"From the first page I was gripped, and delighted to be reading a 'can't put this down' book. The story was funny and inspiring, the warm characters formed clear pictures in my head and the writing flowed effortlessly without a dull moment. There were several laugh out loud moments, and I have to admit an occasional tear."

"...a seriously good read... making it very hard to put down and always a case of "just one more chapter..."

"Mr. Holland will take you on the most entertaining and heart-tugging "round" of your life"

"Like the best underdog tales, this builds momentum beautifully and has a heart of gold"

"This is a genuinely touching story that had me thinking "just one more hole" each time I picked it up. A great read and an even better cause"

"Genuinely one of the funniest and most heart-warming books I have read in years"

Dominic's most recent novel and unlike anything he has published before. A beautiful story for our times and an anti-dote to the increasing divisions of modern society. A provocative and salving story, I, Gabriel is a novel for readers, young and old; for all people with a conscience and a hope that we can do better.

Currently available as a print and eBook. Also available as a print book via dominicholland.co.uk and copies can be signed if you wish.

"Like his novel, Open Links. I read this in one sitting. The best novel I have read in years."

"I just could not put this book down. It is compelling, fascinating and beautifully penned."

"I did not foresee the ending at all and it is so perfect and satisfying that I immediately decided to read it again for any clues that the author leaves. First class story telling."

"Another enthralling book from this wonderful author."

"A perfect heartwarming tale to restore your faith in humanity and make our world seem less heavy."

"I am a notoriously slow reader and I often lose interest and abandon novels. Not so with I, Gabriel. I read it in two days. A record for me and I am disappointed that it is over because it is a remarkable novel."

The Ripple Effect

My second published novel (and last!).

Currently, available as an eBook only and not available in any good book shops.

I do have plans to create a print book version. Bear with me.

"A joyous romp - The Ripple Effect is an Ealing comedy for the 21st Century"
Alan Coren

"Only in America was a step in the right direction, but The Ripple Effect heralds Holland's emergence in to the literary big time."
The Sunday Times

"Proof that Holland is a master of comedy"
Northern Echo

"A belter of a novel. This could be the book of the season."
Danny Baker

"Funny, gripping and hard to put down – what more do you want from a novel?"
The Sunday Times

"An infectious, warm-hearted tale about real people pulling together."
The Mirror

"Not every stand-up comedian manages to be as funny in print as they are on stage. Dominic Holland is one of the few who is."
Liverpool Daily Post

"Proof that Holland is a master of comedy."
Yorkshire Evening Press

Eclipsed

The story of two men and their ambitions to break Hollywood; one as a writer and the other as an actor. The writer is a deluded dad called Dominic and the actor is his eldest son, called Tom.

It is now 2020 and Dominic Holland has yet to hear that seductive word, 'Action'. Tom, meanwhile, is Spider-Man with Hollywood at his beck and call, hence the title of the book, Eclipsed - a heartfelt and funny story on fatherhood written by a dad who is as bemused as he is proud.

Available as an eBook and print book online. Also available via dominicholland.co.uk – where copies can be signed if you wish.

"One might think this is a selfish attempt to gain fame and fortune at the expense of his son. This is the not the case. Eclipsed is written with more brutal honesty and self-deprecating humour than can be expected from anyone with selfish intentions"

"Dominic Holland bravely exposes his hopes and disappointments, his talents and his frailties in a story which is ultimately redemptive in its fearless honesty and open-hearted spirit. 'Eclipsed' is a bitter-sweet tale of great liveliness and warmth; above all, it is profoundly human"

"Dominic Holland doesn't claim 'superior genes', 'unique talent' or 'fate' for his son Tom, but gives credit to his hard work, application and a high degree of natural talent. This is a truly remarkable, balanced perspective given the dizzy heights to which Tom's career has already achieved and which have so far eluded his old man"

"I loved this book as it's funny, honest and heartfelt. My kind of book. Any parent could relate to this and at times it felt like I was reading the script of a movie. I hope you enjoy it, I did"

CPSIA information can be obtained
at www.ICGtesting.com
Printed in the USA
LVHW052046170720
661028LV00001B/45